The Arnold and Caroline Rose Monograph Series
of the American Sociological Association

Protest and participation

The new working class in Italy

Other books in the series

J. Milton Yinger, Kiyoshi Ikeda, Frank Laycock, and Stephen J. Cutler: *Middle Start: An Experiment in the Educational Enrichment of Young Adolescents*
James A. Geschwender: *Class, Race, and Worker Insurgency: The League of Revolutionary Black Workers*
Paul Ritterband: *Education, Employment, and Migration: Israel in Comparative Perspective*
Orrin E. Klapp: *Opening and Closing: Strategies of Information Adaptation in Society*
Rita James Simon: *Continuity and Change: A Study of Two Ethnic Communities in Israel*
Marshall B. Clinard: *Cities with Little Crime: The Case of Switzerland*

Volumes previously published by the American Sociological Association

Michael Schwartz and Sheldon Stryker: *Deviance, Selves and Others*
Robert M. Hauser: *Socioeconomic Background and Educational Performance*
Morris Rosenberg and Roberta G. Simmons: *Black and White Self-Esteem: The Urban School Child*
Chad Gordon: *Looking Ahead: Self-Conceptions, Race and Family as Determinants of Adolescent Orientation to Achievement*
Anthony M. Orum: *Black Students in Protest: A Study of the Origins of the Black Student Movement*
Ruth M. Gasson, Archibald O. Haller, and William H. Sewell: *Attitudes and Facilitation in the Attainment of Status*
Sheila R. Klatzky: *Patterns of Contact with Relatives*
Herman Turk: *Interorganizational Activation in Urban Communities: Deductions from the Concept of System*
John DeLamater: *The Study of Political Commitment*
Alan C. Kerckhoff: *Ambition and Attainment: A Study of Four Samples of American Boys*
Scott McNall: *The Greek Peasant*
Lowell L. Hargens: *Patterns of Scientific Research: A Comparative Analysis of Research in Three Scientific Fields*
Charles Hirschman: *Ethnic Stratification in Peninsular Malaysia*

Protest and participation

The new working class in Italy

John R. Low-Beer

*Assistant Professor, School of Organization and Management and
Department of Sociology, Yale University*

Cambridge University Press

Cambridge
London   New York   Melbourne

Published by the Syndics of the Cambridge University Press
The Pitt Building, Trumpington Street, Cambridge CB2 1RP
Bentley House, 200 Euston Road, London NW1 2DB
32 East 57th Street, New York, NY 10022, USA
296 Beaconsfield Parade, Middle Park, Melbourne 3206, Australia

First published 1978

Printed in the United States of America

Typeset by Jay's Publishers Services Inc, North Scituate, Mass.
Printed and bound by The Murray Printing Company, Westford, Mass.

Library of Congress Cataloging in Publication Data

Low-Beer, John R 1944–

Protest and Participation.

(ASA Rose monograph series; 4)

A revision of the author's thesis, Harvard University, 1974.

Bibliography: p.

Includes index.

1. Electronic industry workers – Italy – Milan – Case studies.
2. Technicians in industry – Italy – Milan – Case studies.
3. Industrial relations – Italy – Milan – Case studies.
4. Social classes – Italy – Milan – Case studies.
5. White collar workers – Italy – Milan – Case studies.
I. Title. II. Series: The Arnold and Caroline Rose
monograph series in sociology; 4.
HD8039.E38I84   1977   331.7'62'13094521   77–80841
ISBN 0 521 21782 2 hard covers
ISBN 0 521 29277 8 paperback

To my mother and to the memory of my father

Contents

Figures and tables

Foreword

The emergence of a massive middle-class, well-educated stratum within the traditional radical movements and the growth of a New Left based on this class has created a puzzling paradox for Marxist analysts of revolutionary politics. Much as classic Marxist thought did not anticipate that movements purporting to be revolutionary socialist would come to power first in less developed agrarian societies, few anticipated that revolutionary politics in advanced industrial societies would draw its sustenance from the more affluent sectors of society, particularly intellectuals, university students, and the more educated workers, including professionals and semiprofessionals. John Low-Beer's important work is a major contribution to the interpretation of the latter group, one which has been largely ignored by American scholars.

Why have technicians become a militant group in Western Europe, supporting strikes and left-wing parties? To answer this, Low-Beer first reviews the literature on the new working class by people such as Serge Mallet and André Gorz and then by Roger Garaudy. The former stress the effect of the structural situation of this group, particularly various contradictions or inconsistencies. These include differences between their actual limited power and claims to superiority along other stratification dimensions, and the notion drawn from Veblen of a "contradiction between the rationality of profit maximization and a higher rationality which is seen in scientific work." Garaudy and others follow in a more orthodox Marxist tradition, emphasizing the "proletarianization of the technician," that his or her job is becoming much like that of the blue collar worker.

Low-Beer seeks to deal with the validity of these and other ideas through a detailed investigation based on survey research and field work. His findings, like much empirical research, upset many of the generalizations derived logically from analysis of macroscopic social trends. The most important factors involved in determining whether technicians engage in militant action turn out to be related to their social background,

xi

not aspects of the job or organization. The middle-class militants are largely of lower-class origin, and come from leftist families. Why then has there been such an increase in involvement in strikes and union action by semiprofessionals? The answer lies in the general set of events that has resulted in the emergence of protest and leftist strength in the entire society and in the large-scale increase in upward mobility brought about by economic expansion, the increase in educational facilities, and the proliferation in the number of white collar, semiprofessional and professional jobs. Many, if not most, of those occupying these new positions had to be drawn from the ranks of the less privileged. This necessarily means that a large proportion of the new class comes from leftist environments in countries with a history of large radical movements. Many of the upwardly mobile move to the right in tandem with their success, but many do not, providing the leadership cadre and mass base for unionism and radicalism among the new working class.

These findings are less dramatic than the comprehensive theories of social analysts who look for explanations in broad structural trends. They reinforce the arguments suggesting that continuities in political traditions stemming from the origin of modern politics in various western nations still inform contemporary political life. In countries with moderate traditions, the left, both working-class and middle-class, continues to follow modern versions of such orientations. In the United States, the activist policies of the new class remain progressive rather than radical. Affluent American reformers advocate conservation, environmental cleanups, improvements in the political process, much as did the Progressives of pre–World War I, or the Mugwumps of the late nineteenth century. In Latin and Southern Europe, with their revolutionary traditions, the sociological equivalents of the American advocates of "cleanliness" support the current *gauchiste* version of radical change.

The presence of so many well-educated persons among the left encourages ideological factionalism, for, as the history of western radicalism demonstrates, increased education is associated with ideological disputation.

John Low-Beer is to be congratulated for an unusually sophisticated study of a major social development. He combines a concern with the most abstract societal theories with the use of statistical analysis, material from in-depth interviews, and field observation. His book should be required reading not only for students of organizational and class behavior, but also for all those who seek to understand the sources of protest. Revolution, as its original meaning derivative from the word *revolve* implies, still involves efforts to move to a new future that is rooted in, to be explained by, the past. Nations and people do not easily escape from their history. Sociologists, as Low-Beer emphasizes, "are often quick to construct theories on the basis of scanty evidence." Here is some hard data with which hypotheses may be confronted. If the findings do not fit the theoretical assumptions, so much the worse for the theories.

Seymour Martin Lipset

Stanford University
June, 1977

Preface

Title notwithstanding, this is a study of a predominantly middle class rather than working class group. Following the usage of Serge Mallet, the term "new working class" has come to refer to technicians and highly skilled workers in the advanced sectors of industry, in research labs, and in certain services. Some are blue collar and some are white collar. The distinction is not very meaningful to the technicians themselves, but in Italy their employers classified most of them as white collar until the union contracts of 1972 and 1973 did away with the dividing line entirely.

Because of the important part they play in Italy's deepening political and economic crisis, the middle classes have received a considerable amount of attention there in the last few years. Yet compared with the large numbers of studies of the working class, there is a paucity of studies of the life and work situations of middle class samples, not only in Italy but elsewhere as well. Considering their pivotal role in the politics of many of the advanced societies (and in those of some less advanced) in the twentieth century, this neglect seems unjustified.

Recent works on the middle classes in Italy have approached the subject from various perspectives, but with few exceptions they contain no systematic information about how the people in question interpret their own situations. This lack may be attributed to the hostility of the Italian intellectual tradition toward the survey research and fieldwork methodologies of sociology. Neither the idealist school of Benedetto Croce nor the Marxist approach lead easily to studies of the ideology, attitudes, and values of individuals. Yet such studies are the necessary complement of studies of political and union action. Although I have been eclectic in my methodology, my primary focus is on the situation of the ordinary member of the new working class and how this situation is experienced by him. I hope I will thereby encourage more empirical work, not only on the new working class, but also on other segments of the working class and other middle class groups.

New working class strikes have by now lost the novelty and some of the creative originality they had in the late sixties and early seventies, but in recent years attention has focused on the labor aristocracy and the white collar employees for other reasons. As the necessity of enacting basic reforms in Italian society has become more urgent, the problem has arisen of constructing an alliance to support such changes, and perhaps even to move beyond them toward socialism. The middle classes are an important element in such an alliance. Their behavior is of special concern, not only because of the support they gave to the Fascist movement in the twenties, but also because the traditional middle classes of small businessmen, shopkeepers, small landowners, and small farmers, who have always constituted the keystone of Christian Democratic support, now often stand in the way of changes whose necessity is admitted by all.

This research was conceived and largely written during a period of optimism and enthusiasm among people working for progressive change in Italy. Their enthusiasm was passed on to me during the year of fieldwork in Milan in 1970-1 and is doubtless reflected in many ways in the text. While I write this preface, the Italian universities are occupied by students once again, as they were during the late sixties, but now the mood is one of pessimism. It may surprise the reader not versed in Italian affairs to hear that even members of the Communist Party are pessimistic, although their party appears to be riding the crest of the wave of discontent. Their sense of foreboding arises from an awareness of the great difficulties involved in trying to bring about fundamental changes in Italian society, even from the seat of government. Although I share this awareness, I have preferred not to change the tone of the text. It conveys, perhaps better than the statistics, the feelings of that time.

This book is a considerably revised and enlarged version of my dissertation, presented to the Department of Sociology at Harvard University in 1974. I would like to thank my advisor, Gino Germani, for his help throughout. It was in his seminar that I became interested in the subject of this study. I have drawn on his knowledge in many of the areas dealt with here. He has been a continual source of intellectual stimulation and enjoyable evenings of conversation.

Thomas Pettigrew was very helpful in clarifying a number of ideas in the early stages of the development of the research.

Proceeding in chronological order, I must express my thanks to the Foreign Area Fellowship Program of the Social Science Research Council for support of the field research and of part of the succeeding phase of this work. The National Science Foundation defrayed the cost of tape transcription. Yale University and its Department of Administrative Sciences provided computer time and funds for general expenses, respectively. I am grateful to them for their support.

A large number of people in Milan made this study possible. Many political and union activists took an interest in it and gave generously of their time. I owe special thanks to the men and women of the Works Councils of three companies: GT&E, SIT Siemens, and Honeywell.

A few people were helpful in ways extending far beyond willing assistance in their capacities as unionists, party activists, or employees. Alberto Milano, Cosenza Fioravanti, Carlo Salvaneschi, and Giorgio Salvini made me feel at home in a new environment.

I hope that the men who gave interviews for this work enjoyed talking to me as much as I did with them. Be this as it may, my debt to them is very great. From them I learned much, and I emerged from my experience with a new sense of the energy, the intelligence, and the possibilities of my fellow men. Needless to say, the names given to them in the text are fictitious.

On the management side, I am thankful to Aldo Cardarelli of GT&E, whose readiness to support even critical research I respect; and to Paolo Zanovello and Caterina Bonati. The findings reported here do not always cast the company in a favorable light. The criticizable characteristics of this company are typical of Italian industry generally. The fact that GT&E was prepared to open its door to an outside observer is in itself a demonstration of a willingness to change and to improve within the constraints of the environment.

Alessandro Pizzorno's house provided me an intellectual haven in Milan. Alessandro opened to me a wide network of contacts bridging the gap between the university and the union movement. Working with him and his research group has given me a new perspective on sociology. Guiliana Carabelli deserves special thanks in this context. Silva Pesso provided sensitive and intelligent help in completing the series of interviews.

Thanks are due a number of people who have read and commented on various drafts of this work: Clay Alderfer, Hilary Beattie, Tom Burns, John Goldthorpe, J. Richard Hackman, Peter Lange, Juan Linz, S. M. Lipset, Riccardo Peccei, John Stephens, Michael Useem, Victor Vroom, and Gerrit Wolf. Gerrit Wolf and John Williamson were very patient in answering my questions on data analysis. Tom Burns, John Goldthorpe, and S. M. Lipset gave much appreciated help and advice concerning publication.

Finally, I am grateful to Maria Maderna, who faithfully transcribed the bulk of the interviews, and to Christine Brousseau, Karen Flowers, Nancy McGuerty, and Janice Seccombe, who were as punctilious as I could have wished them to be in preparing this final draft.

J.L.B.

New Haven, Connecticut
May, 1977

1. The debate on the new working class and the evolution of the class structure

Introduction

Marx cast the working class in the role of the revolutionary force that was to overthrow capitalism. The accuracy of this prediction has been debated ever since. The history of the first fifteen years of the postwar economic boom appeared to refute Marx definitively. It was argued that the working class was disappearing as a distinct entity, merging into the bourgeoisie as its income rose. Theories of integration of the working class came to predominate. Lack of integration seemed to exist only as individual deviance or as alienation.

In the early sixties, however, the embers of class conflict flared up again. Political and labor militancy were on the rise. There was an efflorescence of neo-Marxist writing, placing greater emphasis than heretofore on those humanistic themes in Marx that gave insight into the restless stirrings of affluent societies.

In France and Italy, some of the most remarkable manifestations of the new militancy were the flamboyant and innovative strikes of technicians and white collar workers in the private sector, groups not inclined by tradition toward collective action. Prominent among their demands were those for a greater degree of control over the workplace. A number of observers in these two countries saw in the rapidly growing group of technicians and professionally trained workers the vanguard of a new revolutionary movement. The two most influential statements of this thesis were Serge Mallet's book, *The New Working Class*, first published in France in 1963, and André Gorz's book, *Strategy for Labor*, also first published in France in 1964, and subsequently translated into English.

The phenomena described by Gorz and Mallet were by no means confined to France and Italy. Although the specific forms of white collar unionism varied from country to country, and although they were hardly anywhere so dramatic as in France and in Italy, this unionism has under-

1

gone a spectacular development in most of the advanced capitalist societies. As a theory purporting to explain militancy among comparatively satisfied workers in affluent situations, the new working class thesis has a broader relevance.

The chapters to follow will look in some detail at life in two electronics plants in Milan, Italy, as seen through the eyes of the technicians who work there. Our aim is at once to bring to life the abstract discussions of Gorz, Mallet, and others, and to explore a range of variation in new working class situations as they affect individual attitudes and behavior. In this way, we hope to increase our understanding of the role of the new working class on the political stage of the advanced societies.

In this chapter, we retrace the debate on the role of the working class. This debate has gone in two directions since Marx's time. One of these has been the discussion of the embourgeoisement of the working class. The other has been the controversy over the political significance of the great increase in the number of dependent white collar workers.

These two strands of the debate have historically been separated, but as the blue collar–white collar line has blurred, their referent has come to be the same. One of the groups emerging on this fuzzy borderline is the *new working class*, variously defined as educated labor in general or as technicians in particular. In the new working class thesis, the two strands of the debate are reunited.

The following account retraces the history of the debate. Table 1.1 summarizes the positions of the various authors on the central issues in a relatively orderly fashion, but with no regard for history. The reader interested in comparing these positions may find it helpful to refer back to the table while following the historical recapitulation.

The prewar debate

The first strand of the debate begins with the question of embourgeoisement, discussed by Engels on several occasions in his writing on the English working class and taken up again by Lenin in *Imperialism*. In trying to explain the absence of a revolutionary working class movement in England, Lenin noted that a substantial part of the British working class "merrily share the feast of England's monopoly of the colonies and the world market."[1]

Marx himself did not consider embourgeoisement to be of great importance. It is often said that the pauperization of the working class was an essential postulate in Marx's theory. This is certainly an over-simplification. Marx was well aware that needs are socially determined. He often pointed out that relative deprivation is more important than absolute deprivation in the formation of consciousness, that "our wants and pleasures have their origin in society; we therefore measure them in relation to the objects which serve for their gratification. Since they are of a social nature they are of a relative nature."[2] An improvement in living standards need not lead to a decline in class consciousness. Although he maintained that the existence of a reserve army of the unemployed would prevent any substantial increase in the relative share of wages in the national income, he did not rule out absolute increases in the workers' standard of living.[3]

But orthodox Marxism found Lenin's idea of embourgeoisement more useful in seeking to account for the fact that the working classes of advanced capitalist societies have not become agents of revolutionary change. It was only with the resurgence of working class militancy in many European countries in the late sixties that the left returned to the emphasis on relative deprivation, which was seen as leading to a renewal of unionism in the most modern plants.

Until recently, proponents of embourgeoisement theories limited themselves to challenging the economic aspects of Marx's analysis of the development of the working class. Many authors pointed out the dramatic improvements in the standards of living in advanced capitalist countries. Around the turn of the century, Sombart described what he thought to be the effects of a rising standard of living: "On the reefs of roast beef and apple pie socialistic Utopias of every sort are sent to their doom."[4] The debate on the extent of income redistribution has continued to this day, although most authors agree that there has been some leveling.[5] But it is only in the last ten years that some writers have pointed to changes in the organization of industry as leading to embourgeoisement. We shall have more to say on this subject later on.

The second strand of the debate, the controversy over the political significance of the rise of the new middle class, arises from analyses of changes in the class structure. As early as 1899, Bernstein based his political reformism on an analysis of these changes, pointing out the growth of the new middle class, the failure of the old middle class to disappear, and the separation of ownership and control.

Again, it is an oversimplification of Marx to maintain that he completely failed to anticipate these developments. As Bell has pointed out,

Table 1.1. *A summary of various theoretical positions in the debate on the political role of dependent workers.*

Strand in the debate	Theoretical position	Economic situation	Life style	Work situation	Politics and militancy	Authors
White collar	1. Middle class as moderate	Stable or improving	Status conscious – imitative of elite	Closer to that of management than to manual workers. Sometimes emphasize positive consequences of automation	Moderate progressive	Bernstein; Crozier; Bahrdt
	2. Middle class as autonomous: (a) technocracy theories;	Not discussed	Not discussed	Technocrats seen as controlling industry de facto	Support for managerial technocratic solutions	Veblen; Burnham
	(b) theories viewing middle class as potentially fascist	Worsening	Status consciousness	Increasing bureaucratization, squeezing out of old middle classes	Right-wing militancy	Fromm; mass society theorists
	3. Proletarianization theory	Stable or worsening	Declining status consciousness	Emphasis on bureaucratization, negative consequences of automation	Increasing class consciousness and militancy	Kautsky
Blue collar	4. Embourgeoisement theory (working class is becoming like middle class)	Increasing income overlap with middle class	Increasing emphasis on status, consumption	Emphasis on positive consequences of automation	Decline in militancy, radicalism	Bell; Lipset; Mayer

5. Affluent worker theory – sees the working class as distinct both from middle class and from traditional proletarian	Increasing income overlap with middle class	Characterized by privatization and little status striving	Relatively unchanged – importance of work situation de-emphasized	As yet unclear. Interest in wages and potential interest in broader issues	Goldthorpe, Lockwood, et al.
6. Traditional Marxist view	The bulk of the working class is still very poor.	Unchanged from traditional working class. Little status striving	Relatively unchanged	The working class is still the dominant progressive and/or revolutionary force.	
7. New working class theory	Improving	Not much discussed. Assumption that new needs arise in this realm	Emphasis on positive consequences of automation	Increasing class consciousness and militancy – demands for more control over the workplace	Gorz; Mallet

Marx does remark in volume III of *Capital* that the absolute number if not the proportion of office workers may increase with the development of capitalism.[6] In the *Grundrisse* he goes even farther, pointing to a time when, because of the introduction of machinery, "labour in its direct form, ceases to be the main source of wealth, [and] labour time ceases . . . to be its standard of measurement."[7] The contradiction between socially necessary labor time and surplus labor time is here seen as leading to the fall of the capitalist system.

But it must be admitted that the ideas expressed in the *Grundrisse* are not followed in the main arguments in *Capital* or, indeed, throughout Marx's work. Even in the *Grundrisse* he does not refer to an increase in the number of white collar workers and in *Capital* he notes that whatever increase there may be starts out from a number "infinitesimally small compared to the industrial workshop."[8]

The increasingly rapid growth in the number of dependent white collar workers and their mobilization in the years following World War I led to an outpouring of writings on this subject, particularly in Germany. The three positions taken in this debate are still with us today, perhaps because they exhaust the universe of possibilities. As noted above, Bernstein felt that the changes in the class structure invalidated Marx's analysis. Although he did consider the new middle class as a potential ally of the working class, he described it as an essentially moderate group that would not be open to a revolutionary strategy.[9] Lederer, in his first book on the new middle class written in 1912,[10] took a position very similar to that of Bernstein. Pointing out the heterogeneity of this stratum, he argued that their influence would be exerted in favor of a moderate progressive politics.

In response to Bernstein, Kautsky reaffirmed the orthodox Marxist thesis of proletarianization. This position was later supported by many other German writers such as Dreyfuss, Croner, and Lederer himself in his later work.[11] Most of the writers who depicted the white collar worker as already proletarian emphasized economic factors such as rising unemployment and declining wages, although the theme of alienation also made its appearance in the twenties.

The third position depicted the middle class as having independent interests of its own. Those who suggested this theory considered managers, high-level civil servants, and sometimes intellectuals as part of a new middle class which was often described as serving the general interest. The notion of the technocrat whose objectivity derives from the objectivity of science was present in the work of Gustav Schmoller[12] and Thorstein Veblen,[13] and was opportunistically adopted as part of the fascist ideology.

In the postwar period, the character of the debate changed. With economic prosperity and social peace came theories of integration. The alienation of the affluent society became a prominent theme in the mass media as well as in sociological writings.[14] But in the early sixties, industrial and social conflicts were on the rise, and sociologists of the left were quick to find explanations for this trend. It was at this point that some observers assigned a critical role to what they now called the "new working class." Their explanations for the new militancy of the workers referred to a number of social changes, many of which were the same ones noted by observers of the fifties as leading to increasing integration. But still other authors saw different trends and continued to place an emphasis on the proletarianization of white collar workers. Before presenting these various views, we sketch the changes that all agree have occurred in the advanced societies as well as some points on which there is less agreement as to the direction of development.

Changes in class situations

The changes in class situation fall into three categories: (1) changes in the composition of the labor force; (2) changes in the work situation; and (3) changes in life outside the work situation. These three categories will be discussed in turn.

It is hardly necessary to point out that there are great differences among the advanced capitalist societies in the dynamics of their class structures. However, certain broad trends are common to these societies, giving the debate its international character and significance. They are discussed here, whereas the particularities of the Italian case are considered in Chapter 2.

Changes in the composition of the labor force

All parties in the debate were willing to admit that the skill composition of the labor force of the advanced societies is changing. If the rise of the semiskilled, the clerical, and other white collar groups had been the most noticeable change in the nonagricultural labor force before the war, the growth in the professional and technical category has been the most striking change in the postwar decades. As Bell has pointed out,[15] most of the white collar jobs created in the prewar period in the United States were low-grade clerical jobs filled by women. It is in the postwar period that we have witnessed the rapid growth of the professional and technical category, which in the United States passed from 7.5 percent of the labor force in 1940 to 13.6 percent of the labor force in 1968. This must be placed in the context of increasing educational levels of the entire labor force. In 1960, the median years of school completed by 20- and 21-year-old male operatives was 12.0 compared to a median level of 8.2 years among semiskilled males 55 years old and over.[16]

It might be argued that figures on the educational attainments of the labor force tell one nothing, and that the labor force would be equally productive without the dubious benefit of twelve years in the classroom. It is no doubt true that workers are in many instances overtrained for their jobs. However, there is also evidence to suggest that the demand for technical and professional knowledge has increased dramatically since the war. In the United States, government expenditures on research and development rose from 0.07 percent of GNP in 1940 to 2.16 percent in 1965.[17] Employment has been growing rapidly in high-technology industries such as electronics and chemicals, while falling off or remaining stationary in many mass production industries such as the auto industry.[18]

The Italian case is very different in that Italy is at once a developed country (consider Lombardy, Piedmont, and Liguria) and an underdeveloped country (consider Sicily, Calabria, and other southern regions). The coexistence of developed and underdeveloped regions has led to a unique situation of which more will be said below. Here it is relevant to point out that in Italy too, the number of professionals and technicians in the labor force has been rising, though starting from a much narrower base than in the United States. The figures are not useful for years preceding the 1950s, as the census categories change with disconcerting rapidity. Between 1951 and 1975, white collar and managerial personnel increased from 9.5 percent of the labor force to 21.2 percent of the labor force.[19] In Lombardy, where this research was carried out, the increase was just as great, despite the fact that dependent white collar workers in this region already constituted 15.1 percent of the employed labor force in 1959. By 1975, dependent white collar workers constituted 24.2 percent of the employed population of Lombardy.[20]

Italy has long suffered from unemployment and underemployment of educated workers and intellectuals.[21] Yet it is important to point out that the increase in the percentage of white collar workers is not only the consequence of an artificial inflation of the tertiary sector. Employment of white collar and managerial personnel has increased proportionately more in industry than in other activities such as commerce and public administration.[22]

Within manufacturing, the postwar economic boom saw the greatest increases in employment in those industries employing a relatively high proportion of technical labor: photographic and phonograph equipment, electrical and electronics products, assorted machine industries and repair shops, precision machinery, and chemical industries, in order of growth.[23] (Unfortunately, detailed figures on the growth of employment in various industries are available only for the years 1951 and 1961, covering the decade of the economic "miracle."[24])

The electrical (including electronics) industries, of particular interest here, were among the fastest growing, nearly doubling in employment (92,711 workers to 177,583 workers) in the decade between 1951 and 1961. The impact of this rapid growth on labor relations was all the greater because of the concentration of employment in this industry. In 1961, 60.2 percent of those employed in the electrical equipment industry were employed in Lombardy. The percentage of technical labor employed in the Milan area is even greater than this figure suggests. Many of the nontechnical functions connected with the electronics industry are decentralized to less developed areas where semiskilled labor is cheap and plentiful. Employment in the electrical equipment sector is also concentrated in large units. In Lombardy, 49.2 percent of those employed in this industry worked in units with over 500 employees in 1961, as compared with 23.3 percent of those employed in manufacturing as a whole.[25]

Detailed figures on the educational composition of the labor force are available only from 1959 to 1963, although less detailed breakdowns are available for later years as well. In the four years for which detailed information is available, the number of people with scientific and technical training increased 15.4 percent, while the increase in the larger category of people with diplomas or university degrees of any sort was 13.1 percent. From 1959 to 1973, the percentage of people in the employed labor force with secondary or university degrees rose from 7.4 percent to 13.2 percent.[26]

In Italy as in other advanced societies the technical and professional category of the labor force is growing. Although government policy may foster or retard this tendency, underlying trends toward increased planning (both at the level of the enterprise and at the local and national government levels), greater technological sophistication, and the predominance of services over manufacturing give this growth a momentum of its own. In Italy, the rapid development of a few key industries in the postwar period has created concentrations of technicians that did not exist before. The economic and political crisis has slowed or halted the growth of these industries, but technicians have already shown themselves to be important actors within the labor movement.

Changes in the work situation

Discussions of the work situation have always been central in the controversy over the political future of the new middle class. But it is only more recently that some authors have pointed to changes in the work situation of a part of the working class in their arguments supporting or attempting to refute the embourgeoisement thesis. A concern with the effects of automation and technological development has tended to unite the two strands of the debate on the political roles of blue and white collar workers.

As the preceding discussion of the changing composition of the labor force made clear, the number of jobs requiring technical and professional skills is increasing rapidly. These jobs are located primarily in the advanced industrial sectors and in the tertiary. While this change is recognized by nearly all observers, some authors, looking more specifically at the consequences of automation, have pointed out less happy tendencies as well: toward increasing rationalization of work, toward increasing division of labor, toward work involving increasing mental if not physical strain.

The contradictory and inconclusive nature of the evidence on the effects of automation has led to widely differing assessments of the direction in which technology is leading and of the extent to which changes in people's work situations are, indeed, technologically determined.[27] Those who view the advent of automation optimistically (e.g., Blauner, Simon, Taylor, Touraine, and Naville)[28] claim that the introduction of computers leads to the elimination of the more routine tasks and to the reemergence of integrated work groups such as existed in the craft industries. The pessimists (e.g., Bright, Pollock, Hoos, and Blumberg)[29] claim that more often than not automation lowers skill levels and that the jobs in automated plants often lead to psychic strain as a result of the continuous concentration required.

To some extent the lack of agreement about the consequences of automation may be attributed to the failure of many researchers on this subject to place their findings in any theoretical framework at all. Thomas Whisler's study[30] of computerization in nineteen insurance companies is one example of this type of research, in which the "before" and "after" states are compared with virtually no attempt at interpretation. But it also seems likely that automation does not univocally either upgrade or downgrade jobs. First of all, automation of blue collar functions has different consequences from automation of white collar functions. Faunce, Blauner, Touraine, Bahrdt,[31] and others have pointed out that automation at the blue collar level tends to decrease the division of labor, leaving the worker with an enlarged job and more responsibility. The findings for white collar work are more contradictory and on the whole less sanguine. The kinds of tasks the computer can perform least well are those which involve relatively unstructured decisions, that is, higher-level management jobs, and those at the interface between the machine and its environment, that is, routine jobs requiring the use of sensory organs the computer does not possess. It is thus the middle level of white collar bureaucracies that seems to be most affected by computerization. Decision making involving a limited number of alternatives takes place at this level, and it is these decisions that can be more efficiently made by the computer.[32]

Bahrdt and Faunce have both pointed out that the present stage of office automation corresponds more closely to the mass-production stage of industrial production than to the stage of continuous process production. Much of the manpower in the computerized office is employed at semiskilled jobs, putting information into forms in which it can be "perceived" by the computer and executing the demands of the machine. These sensory-motor tasks that cannot as yet be performed by the computer provide the majority of the jobs for people in the automated office.[33]

Despite these generalizations, it seems evident that the structure of white collar work is as yet not so rigidly determined by technology as is the structure of blue collar work. Different uses of the computer can lead to more or less centralized organizations and more or less autonomy for the worker. This is undoubtedly another source of different and contradictory findings in this area of research.

Perhaps the most useful theoretical analysis of the problem is that by

Alain Touraine.[34] He sees the factory as an integrated whole performing certain functions. The organization of mass-production manufacturing industries typically implied an extreme division of the task at hand. This, in turn, meant the radical separation of the function of production from the functions of product design and of planning the execution of production, of manual from nonmanual functions. New nonmanual roles arose to coordinate functions that had been so subdivided that those who executed them no longer understood their place in the process of production. In the automated production process the coordinating role is taken over by the computer, as are many of the subordinate roles involved only with task execution. But the computer creates new subordinate roles at its interface with the environment and new integrative roles for those who must program it. Instead of looking for dramatic changes in the skill composition of the labor force in automated plants, it would perhaps be more useful to analyze the changing loci of skill concentrations in the factory.

Touraine's analysis is also helpful in pointing out the opposing forces at work within organizations, leading to simultaneous pressures for increased bureaucratization and for the transcendence of bureaucracy. Touraine defines bureaucracy as the mediating function between a decision and the implementation of that decision. In this sense a bureaucracy is a tool for the processing of information and for the handling of operating decisions that are made according to predetermined criteria. To the extent that the functions of an organization are predictable, it tends to become bureaucratic. A business enterprise that can control its external environment through market research or because of its monopoly situation is able to bureaucratize certain functions. Similarly, if the internal environment can be made predictable by rationalizing methods of production, standardizing parts, programming, etc., a bureaucracy develops to perform these functions as well. By increasing the predictability of its environment, the organization is able to minimize its risks – risks that become less and less tolerable as the scale of operations increases.

But paradoxically, technological development also sets in motion a process of "debureaucratization." The technology that makes the environment more predictable is itself relatively unpredictable in its increasingly rapid development. As specialized knowledge becomes more important to the everyday functioning of the organization, power comes to be associated with technical knowledge rather than with position in a bureaucratic hierarchy. Decisions are made at those points in the organization where professional knowledge is located. Decision making becomes decentralized, and the more so to the extent that the firm operates in an environment requiring rapid technological change. The distance between decision and execution is, therefore, once again shortened.

With these contradictions in mind, it becomes possible to understand how authors such as Bennis[35] are writing about the demise of bureaucracy as an organizational form while the introduction of new cost accounting and production programming schemes leads to an increasing rationalization of many jobs, or how some authors[36] have emphasized the political implications of the proletarianization of white collar workers, whereas others[37] have based their analyses on the increasing importance (both numerically and in terms of the functions they serve) of technical and professional workers. Even within the category of technicians, there is, as we shall see later on, a fairly sharp division between those doing routine tasks and those doing varied and involving tasks. As we discuss these various positions we must bear in mind that opposing tendencies exist in social reality as well as among various theories.

These considerations lend support to Goldthorpe and Lockwood's thesis of a convergence of the white collar and blue collar levels.[38] Many occupations, particularly technical occupations, are located in an uncertain border area. The spread of claims to professional status, and the fact that even many highly specialized technical jobs involve a measure of "manual" work, in addition to the consequences of automation outlined above have led to a marked blurring of the blue collar–white collar line. This blurring has been accelerated by the decline of a value system in which conspicuous leisure conferred more status than socially useful work.

Changes outside the work situation

There is general agreement among observers that the income gap between manual and nonmanual workers has narrowed in Western Europe and the United States in the postwar period.[39] Data are available for Italy for the years 1962–70 from a yearly salary survey of many of the largest Italian firms in both the public and the private sectors carried out by agreement among them for their own uses.[40] The sample contains no small firms at all. However, it is large enough (18,312 workers in 79 specific job categories in 145 firms) to give a good idea of the *relative* economic gains of the various occupational groups sampled. The average annual income of skilled blue collar workers increased 108.8 percent between 1962 and 1970, whereas that of low-grade white collar workers increased only 86.9 percent. The gains of higher-level white collar workers were even smaller. Overall, the gain for the blue collar categories averaged 105.8 percent, whereas that for the white collar categories averaged 75.6 percent. At the end of the period, there was a considerable amount of overlap between the top level of skilled workers and the lowest level of white collar workers. This overlap, together with the dramatic postwar increase in the absolute levels of income, has led to a homogenization of consumption.[41]

The migration from rural to urban areas and the explosion of school enrollments have contributed, along with the increasing income overlap, to a decline in the importance of the status distinction between blue collar and white collar workers.[42]

These and similar trends have been documented for most West European countries. It is in interpreting their significance that differences arise, and it is to these various interpretations that we now turn.

The postwar debate

Many of the postwar writings on the political roles of dependent workers followed along the paths laid out in prewar writings. Those who talked about the working class debated as to exactly how much improvement there had been in its situation. Those who looked at the situation of white collar workers took positions similar to the ones staked out by the German authors who had considered the question of proletarianization before the war. However, the postwar debate was different in that most writers based their arguments on more than changes in the relative economic situations of various groups. In particular, they emphasized the changes in the work situation and in the life patterns and social structure outside work which have been described.

Continuing the debate on the working class, numerous versions of the embourgeoisement theory were advanced throughout the fifties and early sixties. In support of these theories, many evoked the optimistic view of the consequences of automation. Outside the factory, the working class was seen as decomposing.[43] Then, in the middle and late sixties, several books and articles appeared which, taken together with the rise in strikes and unrest, suggested that perhaps the embourgeoisement theorists had been a little hasty in sounding the death knell for the labor movement. It was pointed out that substantial income differences still exist between blue collar and white collar workers; that, although blue collar workers buy the same consumer goods as white collar workers, the meaning of the pattern is different; and that the breakup of traditional communities does not lead to any immediate change in working class values.[44]

On the whole the critics of the embourgeoisement thesis did not propose alternative interpretations. The work of Goldthorpe and Lockwood and their collaborators was an exception. In their series on "the affluent worker" they suggested that the changes that have occurred in working class attitudes may best be described as the development of an "instrumental collectivism."[45] The affluent workers they studied in Britain tended to lead privatized lives centering around the nuclear family. Work was seen as a means to ends that could be realized after working hours. The union was seen as a means to the same ends. The authors concluded that, although significant differences between white collar and blue collar workers remained, there was a process of convergence in the normative orientations of the two groups. With the increasingly large size of bureaucratic units and reduced chances for upward mobility, white collar jobs were coming to resemble blue collar jobs, and white collar workers were resorting more frequently to collective action. Instrumental collectivism and "family-centeredness" were the central values in this convergence.

The major writers on the situation of the middle class in the postwar period seemed to agree that there was a convergence between white collar and blue collar workers, although there was less agreement on what it was they were converging toward. Of the four most important books published, two described a process of proletarianization which was rendering the job of the white collar worker more and more similar to that of the assembly-line worker; whereas the other two, relying on an optimistic appraisal of the consequences of automation and pointing to the increasing professionalization of the labor force, described a convergence at a higher level.[46] In view of the contradictory tendencies in the organization of work outlined above, this lack of consensus is hardly surprising.

The new working class thesis

All the writers discussed thus far have implicitly or explicitly assumed that absolute deprivation is what accounts for worker militancy. Those who saw a decline in the combativeness and political strength of the labor movement tended to ascribe this decline to improvements in various aspects of the workers' world. Those who did not see any secular trend in this direction or who argued that the embourgeoisement theorists had overstated their case marshaled evidence to show that the improvements had not occurred at all or were less substantial than was claimed. Similarly, for the case of the white collar worker, those who emphasized the increasing unionization of white collar workers pointed to proletarianization as the major reason for this development.

In discarding the absolute deprivation assumption, the new working class theorists broke fresh ground in the debate. These writers saw in the rapidly growing group of technicians and technically trained workers the vanguard of a new revolutionary movement. Serge Mallet gave the most influential statement of this point of view in his book *La nouvelle classe ouvrière* ("The New Working Class").[47] Mallet by and large accepted the analysis of changes in the advanced capitalist countries presented by the embourgeoisement theorists. However, the conclusions he drew were very different. Mallet emphasized the increasing skill and education of the labor force as did Blauner, Galbraith, and other proponents of the idea that labor was becoming less militant. He agreed with these authors that the jobs in advanced industries are usually more involving. But whereas the embourgeoisement theorists argued that the more satisfied worker is less militant, implicit in Mallet's discussion is the assumption that involvement in work leads to increasing involvement in other aspects of life as well. The worker of the new working class will, therefore, be moved to demand a say in all those decisions which affect him. This assumption is supported by research indicating that workers who are involved in their jobs acquire a greater sense of efficacy, their levels of aspiration rise, and they feel freer to give voice to whatever discontent they may feel about other aspects of their job situations.[48] Workers who are committed to their jobs, who are high in status and pay, and who are well integrated into the community are also more likely to participate in union activities.[49] Participation often means conflict. Peace and quiet may mean apathy and withdrawal rather than satisfaction.

Of course, peace and quiet are not always symptoms of alienation and repression. There is a considerable body of evidence to support the contention of the embourgeoisement theorists that involvement in work and the resulting satisfaction lead to integration and moderation.[50] Hackman and Lawler, for example, find that workers doing more interesting jobs tend to do higher quality work, and to be more highly motivated on the job and less often absent.[51] Studies of worker participation in decision making find that increased participation generally yields similar benefits. Survey research shows that skilled workers in most countries (with some notable exceptions) tend to be more moderate in their political orientations than the semiskilled and the unskilled.[52] The problem becomes one of specifying more precisely the conditions under which involvement leads to conflict or to integration.

Mallet agreed with those writers who saw a decline in labor militancy on other issues as well. He too noted that jobs in advanced industries often necessitate teamwork that develops a sense of community among workers. But, he asked, may not teamwork lead to the development of horizontal solidarity and an antimanagement subculture rather than to stronger solidary ties across vertical levels?

Mallet also noted the increased objective need for management to integrate the worker. Much money is often invested in the training of workers in advanced industries, making turnover relatively more costly. Workers may be entrusted with expensive equipment, and lack of commitment or the failure to accept responsibility can lead to grave damages to capital investment. But the delegation of responsibility signifies potential power, and it is not necessarily true that the worker who feels a sense of responsibility for his work feels equally responsible to management. Again, it is necessary to specify more precisely the conditions under which each of these contrasting hypotheses holds true.

The general notion underlying the new working class theories is that inconsistencies in a person's situation lead to attempts on the part of the individual to equalize his position on all the relevant dimensions. Three basic inconsistencies are cited. (1) The technician is skilled and educated, yet remains powerless to affect many of the conditions of his work situation. (2) The technician is in a strong bargaining position, yet has no institutionalized power, as just noted. (3) In social status the technician is close to his superiors, but he is far from them in terms of power. All three of these inconsistencies counterpose rank on the power or authority dimension with rank along some other dimension of stratification. This may explain why many of the demands expressed by the new working class have been power demands, that is, demands for control over work conditions.

Although some of the arguments just cited could be applied to other groups of white collar or skilled blue collar workers, a number of the points developed by the new working class theorists are particularly relevant to the technician considered as a quasi professional. The use of knowledge as power is a familiar theme in the literature on the professions. Those who control knowledge may often have power as a consequence. In other cases, the relationship is less direct: The possession of knowledge leads to a subjective feeling of security, of strength.

A second idea that the new working class theorists have adopted from the sociological literature on professions is the notion that the technician is oriented toward a body of knowledge and a peer group independent of the specific organization in which he works. This "cosmopolitan" attitude may have several consequences. To the extent that the technician's primary identification is not within his organization, he will identify less strongly with the company he works for. In this sense, his attitude may be very different from that of the stereotypical white collar worker. Furthermore, the fact of working within a body of scientific knowledge will make the technician less likely to accept authority based solely on position rather than on technical ability. The subculture of laboratories tends to be egalitarian. Considerations of status are less important than in an administrative bureaucracy. All of these themes are documented in the extensive literature on professionals in organizations, a research topic that received considerable attention during the fifties.

Mallet, Gorz (at least in the early sixties), Bologna and Ciafaloni, and others explain the militancy of technicians by a more abstract reasoning as well.[53] The common theme in these writings is the contradiction between the rationality of profit maximization and a higher rationality said to be implicit in scientific work. Like Marx, the new working class theorists look to the productive process to bring out the contradiction that will lead to the demise of capitalism. The technician "lives in the heart of the contradiction"[54] of capitalist society. He does not challenge industrial society as such nor does he hearken back to a golden age in which man was not dominated by the machine. He accepts the machine, carrying the rationality it imposes to its conclusion.

In taking this position, the new working class theorists differ from

Marcuse and Habermas,[55] who see science and technology as the very basis of legitimation of the capitalist system. For them, the students in the social sciences and humanities, that very same marginal group which Mallet dismisses as reactionary in its emphasis on aproductiveness, are the only possible agents of radical change.

There is one other body of writings on the new working class that takes a somewhat different approach from that of Mallet. This is the view espoused by many of the new working class militants themselves and by the Italian Communist Party, and it has become a cliché in the press of the Italian left.[56] The constant theme in these writings is the proletarianization of the technician. The international division of labor (whereby advanced research is done in the most advanced countries and the most routine and repetitive jobs are relegated to the underdeveloped countries, with various intermediate steps along the way), the rationalizing tendencies of organizational design under capitalism, and the subjection of science to profit maximization are seen as the root causes of the deteriorating position of the technician.

In stressing the worsening work conditions of technicians, many of the Italian commentators on this subject (and many of the French writers as well, e.g., Roger Garaudy) implicitly disagree with Mallet and Gorz, who emphasize the relative autonomy of the new working class at the workplace.[57] In part this difference is only a matter of different comparison groups. Mallet refers to a blue collar new working class and compares its situation to that of other blue collar workers, whereas Italian authors compare the conditions of the white collar technician today with those of his counterpart some years ago. Both Mallet and Gorz, on the one hand, and the Italian new working class militants, on the other, refer to contradictions within the new working class situation. But for the Italian militants, the most frequently cited contradiction is between the amount of education and skill possessed by the individual and the confining character of his job. Their position is basically similar to that of Mills and Lockwood cited earlier: They see the job of the white collar worker as becoming more and more similar to that of the assembly-line worker. For Mallet and Gorz, the contradiction is between a job which is involving and an organizational structure that places very narrow limits on this involvement. Their emphasis is less on the lack of fit between worker and job, and more on inconsistencies within the job situation itself.

It is not necessary to affirm that the one interpretation is correct and the other is wrong, for, as was pointed out above, they may simply apply to different situations. Some jobs are increasingly subject to routinization, bureaucratization, in a word, to proletarianization, but the number of varied, involving, relatively unstructured jobs is also increasing. In the concluding chapter, we propose a typology specifying more precisely to which jobs each of these interpretations applies. However, it should be noted that, whereas Gorz and Mallet have proposed a new interpretation of certain work situations, the proletarianization thesis is not substantially different from what orthodox Marxists have been saying about white collar workers since before World War II. It might also be noted that to the extent that the proletarianization thesis is correct, one might as well predict conservative movements as progressive ones.

The difference between these two approaches directs attention to another distinctive characteristic of the new working class thesis in addition to the emphasis on relative deprivation, namely its casual disregard for the blue collar–white collar division. Mallet nowhere defines the new working class precisely. Furthermore, his use of the term changes from the first edition of his book (1963) to the fourth edition (1969). But his examples make clear that he is referring to workers with professional training employed in the advanced sectors of the economy, particularly the electronics and chemical industries. This group includes white collar technicians as well as blue collar workers with some technical training.[58] Yet his discussion makes reference only to the debate on the working class, not to that on the middle class. Gorz does not use the term "new working class," but he too situates his early discussion of technicians in the context of the debate on the working class. By contrast, Garaudy and the Italian writers refer to a white collar context, although the range of jobs they consider is overlapping.

The failure to deal explicitly with the blue collar–white collar distinction reflects the lack of salience of this issue to the subordinate levels of technicians. The two strands of the debate on the working class are thus reunited. But, as we shall see, the issue has been picked up once again by some of the critics of the new working class thesis.

The idea that technicians might constitute a revolutionary vanguard did not arise from armchair speculations about possible strains and contradictions. Both in Italy and in France, the flood of journalistic and political writings on the new working class and on the militancy of white collar workers was triggered by certain new kinds of struggles that took place beginning around 1959 in France and somewhat later in Italy.

In the early seventies, technicians were displaced from the political limelight by young, semiskilled workers, often immigrants from rural areas. These became the most militant actors in the French and Italian labor movements, leading to a critical reevaluation of the new working class thesis.

From the Marxist perspective, the critics urged a closer look at the nature of technological development and the role of technicians in the division of labor. Gorz himself changed his position. In an article published in 1971, he argued that technology does not follow an objectively determined course of development; it is influenced by the system within which this development takes place. It is the job of some technicians to remove the intellectual component from a task so that the remaining manual part can be performed by a semiskilled worker. Others benefit less directly from the division between manual and mental labor. The position of the technician in the division of labor limits his solidarity with the working class, giving his demands an ambiguous character.[59]

Non-Marxists, such as Jean Daniel Reynaud, formulated their criticisms more empirically. Reynaud made three major points.

1. The new working class thesis is overly mechanistic in its assumption that technology determines the nature of jobs, which in turn determines worker consciousness. The second point follows closely from the first.

2. Referring to recent research on technicians, engineers, and *cadres* (a French title given to middle and upper-middle management, including engineers, line managers above the level of foreman, and upper-level white collar workers) in France, Reynaud noted the complexities of individual and group strategies within the firm, the differences between groups according to their particular jobs and the personnel policies of particular companies, and the ambiguity of the positions taken by the *cadres*. While admitting that technicians appear to be more dissatisfied than *cadres,* he argued that this dissatisfaction arises exclusively from blocked mobility aspirations and that the primary reference group for technicians is the *cadres* above them rather than the manual workers below them. To Reynaud, the variations in militancy within the new working class can better be explained in terms of the narrow interests and strategies of particular groups within organizations than in terms of the general concept of class struggle.

3. Reynaud's third point provides the ground for the entire critique of the new working class thesis. "While the most skilled categories [i.e., the new working class] might have appeared as the most combative in the early sixties, it is the appearance of conflicts among the semiskilled which has characterized the early seventies. . . . It is the economically and technologically backward sectors which are taking first place. The initiative is with expansion's rejects and no longer with its champions."[60]

In the last chapter, we shall take up the various critiques again, looking at them in the light of recent French research and of our own data. Anticipating a little, we can say that the critics have given a needed corrective to Mallet's notion of the new working class as a revolutionary vanguard, but on a number of points they have gone too far. As with so many controversies in the social sciences, an extreme initial position leads to an extreme reaction, whereas reality lies somewhere in between.

The argument to this point has disregarded the differences between Italy and other societies in their general patterns of development. Yet the last few pages have suggested the impossibility of evaluating a thesis such as the new working class thesis without looking more closely at the broader historical and political context within which individual attitudes and behaviors are shaped. Why did Italy and France see a resurgence of worker militancy and Marxist theory in the past fifteen years? What were the particular circumstances leading to new kinds of struggles? In the following chapter we look at the Italian context in some detail, compare it to the French situation, and describe the new working class struggles in Italy.

2. The new working class in Italian society

It was no accident that the new working class thesis and its variants were first formulated and first gained wide currency in France and Italy. We must be critical of those analyses of postindustrial or neocapitalist society which, while pointing to similar trends in all such societies, fail to appreciate the importance of the particular political traditions and the alignments of social forces in each country. Similar trends may evolve into quite different realities in different contexts.

The proponents of the new working class thesis present it as a general one, presumably applicable to all advanced capitalist societies. But even after the recent revival of Marxism, the term "revolutionary vanguard" sounds quaint in most of these societies. Their political and labor traditions are very different from those of Italy and France. The inapplicability of the thesis in the most affluent capitalist societies is troublesome, especially as the thesis pertains specifically to affluent workers.

The peculiarities of the situation in which new working class militancy arose and grew demand our attention. In this chapter, we place new working class militancy in the context of the vicissitudes of Italian society. The Italian and French situations are compared. Explanations are suggested both for the common experiences of new working class militancy and for the subsidence of that militancy in France after 1968 as opposed to its continuation in Italy. The Italian situation is then discussed in greater detail and the new working class strikes there are described.

This chapter is not intended to negate the previous discussion by implying that the new working class thesis is only of interest to students of contemporary Italy and France. The thesis itself has a more general interest. We have already noted its theoretical importance in explaining militancy among workers who are relatively affluent and satisfied with their jobs. We also pointed out the themes of power and control underlying new working class theories. A theory purporting to explain in

23

general terms the centrality of these themes to the protest movements of our time has a prima facie claim to our attention. Although the broader political generalizations of the theory may not be relevant in other countries, discussions of changes in the work situation and the effects of such changes on workers' orientations apply more widely. An empirical study of the new working class may thus contribute to our understanding of the growing white collar unionism in the advanced countries and the related emergence of demands for control and participation.

Italy and France: similarities and differences

Recent developments in Portugal and Spain aside, the labor movements of Italy and France alone among European labor movements have shown evidence of a potential for mobilization around broad political issues centered in the workplace.

The persistence of the radical leftist tradition in these countries must be explained by the particularities of their historical development. Some theorists would link left-wing politics to underdevelopment. But it is absurd to call France, or even Italy, backward in relation to the rest of the world today. A more valid approach stresses the historical unevenness of French and Italian development rather than its backwardness.[1] According to this view, variants of which by now enjoy fairly wide acceptance among Marxists and non-Marxists alike, the continued importance of sectors of the preindustrial elite (particularly large landowners and the church) and the weakness of the industrial bourgeoisie led to a polarization and a radicalization of the struggle, first between the bourgeoisie and traditional elites and, subsequently, between the working class and a coalition of traditional and modernizing elites.

Lipset and Rokkan have given a schematic formal outline of the development of such cleavage structures. In Southern Europe, the Counter-Reformation tied the church to the preindustrial elites. This alliance opposed the nation-building elite and the nascent bourgeoisie. The result was a "polarization of politics between a national-radical-secular movement and a Catholic-traditionalist one."[2] The continuation in power of old elites and the split between old and new elites gave rise to the radical opposition of the bourgeoisie and later of the proletariat. The initial weakness of the bourgeoisie eventually led it into uneasy alliances with the traditional elites it had once opposed, strengthening the positions of the latter in the political system and allowing them to adapt to changing conditions so as to maintain these positions only slightly eroded by the economic transformations going on around them.

Cleavages whose origins may be traced back several hundred years have proved remarkably stable. A radical-secular movement is still pitted against a Catholic-traditionalist one. The basic party structures coalesced with the extension of the suffrage and the accompanying political mobilization. As Lipset and Rokkan point out, even where the organizational embodiment of the political alternatives has changed, "the continuities in the alternatives are as striking as the disruptions in their organizational expressions."[3]

If new movements tend to be assimilated into the existing political configurations, it is not surprising that new movements among workers in France and Italy should assume a radical leftist position, whereas similar movements in other countries, for example in the United States, assume quite different political coloration or no political coloration at all.

The similarities between France and Italy serve to highlight the differences both in the political environments of the two countries and in their social and economic situations. Because of these differences, the dramatic Events of May 1968 in France subsided as suddenly as they had broken out, while the mobilization of Italian workers in 1968–69 has proved more lasting. France too has seen changes in the quality and quantity of industrial action in recent years, but these changes have not been of the same magnitude as those in Italy. Carried forward by the organizations of the left (both parties and trade unions) and institutionalized through new structures of representation at the plant level (the Works Councils), the thrust of the Italian mobilization has continued despite the weakness of the economy in the subsequent years.

A number of reasons may be given for the different courses taken by events in Italy and France in the years since 1968.[4] Starting from a much lower level of development after World War II, the rate of growth of the Italian economy has been more rapid. A mass migration of workers from the South to the North and a precipitous decline in the agricultural labor force have been the partially unintended consequences of this rapid growth. Regional inequalities, always greater in Italy than in France, have if anything increased. In France, employment in industry has expanded more slowly. Many of the new jobs have been filled by immigrant workers from Algeria or other foreign countries who are unlikely to be militant and who tend to divide the working class. Italy, in comparison to France, has experienced greater changes and dislocations of the type that have often been pointed to as sources of relative deprivation and unrest.

Perhaps even more important in explaining the differences between France and Italy are the differences between the left forces in the two countries. These forces include the Communist parties, the Socialist and Catholic left, and the trade union federations associated with these three political groupings.

Unlike the French Communist Party (the PCF), the Italian Communist Party (the PCI) emerged from over twenty years of opposition to Fascism untainted by the Hitler–Stalin Pact, closely allied to the Socialist Party, and the undisputed leader of the long and heroic resistance against the Nazis. Geographically, support for the PCI was more evenly distributed than for the PCF. Whereas the PCI was able to gain power on the local level in several areas of Northern and Central Italy, the PCF was never allowed to establish the same kind of power base in the Paris region where most of its support was concentrated. The strong moral leadership of the PCI, its local commitments, and its closeness to the Socialist Party have contributed to the development of a Communist Party uniquely Italian in its autonomy vis-à-vis the Soviet Union, its openness, its flexibility, and its strong rejection of Stalinism.

The presence in Italy of such a Communist Party, anxious to increase its chances of coming to power with the support of the Catholic left, was one of the elements facilitating remarkable changes in the trade union movement. As a result of the cold war, both the Italian and the French labor movements had been split into three competing union confederations, with roots in the Catholic left, the secular anticommunist left, and the Communist left, respectively. But whereas the French union confederations remained divided and linked to the political parties [with the partial exception of the Confédération Française Démocratique du Travail (CFDT)], the Italian unions began a process of reunification and simultaneously of separation from the political parties. This process, described in greater detail in the following sections, had gained momentum by 1968, so that the union structures were strong and flexible enough to transmit the waves of demands and protests.

A final point of difference is the instability of the Italian government and its seeming, though perhaps not real, susceptibility to pressure from a mobilized labor movement.

The continued militancy and development of the labor movement in Italy made it a particularly likely setting for empirical research on the new working class.[5]

The Italian context

The new working class thesis describes an increasingly militant labor movement within a capitalist society that has met the basic economic needs of the great majority of its members. It may seem ironic that this position should prove to be most applicable to the society where the orthodox Marxist prediction of the economic collapse of capitalism appears closest to fulfillment. But the Italian economic and political crisis does not exemplify Marx's prediction. Per capita income remains higher than it has ever been before. The crisis is, to a large extent, a politically determined one. It is a crisis in which the militancy of the working class (both "old" and "new") has played an important part. Finally, it is a crisis of arrested development, not of mature development. Such a scenario is not inconsistent with the analyses of the new working class theorists.

The Italian system is faced with the problems of advanced capitalism without having resolved satisfactorily the problems of industrialization and the creation of the welfare state. The new working class thesis focuses on the problems of advanced capitalism as they impinge upon unevenly developed societies.

In the following sections we consider the recent changes in industrial relations, the new militancy of the labor movement, and the economic and political crisis of the last few years. Finally, we describe the new working class strikes. Because much of the following discussion is about Italy's crisis, it is appropriate to preface it by pointing out those respects in which Italy is an advanced capitalist society and the forms in which the problems characteristic of such societies have emerged there.

Problems of advanced capitalism

Figures on per capita income provide a summary measure of the overall level of well-being. They show that between 1951, when per capita income regained the prewar level, and 1970 real per capita income increased by 244.7 percent.[6] This growth rate was higher than those for all other advanced capitalist nations except Japan and West Germany.

At the end of this period, Italy's per capita income was still one of the lowest in this group, but the margin had narrowed with respect to most. In 1970, per capita income (in 1963 U.S. dollars) was $1,304. The comparable figures for a few other industrialized nations were as follows: Japan, $1,385; United Kingdom, $1,594; France, $2,162; West Germany, $2,409; United States, $3,836.[7] Although per capita income was still only one-third that of the United States, it was not far below that of Japan or the United Kingdom. Northern Italy, with per capita income levels more than double those of the South, is today above the Common Market average.

This rise in standards of living has brought with it some of the characteristic structural and ideological problems of advanced capitalist societies. One of the structural problems is the compartmentalization, or balkanization, of the labor market.[8] Unemployment among certain groups coexists with full employment among others. In Italy, this has been the case since the late sixties. Unemployment remains low among men between the ages of 25 and 45, while other groups are pushed out of the labor force. Unions are able to maintain pressure on employers despite an overall increase in the level of unemployment.

Massimo Paci has described the labor market under advanced capitalism as divided into three relatively separate compartments: the marginal labor market; the large-firm, blue collar labor market; and the white collar, "intellectual" labor market.[9] The first two correspond to what U.S. researchers have called the secondary and the primary labor markets, respectively.[10] Jobs in the primary labor market are usually unionized, relatively well paid, secure, and with some chances for promotion. Firms are large and productivity is high. Jobs in the secondary market are badly paid, often temporary, with no chances for promotion. Firms are small with low productivity. Some are independent, but many are linked to the large corporations as suppliers, subcontractors, and sales or service organizations. In Italy, a larger portion of the secondary market consists of small firms in traditional types of production and marginal services. There is also a rebirth of extralegal cottage industries as the large corporations' attempt to cut their labor costs by decreasing the number of workers listed on their payrolls, thereby decreasing their contributions to welfare programs.

The third labor market, that for intellectual labor, is of particular interest to us here.[11] The changing educational composition of the labor force was outlined in Chapter 1. Although the demand for white collar workers and technicians has grown rapidly, school enrollments have expanded even more rapidly. This expansion was facilitated by laws creating a single-track "middle school" (roughly equivalent to the U.S. junior high school) and liberalizing access to the university. Between 1954 and 1971, the number of graduates from secondary schools increased more than fourfold, reaching 312,000 in the latter year. The number of graduates from technical secondary schools increased nearly tenfold during this same period, from 3,620 graduates in 1954 to 35,635 graduates in 1971. The annual number of university graduates began its steep climb a few years later, going from 24,000 in 1963 to 60,000 in 1971.[12]

For the first time, large numbers of children of the lower classes entered the higher levels of the educational system. The expansion in school enrollments has been spurred by the changing requirements of the economy, by the increasing incomes of the parents, and by the legal changes just noted. However, Marzio Barbagli has shown that unemployment too has caused youths to postpone their entry into the labor market. This hypothesis is supported by analyses over time as well as by comparisons between provinces. Whereas the most developed provinces have higher percentages of the relevant age groups in elementary school, the least developed provinces have higher percentages going on to secondary school and university. As Barbagli says, the trends in enrollments in both secondary schools and universities may be explained as "the singular and contradictory result of economic expansion and crisis, of increased per capita income and declining employment of youth, of the mobility aspirations of the lower classes and the fears of downward mobility of old and new middle strata."[13]

Barbagli documents the improvement of the labor market position of university and secondary school graduates up to 1963 and its gradual worsening thereafter. Although the excess of supply over demand is particularly great for secondary school graduates (a category that includes technicians), much of this excess is rendered invisible as more and more secondary school graduates continue on to the university. So far, university graduates have not experienced a major decline in their positions, but this decline is not too far off if present trends continue.

In Paci's view, the worsening of the labor market situation of intellectual workers and the further development of the separate labor market of the marginally employed are characteristic of advanced capitalism. Employment in industry stops growing as productivity is increased through investment in labor-saving machinery. Growth in employment is confined primarily to the service sector. The balkanized labor market not only impedes certain workers in getting jobs, but also enables other sectors to maintain their bargaining power in spite of high unemployment.

Clearly, there are many parallels to the United States, where the dual labor market thesis was first formulated and where unemployment and underemployment of highly educated labor as well as of marginal labor are increasingly visible.

It is difficult to predict the effect of the excess of supply over demand on the militancy of educated labor. Technicians may be forced to take jobs below their customary levels of employment. This would be likely to lead to greater militancy. Considerable unemployment would not necessarily reduce their bargaining power.[14]

Even in the late sixties, when new working class militancy was most visible in Italy, the labor market situation was not favorable to technicians.[15] In fact, the "stickiness" of the market in this area is such that an excess of supply is unlikely to reduce the bargaining power of technicians significantly, particularly so long as demand is increasing. Stickiness results from the costs invested in training workers in the very specialized industries where technicians are employed as well as from the legal difficulties in firing workers for union activity. As we shall see, the technicians themselves are optimistic about finding another job once they have some work experience.

Another problem area for the advanced capitalist societies has been the realm of values. The development of mass education and the growth in absolute standards of living together with the persistence of social inequality has led to a questioning of the value systems of these societies. Focus has moved away from possession of resources to distribution of resources. Among the resources whose unequal distribution is challenged are power, money, and jobs themselves. The student movement and the militancy of the new working class and young semiskilled workers express this challenge to the value system in Italy. In the United States, the hippie movement and the rising crime rate were less articulate expressions of the same challenge, which also received a more explicit, although short-lived, political formulation in the protest movements of blacks and students.

The growth of rank-and-file labor militancy is common to many of the advanced capitalist nations. It reflects the increased willingness of all groups to organize and to press their claims through direct action. The greater visibility of the hand of the state and of nonmarket mechanisms in allocating resources has created counterparts against which claims can be pressed. The questioning of legitimizing values has played its part, as have the changes in labor markets just described. Although the new militancy of the Italian labor movement appeared to come suddenly, it was the extension of a number of changes in the system of industrial relations beginning in the early sixties.

Changes in industrial relations

There are three labor union confederations in Italy, corresponding to the three major political groupings. The largest of these is the Italian General Confederation of Labor (CGIL), linked to the Marxist left, that is, the Communist and Socialist parties. Somewhat smaller is the Italian Confederation of Labor Unions (CISL), originating in the Catholic left and formerly tied to the Christian Democratic Party. The third confederation, the Italian Union of Labor (UIL), is much smaller than the other two, and is associated with the non-Marxist lay parties of the moderate left, namely the Social Democrats, the Republicans, and elements of the Socialist Party.

Three major changes occurred within the labor movement during the 1960s: Collective bargaining was decentralized, so that plant-level bargaining came to supplement the industrywide national contracts; the union confederations, formerly hostile and competitive, began first to act together and then to take concrete steps toward merging their organizations; and the unions began to sever their formal ties to the political parties. These changes have been accompanied by a growth in the strength of the Italian unions, now a major political as well as industrial force, negotiating directly with the government over reforms in the areas of pensions, housing, health care, taxation, and economic policy, and prodding and challenging the political parties.[16]

The new working class theorists have pointed out one cause of the decentralization of collective bargaining in many countries during the sixties. The increasing technological sophistication of production processes and the tightening of labor markets in the early sixties made the costs of labor turnover very great. Integration of the worker into the firm became a necessity from management's point of view and a fact, rather than a paternalistic gesture, from the worker's point of view.

Thus the worker acquired greater power on the shop floor. Both management and labor became interested in productivity and, hence, in investment policy, planning, and the organization of production within the firm. These were issues that could not be addressed in centralized bargaining.

At the same time, the thaw in U.S.–Soviet relations made political changes possible. The right wing of the Christian Democratic Party lost some of its influence, the Socialist Party began to drift toward its alliance with the Christian Democrats, and the Vatican under John XXIII moderated its anticommunism. The Communist Party, interested in stimulating ever-broader alliances on the left and confident of its own organizational strength, was willing to see the "transmission belt" relationship between party and union modified.

The Socialist Party's entry into the governing coalition in 1963 proved a decisive factor in loosening the unions' ties to parties. The largest union confederation, the CGIL, could not continue to operate as the transmission belt of the Communist Party when it was also linked to the Socialist Party. The new coalition formula and the Communists' desire to maintain their good relationship with the Socialists implied the attenuation of the ties between the confederation and the parties. Rank-and-file pressure also led toward greater autonomy. In 1969, the CGIL Congress formally sanctioned the autonomy of the union by establishing the principle that union leaders could not hold party offices above the lowest levels.

Equally important were the changes at the rank-and-file level discussed below. Militancy grew fitfully throughout the sixties, culminating in the famous Hot Autumn strike wave of 1969. The new level of militancy was consolidated through the creation of broad structures of union representation within the factory, the Works Councils. Young workers had little patience with ideological scissions dating back to the cold war. Within the CISL, the young activists became disenchanted with the Christian Democratic Party. They were ex-Catholics, now extreme leftists, educated in a tradition of American business unionism now transmuted into a kind of syndicalism. Under pressure from these activists, the CISL broke its ties with the Christian Democratic Party in 1969.

The Italian labor movement has been transformed since the fifties. Unity at the base level, autonomy from political parties, and decentralization of bargaining have been accompanied by a revitalization of top-level leadership and a mobilization of the base in support of reforms and an economic policy capable of reducing unemployment and developing the South. Despite the difficulty of the present economic situation, the unions have largely been able to maintain their newly acquired strength.

The new militancy

The new militancy of both blue collar and white collar workers was noteworthy not only in contrast to the years of relative industrial peace in the fifties, but also because of its new tactics and content. Demands were typically egalitarian in seeking to reduce the wage differences among skill levels. They frequently challenged the supposedly objective dictates of technology and the existing organization of work. New tactics included widespread use of "checkerboard strikes" (strikes in which each workshop within the plant goes on strike for a different period during the day), dramatic appeals to public opinion, blockades, and demonstrations.

How is this new militancy to be explained? Two elements common to many European countries have been noted: technological changes that give greater power to the worker and the tightening of the labor market, which has the same effect. But there are also elements peculiar to Italy, or at least more important in Italy than elsewhere.

A number of observers have pointed to the prominence of young workers and immigrants from the South among the militant. The immigration of large numbers of workers from depressed rural areas to a small area around Milan and Turin and the rapid growth of industry during the period of the "economic miracle" (i.e., the postwar years up to 1963) led to a demographic change in the labor force. Alessandro Pizzorno has hypothesized that the mass of new workers who entered the industrial plants of Northern Italy during these years were not socialized as to the modalities and limits of union action.[17]

The cost of living for the working class, and especially for the immigrants, was increased by the inadequacy of publicly supplied means for the satisfaction of basic needs in the areas of housing, health, and other social services.

The unions' gains in the 1963 contract led to a substantial increase in labor costs in manufacturing. Employers reacted by increasing labor productivity, not through investment in new machinery, but through rationalization of production, placing greater pressure on their employees. In 1968, the cost of labor actually went down 4 percent.[18] In 1969, when the metalworkers' contract expired once again, the upturn in the economy put labor in a strong position. (The metalworkers' unions organize white collar and blue collar workers in most of manufacturing.) The stage was set for the Hot Autumn.

The student movement was an important influence on the ideological content of worker militancy. There was a considerable amount of contact between workers and students, and among white collar workers there were many who had themselves been active in the student movement. Technicians and other new working class elements conducted some of the most creative strikes of these years.

In Northern Italy in the 1960s, the contradictions of advanced capitalism, which spawned the student movement, reinforced the contradictions of an earlier phase of growth of mass production industry and migration from rural areas. The resulting social movement fused a demand for a decent standard of living outside the plant with a demand for power within the plant and a rebellion against bureaucratic rationalization and the constraints of mass production technology.

The economic and political crisis

The period since 1969 has been characterized by the continued strength of the labor movement, together with continued stagflation and political crisis. Stagflation and crisis are the results of the inability of political and economic elites to overcome the contradictions of a dual economy and to respond to the universally recognized needs for reforms in the areas of public administration, health care, and public housing, for expanded employment at living wages, and for the rationalization of agricultural production and distribution.

The outlines of Italy's crisis are emerging from the intellectual debate over its causes and possible remedies.[19] A full discussion would be a book in itself. Here we can only list the most important aspects. Some are obviously prior to or more important than others, but they are so intertwined that our listing cannot follow any strict temporal or logical sequence. The aspects we will touch upon are (1) the dualism of the Italian economy, (2) the orientation of the advanced sectors of the economy toward exports, (3) the deflationary monetary policies of the Bank of Italy, (4) the decline in the percentage of the population in the (legal) labor force, (5) the excessive growth of the tertiary in certain directions dictated by the political needs of the Christian Democratic Party, and (6) the militancy of the labor movement.

1. The dualism of the Italian economy is the root cause of many of the other problems of Italian society. This dualism is first and foremost a regional phenomenon. Per capita income in the South (including Sardinia) was only 62.7 percent of the national average in 1970, whereas per capita income in the Northwest was 143.3 percent of the national average.[20]

There is also another kind of dualism, partially overlapping with regional dualism, dividing the economy into a high-productivity, capital-intensive, high-wage sector oriented toward the export market and a low-productivity, small-scale, low-wage sector producing for the domestic market, or, in some instances, as suppliers for the large firms. The growth process has accentuated rather than diminished these forms of dualism over the last twenty years.[21]

2. Augusto Graziani has developed a model of export-led growth to suggest how Italy's economic dualism has worsened with development. The dynamic export-oriented sector of Italian industry has become specialized in the areas of consumer durables and, to a lesser extent, investment goods, whereas other sectors, most importantly the food industry and traditional agriculture, have remained backward and inefficient. In order to meet international competition, the advanced sector increased productivity through capital investment, leading to little growth in employment in this sector.[22] Meanwhile the sector producing for the domestic market, where demand was relatively low and foreign competition was less pressing, grew increasingly backward.

3. The dependence of the advanced sector on exports has meant opposition of this sector to expansionary monetary and fiscal policies and greater concern with wages as costs rather than as income leading to consumer demand.

Gordon Ackley has pointed out that there were other reasons as well for the generally cautious monetary policy of the Bank of Italy and the complete absence of fiscal policy designed to offset the business cycle.[23] Expansionary policies along Keynesian lines are possible only if the economy is able to respond to a general increase in demand. There must not be bottlenecks in certain industries. If demand should outstrip supply in a given sector, there must be ways in which new resources can enter that sector. These conditions have never existed in Italy. There are rigidities on the supply side in large industries controlled by cartels as well as in small-scale industry and in agriculture. An increase in aggregate demand under these circumstances would have led to inflation, increased imports, and the sacrificing of the more inflexible and backward industries. In addition, the labor market would have tightened further, leading to increased worker militancy and higher wage costs. These were consequences no postwar Italian government could contemplate.

4. Official statistics show a decline in the number of jobs in the Italian economy since 1963. The percentage of the population in the labor force (i.e., either working or looking for work) also has gone down, from 42.1 percent in 1962 to 35.9 percent in 1972. This is one of the lowest activity rates in Europe. Comparable figures for other countries for the same year are France, 42.1 percent; West Germany, 43.3 percent; Japan, 48.9 percent; and the United States, 42.6 percent.[24]

Although there has been a slight increase in employment in industry, it has not been sufficient to compensate for the exodus of labor from agriculture. Despite the low activity rate, the labor market for men between the ages of 25 and 40 remains favorable to the worker. Those who are expelled from the labor force tend to be women, the very young, and the old. Many young men, unable to find jobs, are taking advantage of the educational reforms liberalizing access to university and secondary education by staying in school. This is one of the causes of the explosion in enrollments noted earlier.

Very recent research indicates the existence of a large extralegal labor force conservatively estimated at well over 2,000,000 workers.[25] If these are included, the percentage of the population that is active goes up to between 40 and 47 percent. Although other advanced countries also have clandestine workers, the evidence suggests that in Italy this phenomenon is far more widespread than elsewhere. The reasons are not hard to find. Although the productivity of labor is considerably lower than in most other European countries, the costs of legal labor are about equally high. These high labor costs can be attributed to the strength of the unions in collective bargaining as well as to Italy's tax system. Almost all social welfare programs are financed through payroll taxes. The price of welfare benefits is, therefore, paid entirely by workers and employers, giving both, but especially the latter, a strong incentive to extralegal employment.

The extralegal labor force consists primarily of housewives working at home, young people, and old-age pensioners. These workers pay no taxes, but they are completely unprotected against exploitation of all sorts. A distortion is also introduced into the economy as a whole, because employers who take advantage of this type of labor face strong financial and legal disincentives against upgrading jobs or increasing productivity.

5. Although the growth of the white collar categories and the tertiary is generally a response to the expanded functions of public and private bureaucracies and the rising demand for services, in the Italian case such growth has been further stimulated by what may broadly be termed political considerations. This has occurred through two mechanisms. First, the Christian Democratic Party, in power continuously since World War II, has placed people on the public payrolls in response to pressures from numerous clientele groups within the party, all seeking to do favors for supporters or potential supporters in need of jobs. While it is difficult to estimate the extent to which such practices have inflated the public administration above and beyond the functional requirements, it is common knowledge and has been confirmed by a number of studies that these practices occur.[26]

A second mechanism leading to the inflation of the tertiary has been the support given by the government to small businesses through tax breaks and other concessions. Suzanne Berger has outlined how such support not only provides votes for the Christian Democrats, but also serves as a "shock-absorbing" sector, dampening the jolts of unemployment in large-scale manufacturing during cyclical downturns and thus mitigating the effects of the inadequacy of the welfare system.[27]

The politically motivated inflation of the tertiary has created large interest groups opposed to rationalizing reforms of their domains. Paolo Sylos-Labini argues that the petite bourgeoisie has constituted a barrier to reforms in many areas where the advanced industrial bourgeoisie is now anxious to see these reforms enacted. In this area, Italian government policy has been weaker than French policy under Gaullism, which was oriented toward big business and rationalization above all.[28]

6. Worker militancy has been both a cause and a consequence of the crisis. It has been a consequence insofar as the government's inability to enact reforms has raised the cost of living for all wage earners, and especially for immigrants from the South to the industrial North. This has led workers to demand higher wages than they might have otherwise and to strike for reforms as well.

Militancy has been a cause of the crisis in that the very high rate of strike activity (the highest among the industrialized countries in the years following 1969) has forced an extremely rapid increase in labor costs. The labor movement has placed the political and economic system under constant pressure since 1969.

A debate has been carried on in the Italian mass media since 1969 as to whether the labor movement is to blame for the crisis. Casting all blame on the labor movement ignores the factors leading up to the present situation and the possible solutions that the government has been unable or unwilling to implement. It also ignores the effects of attempts by the major employers' organizations and the government to break the unions through needlessly tough stands in collective bargaining (particularly in the national metalworkers' contract in 1972) and through the use of instruments of economic policy. These tactics had proved adequate to deal with the militancy of 1963, but were no longer adequate to quell the stronger wave of militancy of 1969 and its subsequent institutionalization in the Works Councils. A meaningful response to some of the substantive demands of the labor movement would now appear to be necessary.

Although the militancy of the labor movement has been among the proximate causes of the present crisis, the mediate cause is the inability of the government to set Italy upon a different course of development, to overcome the crippling dualism of North and South, and to enact basic reforms. Italy's crisis is not the inevitable outcome of capitalist development, but the result of particular political and economic choices made under particular historical circumstances.

New working class struggles

Some of the new working class struggles in France have been described by Mallet and others.[29] We shall concern ourselves only with the Italian situation here. In Italy, certain groups of white collar workers had been unionized for some time, although their organizations were not closely tied to the labor movement. In the sixties, for the first time, white collar workers in the private sector began to participate in strikes without promptings from blue collar pickets. In a few clamorous cases, such as that of the Olivetti computer labs, the workers – engineers, technicians, and blue collar workers – mobilized to demand an alternative course for the enterprise to that which top management had in mind.

In 1968, amid the atmosphere of increasing militancy of various groups, white collar workers first began to strike in large numbers. Technicians were prominent in all the white collar strikes. The most notable of these struggles occurred in companies in the advanced sectors that employed predominantly technically trained labor: companies such as SNAM Progetti (oil prospecting, drilling, design and construction of oil refineries and chemical plants); Italimpianti (design and construction of steel mills); SIT Siemens (telephone and telecommunications equipment); Selenia (electronic equipment); and some of the installations of the CNEN (National Committee for Nuclear Energy).

In these struggles, as in the struggles in the mass production industries, new demands were voiced and new tactics were devised. There was an air of creativity and boldness that seemed to surprise even the protagonists and rekindled a new enthusiasm in all those who had watched with sad pessimism the travail of the labor movement in the preceding years.

In the fall of 1968, with the failure of the unions' attempt to negotiate over the introduction of a job evaluation scheme and over salary increases, the engineers, technicians, and blue collar workers of SNAM Progetti went on strike. What was unusual about this strike, apart from the effervescence of theoretical and ideological statements that accompanied it, was its procedural aspect: All decisions were made by the employees gathered in a Permanent Assembly in one of the company buildings. The Assembly lasted for ten days. The company quickly dropped its job evaluation scheme. The remaining demands of the workers were (a) equal fringe benefits for blue collar and white collar workers; (b) reduction of the work week to forty hours; (c) pay increases; (d) institution of internal training courses and special privileges for workers going to night school. These demands seem rather modest, particularly when compared to the rhetoric of the Permanent Assembly. Nonetheless, very little was obtained. As in many of the subsequent cases, management was able to divide the workers by offering concessions on pay while remaining inflexible on the more "political" demands regarding control over the workplace.

A few of the later struggles were more successful. In 1971, for example, after six months of struggle, the workers of the Selenia electronics company in Rome obtained (a) study time to be set aside during work hours for those attending night school; (b) a promise to "eliminate" the semiskilled jobs and to promote their present occupants; (c) equalization of fringe benefits between blue collar and white collar workers; (d) pay increases inversely proportional to present pay. Here too original tactics were developed: "counterpickets," not letting out for some time those workers who persisted in doing overtime during this period when overtime was banned by the unions; a blockade of outgoing goods; checkerboard strikes; and control of the struggle through assemblies of all the workers.

The more flamboyant struggles occurred in cases where there was no existing union organization. In these companies there was often a backlog of grievances. The strike leadership tended to be heavily influenced by the student movement and various political groups to the left of the Communist Party.

Often too, the more notable cases of new working class unrest followed histories of mismanagement. Thus, at Telespazio, the state-owned company that manages communications via satellite, the workers went on strike to demand control of all personnel mobility and hiring, the institution of internal training courses, and the right to be consulted on future changes in the company. No wage demands were made. The strike was prompted by the clientelistic and politically motivated personnel policies pursued by management. The workers justified their demands solely on the grounds that they were interested in "a healthy, prosperous company," whereas the management was not. There are numerous other examples (CTIP, SAES, Italimpianti, Olivetti–General Electric) of workers striking or occupying factories and labs to resist dismemberments and layoffs resulting from mismanagement or from the sale of the company to U.S. or other foreign interests. These struggles unite all levels of workers from blue collar to engineers in the feeling that "we could do it better."

The major demands of the white collar struggles between 1968 and 1971 were (a) reduction in the number of categories of employees and reduction in pay differences among the remaining categories; (b) publication of the criteria by which merit raises are awarded, and publication of the raises themselves (this demand eventually became a demand for the abolition of merit raises as discriminatory and divisive); (c) the development of careers where mobility is blocked, using outside recruitment only as a last resort; (d) the granting of special privileges to employees going to night school; (e) the right to hold a certain number of paid union assemblies during work hours and recognition of a Works Council, consisting of delegates elected by the employees, to replace the much smaller Internal Commission; (f) abolition or reduction of overtime.

There was much debate within the left as to the precise forms these demands should take and as to whether some of them should be made at all. Some groups argued that one or another of them were overly reformist or incompatible with a broader view of working class interests.

It should also be pointed out that not all of these demands originated with technicians or white collar workers. Semiskilled blue collar workers demanded a reduction in pay differentials and in the number of categories of workers very early in 1968. During this period, blue collar workers also raised other egalitarian and "antiproductivistic" demands, such as those for automatic promotions based on seniority, abolition of piece rates, and modifications of work situations where there are health hazards, rather than compensatory pay supplements.

At least partial successes were obtained with respect to most of the white collar demands (and with respect to the blue collar demands as well). However, those which conflicted seriously with what management regarded as its prerogatives were not met. This was particularly true with regard to merit raises, which remained as rewards to be handed out by management.

When compared with the language and analysis of the militants, what is most striking about these demands is their moderation and their rationalizing character. Strikes based on these types of demands are a long way from Mallet's strikes for worker control. Yet it is hard to imagine what kinds of demands could be made that would constitute more positive steps toward workers' control. This has been and remains the dilemma of any revolutionary strategy centered solely on the workplace.

Quite apart from one's judgment as to the "revolutionary" character of the new working class struggles, there is much in them that is new. If we compare the events of 1968–72 with the history of previous years rather than with the new working class theorists' notion of a revolutionary vanguard, it becomes apparent that there has been a great change in the behavior of technicians and white collar workers. First, there is the important fact that workers who had never engaged in independent collective struggles at all are now striking on a large scale. Second, the contents of the demands pertain primarily to the organization of work rather than to questions of salary alone and are aimed at reinforcing solidarity at the expense of individual competitiveness. Third, the procedural aspects of these struggles have expressed a new demand for participatory democracy within the firm.

Before discussing the significance of these struggles, it would be well to look at the data we have collected. In the pages that follow, we shall consider the new working class hypotheses in the light of what the technicians themselves, who are the subjects of these hypotheses, tell us.

3. Design, methods, and locales of the study

The design of the study

This study was designed with the intention of showing that the new working class theories provide accurate explanations for at least some situations. At the same time, it proposed to test a number of more specific hypotheses, outlined in Chapter 1, on which there is disagreement between new working class theorists and others.

The arguments on the militant and/or revolutionary character of the new working class have usually been supported by case histories of factory struggles. These case histories generally consist of descriptions of the economic vicissitudes of the companies concerned, their patterns of growth and concentration, and accounts of their labor struggles. Even though the arguments of the new working class theorists hinge upon hypotheses about how individuals react to their work situations, until recently there has been little effort to examine how the members of the new working class perceive their own situations. Perceptions and objectives have been imputed to workers on the basis of their actions and what their leadership has said without any close examination of their situations or motives.

Data derived from observation of behavior have biases just as do attitudinal data. Our feeling was that the existing literature suffered rather badly from the former biases. This is, therefore, a study of attitudes. However, realizing the weaknesses of many attitude surveys, our method has been not to study attitudes in a void, but rather to relate them very closely to the structural realities to which they are reactions. This implies careful study of the context within which they have meaning, in this case the workplace. Attitudes cannot always be taken as indicative of "objective reality," nor can they always be seen as reflections of personality characteristics. Sometimes they must be taken at face value, and at other times they must be interpreted. In all cases an appreciation of the context is essential.

43

Although most of the data referred to in the succeeding chapters come from interviews, it was recognized that the research design would entail the use of historical and observational data as well. Union organization and labor history of the particular settings would obviously be important. Even more important to our hypotheses was a clear picture of the organizational structures within which people worked. Material on these and other subjects was collected and has been used throughout. The interview data are in addition to, rather than substitutive of, the kind of data Mallet and others have adduced.

The need to have a clear picture of the structural context of attitudes and to draw on historical and observational data suggested that the interviews be done within the framework of organizational case studies.

Two kinds of variables, aside from education, were hypothesized to be particularly important in their effects on militancy: variables related to the type of work task and organizational variables that affect the work situation. The most important organizational variable that bears on the hypotheses in which we are interested is the degree to which the organization is *organic* (i.e., open, decentralized, encouraging autonomy, and the delegation of responsibility) rather than *mechanistic* (i.e., hierarchical, centralized). In order to be able to look at the effects of this variable, it was decided to do two organizational case studies. One of the organizations was to be relatively participatory, the other one more hierarchical. The factories chosen would have to include several different kinds of work, ranging from fairly routine, "proletarianized" jobs to more involving jobs. But it was important that within each of the two factories the same set of jobs should be present. This would make it possible to compare people doing similar jobs in different organizational structures as well as people doing different jobs within one organization.

The research design required, then, that two factories be found in the same industrial sector (so that the same jobs would be present in both) that were different in terms of organizational structure. An additional requirement was that at least one of the factories must have had new working class-type labor unrest in the recent past.

It will be objected that in choosing factories that exemplify what the theories refer to, the case is prejudged. But our aim here is not to generalize from two factories to a universe of factories. The unit of analysis is the individual: Our aim is to understand how the individual experiences the new working class situation and how variations within this situation affect militancy and political attitudes. Two factories were to be chosen so as to make possible the study of a wide range of organizational and work situations, all of which still can be described as new working class. In a more general sense, this research may be seen as documenting the existence of situations such as those described by the new working class theorists. It is within this larger category of situations that our analysis takes place.

It would be presumptuous to assume that the findings of a small-scale survey of individual attitudes could be decisive in adjudicating between different theories as to the historical role of a collective subject such as the new working class. Even a large survey, using organizations as the unit of analysis, or using individuals *and* organizations as units, could not be presumed to be definitive. The new working class theory does not rest on a count of the number of workplaces to which it applies at a given moment in time. It is a historical theory and as such can only be finally evaluated over time. While we await the verdict of history, however, a sociological analysis will give some indications from which to draw more immediate conclusions. It will also allow us to examine the more general question of what the processes are by which some workers become militant and/or class conscious while others remain apathetic.

The factories

A number of the more spectacular cases of new working class unrest were eliminated as possible research sites after some investigation indicated that they were too atypical in the type of work performed or in the managerial situations they represented to allow even the most speculative generalization.

This is not the place to tell of the difficulties encountered in trying to find suitable research sites. Suffice it to say that it soon became evident that managements were very wary of granting access to do research on this sort of topic. Formal permission to carry out the project was eventually obtained from the Società Generale di Telefonia ed Elettronica. It is ironic that gaining access to the participatory organization, the Special Systems Laboratory of the Società Italiana Telecomunicazioni Siemens, proved more problematic. In fact, formal permission was never granted by the Siemens management. However, people within the Special Systems Laboratory were willing to help the researcher on an informal basis despite management's veto.

Both organizations are in the telecommunications industry. Both are within a ten-mile radius of Milan, Italy's most industrial city. The kinds of jobs that exist in both are similar.

The Società Generale di Telefonia ed Elettronica

The Società Generale di Telefonia ed Elettronica (GT&E) was chosen as an example of a traditional, nonparticipatory organization, in which communications and power tend to flow along strict vertical lines. GT&E is a subsidiary of a multinational, U.S.-based parent company, General Telephone and Electronics, which is one of the largest producers of telecommunications equipment in the world.

The Italian subsidiary has three plants, two in the Milan area and one south of Naples, and employed a total of 4,788 persons in February, 1971. Of the three factories, the Cassina dè Pecchi plant outside Milan, one of the sites for this research, is the largest: It employed 2,269 persons at the same date. It houses many of the central administrative offices for all of Italy. Its production is the most technically sophisticated, consisting primarily of microwave transmitting and receiving equipment. Most of this equipment is used in long-distance telephone systems. This includes transmitting and receiving stations for satellite communications. The plant also produces a few smaller systems, mainly for the Italian armed forces and police. A major proportion of the production of the Cassina plant is exported. In 1970, for example, contracts were won to build stations in Argentina, Trinidad, Barbados, Venezuela, and New Zealand as well as in Italy. The company carried on contract relations in forty-seven countries, from Western Europe to Asia.

Despite U.S. ownership, GT&E–Italia is an entirely Italian organization. Only the administrative director (who is in charge of financial matters) is American. The Cassina plant originated at the end of 1960 with the creation of the Marelli-Lenkurt Company, a joint venture of an Italian company, Magneti Marelli, and Lenkurt Electric Co., a GT&E subsidiary. Lenkurt provided the capital, while the organization itself was based on the old transmitter and receiver sections of Magneti Marelli. By 1963, the new company, employing a little over 1,000 persons, had moved from Sesto S. Giovanni, where the parent Marelli plant was located, to a new plant in Cassina dè Pecchi, a few miles away. After 1966, the company experienced rapid growth, so that by 1970 the number of employees had more than doubled at the Cassina plant.

The labor force is highly skilled. Of the 2,269 persons employed at Cassina 661 (29%) have some kind of technical training. One hundred and twelve (5%) are engineers; another 549 (24%) are the technicians from whom the sample was drawn. There are 1,195 (53%) blue collar workers of whom 135 (11%) are technicians and 490 (41%) are semi-skilled women who assemble electronic components. The remaining blue collar workers are mostly skilled machine-tool operators fashioning the mechanical components of the equipment. About 260 white collar workers who are not technicians carry on purely administrative work.

The plant has had an active union organization since its inception. The nucleus of the labor force came from Sesto S. Giovanni, a town known as the Stalingrad of Italy because of its strong communist traditions. In 1962, when the company was still located in Sesto, 48 percent of the employees voted for the Communist and Socialist union (Federazione Italiana Operai Metallurgici or FIOM) in the election for the representatives who were to form the Internal Commission handling all factory-level union contacts with management. The new plant was built in a "white" (i.e., Catholic) area to the northeast of Milan. The move led to a sharp decline in support for the FIOM. In 1969, the last year a comparable election was held, FIOM received only 38 percent of the vote. The effect of this decline in support was mitigated by the fact that the factory-level activists of the Federazione Italiana Metallurgici (FIM), the union nominally tied to the Christian Democratic Party, were already fairly militant and willing to cooperate with the FIOM activists during these years. The Unione Italiana Operai Metallurgici (UILM), the Social Democratic and Republican union, was the most hesitant partner in this alliance for common action. Nonetheless, whereas in other plants the unions were unable and/or unwilling to bargain aggressively, at GT&E the unions signed numerous plant-level agreements throughout this period. Compared to the unions at other plants, those at GT&E maintained relatively good relations among themselves and were effective as bargaining agents. The hiatus in the union organization within the plant, which Pizzorno, Reyneri, and others have seen as one of the causes of the spontaneous "revolts" of 1968-9, was not present here.[1]

Individual strike participation at GT&E, 1967-71. We were fortunate to come by a copy of GT&E Personnel Office statistics on individual strike participation from 1967 to 1971, documenting the dramatic jump in white collar participation during this period. It must be pointed out that in Italy, unlike in the United States, it is meaningful to discuss individual strike participation. Strikes are generally only one or two hours long. Collective bargaining involves a series of such strikes (which we have called a "struggle" in rough translation of the Italian *lotta*) spread over a period of several weeks or even months. In periods of increased militancy such as the years from 1968 to 1973, strikes are organized so as to create the maximum disruption of production with the minimum cost to the workers. One example of such a tactic is the checkerboard strike, in which various units of the factory walk out for short consecutive periods rather than all walking out simultaneously. Short strikes, particularly checkerboard strikes, rely on the more or less voluntary participation of a majority of workers. Every time a strike is declared, the worker has the option of walking out or not walking out. Among blue collar workers there are, of course, strong pressures to participate, but until recently this was not true for white collar workers. The fact that the amount of participation does, indeed, vary considerably from strike to strike confirms that, even for blue collar workers, to strike or not to strike involves an individual decision. The one partial exception to this rule concerns strikes that are scheduled for the early morning, with the express intention of using pickets to keep scabs from entering the factory at the start of the workday. In the case of GT&E, early morning strikes became less and less frequent as the spontaneous participation of white collar workers increased.

The statistics show a spectacular leap in the participation of white collar workers, suggesting a qualitative change in their behavior. Although there has also been an increase in the participation of blue collar workers, their participation was at a high level from the start.

In six of the seven strikes over factory-level collective bargaining issues that took place in the fall of 1967, white collar participation was below 10 percent. On only one occasion did it approach 40 percent. In the series of fourteen strikes over similar issues in the fall of 1968, white collar participation was substantially higher, averaging 32 percent. However, it must be pointed out that in those eight cases in which the strike occurred after the workday had begun, white collar participation was never over 30 percent. The other six strikes were scheduled for the morning, and it may be assumed that pickets attempted to prevent the white collar workers from entering the factory. Taking into consideration the histories given by activists, we can say that during the fall of 1968 a substantial group of white collar workers participated in the whole series of strikes for the first time.

But it was not until the fall of 1969, the now famous Hot Autumn, that a large increase in spontaneous white collar strike participation took place. Although many of the strikes during this period occurred in the mornings, many did not. There was no great difference in participation between the morning strikes and some of the others. The highest level of participation in a morning strike was 79 percent, the lowest 63 percent. Two afternoon strikes received 74 percent participation, and the average participation of white collar workers in the late morning or afternoon strikes of the fall of 1969 was 53 percent.

During the struggle of the fall of 1970, participation increased still further, while the practice of early morning strikes became infrequent. Excluding early morning strikes, the average level of participation was 76 percent.

If we turn from consideration of participation in strikes over collective bargaining issues to participation in politically motivated strikes, we find a similar, if much less dramatic, upward shift.

Within the general category of political strikes, it is necessary to distinguish between strikes for specific reforms and demonstrative strikes. The strikes for specific reforms constitute a kind of collective bargaining with the government, whereas the demonstrative strikes are stands taken to show a determined opposition to some other political force (e.g., strikes against neofascist activities).

Not surprisingly, the demonstrative strikes do not receive the same amount of support as do some of those oriented toward specific demands. The number of political strikes is small and, hence, there is less evidence from which to deduce a trend. Nevertheless, there has been an upward shift in the level of participation in both types of political strikes, and particularly in strikes for specific reform demands. In April of 1970, for the first time in the period for which we have data, participation in strikes for specific reforms went over the 50 percent mark. In December of that year, a strike for reforms that occurred in the course of a factory-level struggle drew out 73 percent of the white collar workers. In April of 1971, 73 percent of the white collar workers struck for reforms when there was no company struggle going on. Before 1971, only one demonstrative strike had over 5 percent of white collar participation. The afternoon strike against neofascism and repression on February 5, 1971, was supported by 21 percent of the white collar workers.

We have looked at these GT&E statistics in some detail because they constitute a rare piece of behavioral evidence for one aspect of the change that is the subject of this research. The upward shift in participation in all kinds of strikes suggested by these figures is more than a temporary outburst of militancy. Particularly in the case of white collar workers, who had never before participated in strikes en masse, what has occurred in these years has been a change in the norms regarding the propriety of participation in collective actions, a change unlikely to be reversed.

Data on union membership at the Cassina plant, available for the two major unions, FIM and FIOM, from 1968 to 1970, support the contention of the institutionalization of a higher level of participation. In three years, the FIM increased its membership by 78 percent, and the FIOM, which had more than twice as many members as the FIM in 1968, increased its membership by 60 percent. In 1971, there appears to have been a slight decline in union membership, but definite figures were not available when the fieldwork was concluded. National-level data are available for FIOM. The increase in FIOM membership in GT&E is about the same as that in the FIOM nationally.[2]

For 1970 we have a detailed breakdown of union membership by unit within the plant. These figures, supplied by management, tend to underestimate membership[3] because they do not include those who pay their union dues to the union directly rather than having them deducted from their paychecks. Direct payments are made by workers who wish to prevent management from knowing that they have joined one of the unions. If it is assumed that the underestimation is relatively uniform throughout the factory, some rough comparisons can be made between the different units. The data support the contention that technicians are more militant than administrative workers. Whereas 7 out of 141 employees of the administrative offices (0.05%) are union members according to these figures, 97 out of 380 employees in the labs (23%) are union members. If we add the testing department, consisting of low-level technicians and a few semiskilled women workers, the percentage goes up to 37. The testing department alone is 54 percent unionized. By comparison, the production departments, which employ semiskilled women and skilled men, are about 58 percent unionized. Even taking into account the bias in the data, it is clear that technicians are much more likely to join unions than are clerical workers, although considerably less likely to join than are traditional blue collar workers.

The 1970 conflict at GT&E. Thus far we have described the quantitative changes in the pattern of participation with little reference to the content of this participation. Some of the demands first raised by workers in 1968 and 1969 were outlined in Chapter 2. It is evident from the data presented that GT&E was not one of the factories in which these demands first emerged. It was not until the struggle for the national-level metalworkers' contract that a new level of participation was clearly apparent at GT&E, and it was not until the fall of 1970 that this higher level of spontaneous participation became the norm among technicians.

The issues raised by this last struggle and the subsequent agreement with management were still being debated during the time of the field-work. A brief description of the events of the fall of 1970 will give some meaning to the figures previously cited and will introduce the reader to some of the topics developed further in later chapters.

The development of a bargaining platform began in June of 1970, with meetings of the Works Council and assemblies of all workers held after work hours. The Works Council is a body of approximately fifty representatives of the workers, which, in GT&E as in other factories, supplanted the much smaller Internal Commission during the struggles of 1968 and 1969. It emerged as an expression of the demand for a more direct participation of workers in matters of labor relations and was accepted and encouraged by union leadership as a means of insti-tutionalizing and controlling the waves of protest during this period. One of the issues in the struggle in the fall was to be the recognition of this council as the legitimate representative of the workers.

The development of a company platform following the conclusion of the national contract was in accordance with the union directives of the time. The issues discussed in June and July led to the formulation of the demands presented in the fall. These demands, in their final form, were as follows.

1. Salary increases of 75 lire per hour (equal to about $21 per month) for hourly paid workers and 15,600 lire per month (about $26) for white collar workers. This request for a pay in-crease arose out of a discussion of the desirability of prohibiting any regular overtime work. Among the demands won in the 1969 national contract had been the gradual reduction of the work-week from forty-four to forty hours over the three-year contract period. This demand had been one of a number of antiproduc-tivistic demands noted previously. But it was also intended as an incentive for companies to invest in Southern Italy. If regular overtime work could be stopped, the labor shortage in the North

of Italy and the inducements for investing in the South would lead to the construction of new factories in the South. At GT&E, the workers were willing to stop doing overtime work only if this did not mean a decline in their incomes. The demand for a pay raise was originally seen as a step along the way toward limiting the number of hours of overtime. The pay raise requested took the symbolically egalitarian form of an equal increase for all categories of workers rather than an increase proportional to present pay. (The increase was to be equal for all white collar workers and equal for all blue collar workers, although white collar workers were to get a greater increase than blue collar workers.)

2. Recognition of the Works Council, with 3,000 hours at the disposal of the representatives.
3. Abolition of the lowest categories of white and blue collar work. For blue collar workers, the fourth category was to remain as a transitional category, out of which every worker would automatically be promoted after six months.
4. Changes in certain unhealthy work situations.
5. Reduction of the white collar work week by one hour.

The demands were presented at the beginning of November. Management said it would not negotiate with the Works Council. Finally a compromise was worked out: The workers were represented at the first meeting on November 18th by the old Internal Commission and a number of union-appointed delegates. Management's counterproposals were judged to be unacceptable. Their offers sought to divide white collar and blue collar workers by acceding to most of the demands of the blue collar workers while maintaining that the white collar workers were already sufficiently well treated. That this tactic was largely unsuccessful is evidenced by the high strike participation figures for blue collar workers.

The struggle continued throughout December with almost daily strikes, many of them checkerboard strikes. Although all decisions were nominally made by the Works Council, in actual fact they were made by a small group of union activists. All overtime was refused during this period, and pickets were posted after work hours to discuss with those employees who persisted in working overtime, and to keep them in longer if possible. This picket also prevented any goods from going out between 6 P.M. and 8 P.M.

During the second week in December, some of the women, impatient with the thus far unsuccessful tactics of the unions, proposed a more militant action: a round-the-clock blockade of outgoing goods. This proposal quickly gained the support of a large number of workers, particularly among the women. Over the objections of most of the union activists, a tent was set up at the factory gate. For three weeks of the cold and foggy Milan winter, workers were camped at the gates day and night. A fire was kept going to provide some warmth, and when, by Christmas Eve, the dispute still had not been settled, the media began to pick up the story. But the workers were weakening. The union activists had initially opposed the blockade on the grounds that it was an effort that would be difficult to sustain. As the group of people manning the tent grew smaller, it appeared that they may have been right.

Just after Christmas, a march through the factory was staged, ending with a sit-in in the corridor outside the top managerial suite. Apparently management had had enough as well. On December 29th, an agreement was signed. It provided for the following improvements: (1) a 50 lire per hour raise for all blue collar workers and raises between 4,000 and 6,000 lire per month for white collar workers, the raise being inversely proportional to present salary; (2) recognition of the Works Council, with 1,500 hours at the disposal of the representatives; (3) the lowest categories of blue collar and white collar work to become transitional; (4) the creation of a joint committee to deal with problems of the work environment. Other minor provisions were also included.

Although all the workers' demands were at least partially met, some felt that the gains had not been worth the sacrifice. These people felt that management had conceded relatively little beyond its first offers presented early in December and that the workers would have done better to settle at that time. Many of the white collar workers in particular felt that their gains were insignificant and rapidly eaten away by rising prices.

None of the demands were in any sense revolutionary. Nonetheless all the demands, even the wage demand as it was presented, embodied a spirit broader than the bread-and-butter trade unionism of previous years.

In its labor history, the GT&E Cassina plant is not atypical of plants in advanced sectors employing large numbers of technicians. The workers have shown more militancy than those of some firms, particularly in the private sector, and less militancy than those of other firms, particularly in the public sector. It is impossible to choose one or two factories and call them typical. Each plant is characterized by its own labor history, its own union organization, its own management. In GT&E we found a plant that had had new working class labor unrest, had employees engaged in various kinds of technical jobs, and was relatively hierarchical in its organizational structure.

The Special Systems Laboratory of SIT Siemens

The Special Systems Laboratory of the Società Italiana Telecomunicazioni Siemens (SIT Siemens) was chosen as a participatory organization comparable to GT&E in the types of jobs it offered. SIT Siemens is one of the companies that together form the government-controlled holding company STET. The companies of the group produce telecommunications equipment and other electronics products, and manage the Italian national telephone system. Before the war, the Italian Siemens plant belonged to the German Siemens firm. The factory was taken over by the government as enemy property. Because it was the main supplier of the national telephone system, it was retained under governmental control. As with other state-controlled companies such as Alfa Romeo, Alitalia, and Montedison, the role of the state is an indirect one, state ownership being mediated through a holding company. In most respects, these companies are operated exactly as would be any large private enterprise. Their personnel policies are not exceptionally enlightened; but they are generally not extremely reactionary.

Because we were refused permission by management to conduct this study, our data on SIT Siemens are considerably less complete and less accurate than those on GT&E. They were obtained from published sources, from the Personnel Department Research Office before the researcher's request was turned down, and from union activists and lower-level personnel officers after the request to do the study was turned down.

In 1971, SIT Siemens employed 16,300 people. About 10,500 of these worked in Milan. The remainder worked in Siemens's two southern factories. There were also about 1,750 persons who traveled around the country installing equipment.

In Milan there are two factories. The largest one is the old plant, employing 7,600 people in a complex situated in one of Milan's more fashionable neighborhoods. The company has just completed the construction of a new complex in Castelletto, a few miles west of Milan on the same side of town as the old plant. The new plant housed 2,880 people at the time of the study, but more and more units were being moved to the new location throughout the year.

SIT Siemens produces all kinds of telecommunications equipment: telephones, switching stations, and transmitting and receiving equipment for radio and television as well as for telephone communications systems. Most of their production is sold on the Italian market. Switching stations are by far the most important product and account for 50 percent of sales.

At the time of the study, the labor force of the Milan and Castelletto plants was about 30 percent white collar. The blue collar workers who made up the remaining 70 percent were almost equally divided between men and women. The high proportion of women workers is one important determinant of the volatile union climate pervading the plant.

The Special Systems Laboratory (the Lab) is one of eight Siemens research laboratories. It began in 1967 as a small research group. In 1968 it employed 40 people, and in 1971 there were 250, with further expansion expected. One-third of the employees are engineers, one-third are technicians, and one-third are blue collar workers. Many of the blue collar workers do technical work: testing, drafting, etc. Many of them have attended a special Siemens company professional school for three years. There is only a small group of semiskilled women workers.

The origins of the Lab, recent as they are, are shrouded in myth. These origins, together with the charismatic quality of its leadership, account in part for a participatory organizational climate exceptional for Siemens and for Italian industry. As the story was told to the researcher, two engineers who worked in one of the other laboratories designed on their own an electronic commutation system which was so well received by high-level management that they were placed in charge of developing the project further. This project was determined to be sufficiently important to justify the establishment of a new laboratory. The Lab is thus seen as having been born through an idea developed by a small group of devoted enthusiasts. The two engineers responsible for the idea were open-minded, egalitarian, and sympathetic to the political left. One of them, DeVarda, is still seen as the head of the Lab despite the fact that it is nominally run by a committee. His informality and flamboyant geniality stand out in contrast to the distant and formal behavior of most Italian higher-level management. Some people in the Lab perceive DeVarda as being engaged in a continuous battle with "the factory" to preserve the autonomy of the Lab and the participatory practices that have developed there.

A more cynical and perhaps more realistic view of the origins of the Lab is given by some of the union activists. They see the creation of the Lab, with its rather unusual organizational structure, as a deliberate experiment in the integration of technicians, promoted by top-level management in the wake of the 1968 disturbances among white collar workers. Be this as it may, the myth of the origin of the Lab is interesting in that it emphasizes the feeling of separation of the Lab from the rest of the factory.

The Special Systems Laboratory as a participatory organization. The logic underlying the choice of the Special Systems Laboratory as a participatory organization does not require us to argue that the Lab is an example of workers' control. Nor would we want to. It is only necessary to convince the reader of a much weaker conclusion, namely that, compared to most Italian firms and to GT&E in particular, the Lab allows the individual worker a good deal more freedom and autonomy on the job.

To the minds of those in charge of the organization of the Special Systems Laboratory, it represents a unique experiment, an attempt to overcome, insofar as possible, the contradictions between individual needs and organizational goals. They are steeped in the language of Argyris, Likert, and others of the human resources school. They see their goal as the creation of a humane, flexible, dynamic organization. Although the reality may fall short of their expectations, it is dramatically different from the organization of GT&E.

The most noticeable difference between the Lab and GT&E is that in the Lab it is impossible to monopolize information and use it as power. The Lab is characterized by an informal atmosphere that encourages cooperation and the flow of information. "Bosses" have been replaced by "coordinators." Everyone uses the familiar form of address. The formal structure provides for numerous meetings. Each work group, consisting of about thirty people, meets weekly to discuss technical and personnel problems that arise within the group, and has decision-making power to resolve some of these problems. The Lab also meets as a whole each week – one week to discuss technical matters, the following week to discuss other matters. The large meeting does not usually take on a decision-making role, although it may do so in exceptional cases. Each work group also has a technical secretary who attends a weekly meeting of all the technical secretaries and reports back to his group. There are committees for handling various specific topics, such as internal courses, exchange of information with outside sources, and lectures. Although none of these bodies has much power, they ensure that every problem gets a hearing and thereby limit the arbitrary exercise of power by bosses.

Other rules and practices also evidence an unusual degree of freedom. Workers are allowed to spend up to 10 percent of their time studying. Because many of them attend technical school or university at night, this rule is particularly important. Courses on various subjects are also given within the Lab during working hours. Unlike at GT&E, horizontal mobility is in theory encouraged in the Lab. In practice, it is not impossible to change one's job if one is bored, feels a need for more challenging work, or simply does not get along with one's workmates. Merit raises are discussed by each work group, which makes recommendations to the heads of all the work groups within the Lab. For technicians, all raises are fixed and automatic for the first three years.

Decision-making power within the Lab is formally vested in two bodies. The highest body is the *Direzione Coordinamento Laboratorio* (DICOL), a committee consisting of one person appointed by top-level management and three people appointed by an enlarged group representing the whole Lab. Under the DICOL is another body, the *Assemblea dei Capiufficio* ("Assembly of Office Heads"), a group consisting of the heads of all work groups that meets weekly. At a still lower level, within each work group the head of the group is far from powerless, although he generally must try to preserve a semblance of consensus.

The formal mechanisms of participation are viewed with a good deal of skepticism by most of the employees. Nevertheless, there is a considerable esprit de corps and channels of communication are sufficiently open to prevent the bottling up of grievances common in more hierarchical structures.

One instance of conflict between one of the work groups and the top management of the Lab will illustrate the scope and limits of the employees' autonomy. The software group, the largest work group in the Lab, had decided that no merit raises would be given to technicians within the group. In order to avoid the kind of competition that pits individuals against one another, all raises were to be determined by seniority. The total sum allotted for increases would thus be distributed according to a plan in which productivity played no role. A case arose in the fall of 1971 of a technician who, according to management, had done nothing but study for his university courses for the past six months. According to one version of the story, the accusation was true, but there were mitigating circumstances: He had been waiting to be drafted and had not wanted to begin a new project. According to another version, the accusation was only partly true. In any case, his work group came out in support of his right to a raise (the benefit of which he would reap upon his return from military service), citing the agreement to disregard individual differences in awarding raises. Top management claimed that those who had done no work at all were excluded from the agreement. The employees argued bitterly that management was saving money by reneging on its promise. After having leveled off the peaks in the salary curve, the management was now restoring the troughs. The debate ended with no raise for the technician in question.

Recent conflicts at SIT Siemens. We have described the organizational structure of the Special Systems Laboratory at some length because of its rather unusual nature. We shall be much briefer in our discussion of union organization and history at Siemens. To the minds of most of the employees in the Lab, the union is an external body that bargains for demands concerning "the factory." As we shall see, the technicians in the Lab are relatively uninformed about what the union is doing in the factory as a whole. In part this is a result of the size of the organization. The Lab, with 250 employees, has only two delegates in the Works Council. It is much more difficult to follow the labor disputes of an industrial complex of 10,500 people such as Siemens than those of a plant of 2,500 such as GT&E. The fact that the Special Systems Laboratory has a strong identity and an esprit de corps of its own as well as particular problems of its own also leads its employees to focus on the affairs of the Lab rather than on those of the factory as a whole. Many of the unions' demands are not relevant to the Lab or seem relatively unimportant in view of the generally privileged position of the employees of the Lab. Finally, because of the recent origin of the Lab, many of its employees did not experience the events at Siemens in 1968.

The struggle of the white collar workers of SIT Siemens in 1968–9 was one of the more notable of a succession of dramatic white collar struggles during that period. The struggle grew out of the activity of a study group formed in the spring of 1968 to analyze the problems of the white collar employees. The study group consisted primarily of people sympathetic to the student movement and the political groups of the extreme left.

In November, a series of demands were presented. They were (1) that those currently employed be given first chance at any positions to be filled, (2) that the results of employee evaluations be made known to those being evaluated, (3) that merit raises be announced publicly, (4) that 10 percent of employees' time be free to use for study in areas broadly defined as being of interest to the company, (5) that university graduates and technicians be promoted automatically to a higher-salary category after a certain period of time, and (6) various salary and other financial improvements.

Participation in the strikes following rejection of these demands was very high. During the strikes, assemblies were held to vote on subsequent actions. Among these actions was the peaceful occupation of a subway train from which leaflets were distributed at every station.

The struggle became bitter. Thirty strikers were charged with various criminal offenses by management. As at GT&E in 1970, management's tactic was to try to divide blue collar and white collar workers by giving in to the demands of the former while resisting those of the latter. At Siemens this tactic proved relatively successful, as the blue collar workers were unwilling to continue to strike for the white collar workers.

When the accord was finally signed, almost none of the nonmonetary demands were met. The salary demands were met in part. As if to deny the effectiveness of collective bargaining for white collar workers, management distributed a far greater amount in merit raises in the succeeding months than the unions had won through the struggle.

In the light of later events, and because the white collar workers struck without blue collar support, some commentators dismiss the 1968 white collar struggle as an attempt to maintain the differences in pay and status between white collar and blue collar workers. In fact, after 1969, a reaction set in among the white collar workers at Siemens. By September of 1970, they were staging a "counterdemonstration" in protest against the militant picketing by blue collar workers and students which was occurring at the time. In November, the highest category of white collar workers (a category that includes top management) went on a "counterstrike" in protest against a supposed "atmosphere of violence" in the factory. The Special Systems Laboratory registered its disapproval of this action by voting a unanimous resolution condemning it.

This history illustrates the basic ambivalence rather than the conservative or narrowly group-oriented character of white collar struggles. As in many other cases, the leadership of the 1968 struggle at Siemens went far beyond the followers, elaborating basically trade-unionist aspirations as ideological demands.

At the time of the study, the union organization at Siemens was much more fragmented than that at GT&E. At GT&E, the two major unions, the FIM and the FIOM, were allied against the more moderate UILM. At SIT Siemens, although the figures for the Internal Commission elections look remarkably similar to those for GT&E,[4] a much broader political spectrum was present, ranging from the extreme leftist groups to the UILM. The tensions following from this political diversity were accentuated by the centrifugal tendencies of the various units of the factory, each one of which had its own grievances and problems. Many of these units were fighting for their demands on their own, paying little attention to the Works Council or the union organizations. This somewhat confused situation contributed, along with the other factors already mentioned, to the lack of awareness of union activities of the employees of the Special Systems Laboratory.

The situation of the Special Systems Laboratory inevitably makes its employees an elite. To what extent does this fact in itself affect their attitudes and behavior? We will show in Chapter 4 that the privileged situation of the Lab does not guarantee the quiescence of its employees. On the contrary, under certain conditions the participatory situation makes them more militant then they would otherwise be. Their reference groups tend to be within the Lab rather than outside.

Perhaps, these effects would be magnified were it not for the privileged situation of the Lab as a whole. This hypothetical question is unanswerable. As long as a participatory organization is exceptional, it will be impossible to separate the effects of such an organization from the effects of its exceptionality. But it is at least in part because the organization is exceptional that it is an interesting object of study.

In what follows, we shall be treating the Lab as a self-contained unit, which it is to the minds of most of its employees. The technicians we interviewed had no regular contacts with the rest of the factory at all. On a much smaller scale, the Lab parallels the organizational functions and the jobs with which we are concerned in GT&E. It is primarily in terms of its organizational structure that the Lab is different and exceptional.

The interview sample

Given that the number of persons interviewed was not going to be sufficient to allow as many controls as might be made with larger samples, it was thought to be more fruitful to concentrate on gaining in-depth information on a smaller number of people and on the context within which they lived and worked.

The sample includes only technicians, defined according to their education as people who either had completed five years of technical school (i.e., thirteen years of schooling altogether giving the title of *perito*) or had taken some courses on radio or TV repairing, electronics, or drafting. In Siemens, many of the lower-level technicians had gone to the company school. This was a three-year course leading to a diploma not recognized outside the company. Thirteen people in the sample had finished technical school and were attending night courses at the university in the hope of taking an advanced degree.

Engineers and other university graduates were excluded. Although a few engineers are both militant and radical, and sometimes constitute the body of the union leadership, the great majority of them do not participate actively in union struggles. From their point of view, this inactivity is not difficult to understand. Though their position in the factory has declined as their numbers have increased, they are still in a relatively privileged position. If someone is to be promoted, it is almost always going to be an engineer or other university graduate. Two necessary if not sufficient conditions for collective action missing in the case of the engineer are a common situation and common prospects for the future.

The data analysis is based on 88 interviews, somewhat less than the target number of 100. Six pilot interviews, carried out in a different factory, are not included; nor are 4 interviews with people who turned out not to be technicians according to the definition given here. Three interviews had to be discarded because the tape recordings were unintelligible. Of the interviews used in the analysis, eight were carried out by a paid interviewer, the remainder by the author.

The sample was drawn differently in the two factories. The GT&E

sample was stratified so as to include a meaningful number of people from each of several sections of the factory. A meaningful number was operationalized as at least ten. The sections of the factory included were the labs, the testing department, and the sales department. Draftsmen are included within the labs. Altogether, 62 interviews were obtained from a universe of 322 technicians. The production departments were omitted as they have no technicians apart from a handful in supervisory positions. The installations department was also omitted. The 30 technicians employed there are only in Milan for relatively brief periods, spending most of their time abroad or in other parts of Italy. Needless to say, it would have been difficult to obtain interviews from these men. In any case, their impact on factory life was slight.

In Siemens the small size of the universe (about 100 technicians) suggested the simpler procedure of picking every third name from the list of employees. The list in this case was provided by category. The highest categories, nearly all university graduates, were excluded, as was the lowest level consisting of women doing semiskilled jobs. Twenty-six interviews were carried out in Siemens.

Although the Siemens sample was not stratified according to type of job, it included people from all sections of the Lab. The sections at Siemens correspond to those at GT&E, with the exception of the sales group which does not exist in the Special Systems Laboratory. Unfortunately, the Siemens testing group is only represented by six people in the sample. This reflects the very small size of the group in the Lab (approximately fifteen people).

The interviews lasted from two to three hours. They were usually carried out after dinner or on weekends in the homes of the respondents. In nearly all cases the conversation went beyond the questions in the interview guide, often leading to lively discussions that were learning experiences for both the interviewer and the person interviewed.

4. Life at work

In this chapter we consider the effects of the job a man does on his orientation to various aspects of his life at work: the job itself, the organization, his fellow workers, his boss, and collective actions such as strikes. In the last sections we consider briefly the effects of the job on life outside work and of prior orientations on workplace behavior.

The jobs

We begin with a description of the jobs in the sample. There are four different types of jobs: sales, testing, drafting, and laboratory work. As noted in Chapter 3, all of these jobs exist in both organizations, with the exception of sales which exists only at GT&E. After a brief description of the content of each of the jobs, we shall go on to discuss job satisfaction. Despite the general similarity of jobs with the same labels in the two organizations, the differences are sufficient to warrant a separate description for each job in each factory.

GT&E – commercial (sales) offices

One hundred and seventy-six people work in the commercial offices of GT&E. Of these, thirteen are engineers and fifty-one are technicians. The others are accountants, clerks, and typists. Nine technicians from these offices are included in our sample.

The commercial offices handle the sales aspects of most of the products made by GT&E in Italy, including the switching equipment manufactured by the GT&E-Autelco factory in Milan. Small switchboards are the only products that are sold to private companies. Various governments, Italian and foreign, are the clients for other kinds of equipment. These orders are usually obtained after competitive bidding by companies throughout the world. The commercial offices prepare the offers. After an order for a system or a piece of equipment is placed, they continue to perform a liaison function between the client and the factory.

The work in the commercial offices is primarily paperwork. One older technician who has several people working under him described his job:

Orders arrive for the equipment we make. The productive capacity of the company is only so much. Let's say the company can produce 500 transmitters a month. If our orders are under 500, we only have to arrange them in succession. But if the demand is greater, we have to rank the various orders on the basis of the importance of the customer or whether there are fines or other penalties for lateness, to decide which one the company must fill on time. . . . (Vassallo)

The jobs of the young technicians have even less discretion:

I make up bills for replacement parts. You ask me the price of a certain module installed on a certain piece of equipment. I say, "The price is such and such, delivery is so and so much, the tax is at our expense, or at your expense," depending on whether or not you are a state agency. . . . The catalogue has the price for every part. . . . (Guerrieri)

As we shall see later in this chapter, the technicians in the commercial offices are lower in job satisfaction than any other group in the sample.

GT&E – testing

Two hundred and seventy-six people work in the testing department at GT&E. Sixty-six percent of these are white collar workers. Of the blue collar workers, 44 percent are women assigned to the simplest testing jobs and the lowest union categories. The sample includes nineteen testers, of whom eleven are blue collar workers.

The GT&E testing department exemplifies the blurring of the blue collar–white collar line. Although the white collar workers tend to do the more complex testing jobs, there are many instances in which blue collar and white collar workers do the same jobs side by side. Seniority and formal education are more important in attaining white collar status than type of job. The distinction between white collar and blue collar workers is seen by the testers as arbitrary. People "pass" frequently. White collar status is seen as desirable because of the better fringe benefits it carries with it, but this attitude is purely instrumental. There is no awareness within the testing department of the white collar–blue collar distinction as a status barrier.

The department is divided into various subunits in charge of different kinds of testing: testing of incoming material, quality control, and testing of finished products. The last subunit is by far the largest, employing 237 people. It is itself broken down into seven different groups, some of which correspond to product lines, while others concern themselves with the testing of elements common to a variety of products, for example, transformers.

Most of the testing department is housed in one section of the production shed. This section consists of a single huge room with parallel lines of work tables and aisles running between them. Oscilloscopes and other pieces of testing equipment rest scattered on the tabletops along with printed circuits and subassemblies of electronic equipment being tested. In certain parts of the room, the larger units ready for final testing stand high off the floor, blocking the view across the work tables. To one side, near the door, the supervisors' and secretaries' offices are partitioned off by transparent plastic barriers that create a fragile shield between the frenzied world of the testers and the seemingly more ordered world of the clerks who busy themselves with the paperwork related to testing.

Testing is done in two or more phases. First individual elements such as printed circuits and wave guides are tested. These are then combined into larger units that, in turn, are tested. Finally the entire apparatus is tested as a whole. For the simpler pieces of equipment, testing is limited to two phases. The final testing of the complete piece of equipment is generally considered to be the more desirable job, but this is not always the case. For some types of equipment (e.g., multiplexes), the tester at the final stage merely ascertains whether the apparatus meets specifications. If it does not, he returns the defective or improperly adjusted circuit board or filter to the tester who was responsible for testing that component.

Testing jobs vary a great deal in complexity. Testing coils requires much less knowledge than testing a complete transmitter. The simplest tests require only a pass–fail judgment based on reading a dial. If the volume of production were larger, these tests might be done by machines. At GT&E they are done by women. The tests of other elements such as filters, channels, heterodynes, and transformers, require a series of measures with an oscilloscope. These units almost always need some adjustments and/or repairs. For those doing the most complex testing jobs in the sample, the time allotted for the testing of one unit may be as much as five or six hours, whereas for the simplest jobs the time allotted may be only fifteen minutes.

Siemens – testing

The testing section in the Special Systems Laboratory employs about fifteen people. It constitutes one section of a larger unit, including draftsmen, office workers, and blue collar workers, whose job it is to construct the prototypes designed in the development sections of the Lab and to prepare them for mass production. The sample includes only six people from the testing section.

The testers do a variety of jobs in the Lab, ranging from the simple testing of printed circuits to the design and construction of automatic equipment for the testing of circuits. Five of the six testers interviewed described their current work as involving study. Two were in a maintenance and testing group engaged in trying out a new type of switching station and performing maintenance jobs on the prototypes already installed. Two others had just begun to work in testing, and felt that, although the job might eventually come to seem monotonous, they were still learning.

GT&E – draftsmen

There are about eighty draftsmen at GT&E. A few of these are scattered throughout the labs, and work in direct contact with the electronic engineers and technicians. Others work in the production department offices. However, the majority of the draftsmen work in two offices, namely, the mechanical drafting office and the electrical drafting office, both of which are subunits within the development labs. The sample includes nine draftsmen, of whom seven are in one or the other of these two offices.

There are three ranks among draftsmen: designing draftsman, assistant designing draftsman, and detail draftsman. The significance and importance of these distinctions vary from office to office and from group to group within offices. In the large offices the most junior draftsmen (the detail draftsmen) spend much of their time working on variants of old projects. This rather tedious job involves copying existing drawings and filling out forms specifying the changes that have been made. "We aren't draftsmen, we are almost like clerical workers – provisional variant, definitive variant, labeling, etc. – in short, we are full of paper. A draftsman who does his drawing in ten hours has to spend between two and five hours on nomenclature. . ." (Valachi). Even the most junior people are not left doing only these jobs for very long. If the office is not taking in new draftsmen, the variants are divided up equally.

The mechanical and electrical draftsmen do somewhat different work. The job of the electrical draftsman is less skilled and varied. He receives the schema of an electric circuit from the electronics engineer or technician:

> In practice all we do is to make a good copy. They [the electronic designers] give us a schema which is finished as far as conceptualization goes, and we have to make it intelligible to the production workers. Just about all we do is to straighten out the crooked lines, because they draw them freehand, but we don't contribute anything conceptual. Sometimes it can even be a matter of tracing a drawing. . . (Mei)

In this situation there is little distinction between the work of the designing draftsman and that of the detail draftsman.

The mechanical draftsman does technical drawings of the mechanical features of the equipment: various kinds of containers, some of them cast; frames; circuit boards; etc. The designing draftsman must agree with the electronics engineer on an appropriate design that will allow mass production while preserving the electrical characteristics of the equipment in question. In this negotiation, the electronics engineer always has the final word. After the designing draftsman has sketched out the project in consultation with an engineer, he passes it on to an assistant designing draftsman and a detail draftsman, who execute the final copy. It is only after the mechanical aspects of the project have been fully worked out that it goes to the electrical draftsmen.

Siemens – draftsmen

As at GT&E, the draftsmen in the Special Systems Laboratory are divided into two offices – mechanical and electrical. There are fifteen mechanical draftsmen, all categorized as white collar workers, and eighteen electrical draftsmen who work in an office called the "printed circuits office." Most of the latter are young blue collar workers. Many have come straight out of the Siemens school.[1] Within a few years they are all expected to pass into the white collar categories. The sample includes five mechanical draftsmen and four draftsmen from the printed circuits office.

The electrical draftsman receives the rough schema of an electrical circuit from one of the technicians or engineers of the development sections. From this rough schema, he must develop an exact picture of the layout of the circuit as it will appear on the printed board. While abiding by certain rules regarding minimum distances between paths, he must connect all the points listed in the rough schema, avoiding crossovers and minimizing the amount of empty space. The work is rather like certain spatial puzzles.

Because the frequencies dealt with here are much lower than those in the equipment made by GT&E, the layout does not affect the functioning of the system so much. Thus, more is left to the discretion of the electrical draftsman at the Lab than at GT&E.

The work of the mechanical draftsmen is even more varied. Some work on the mechanical structure of a computer, others design the casings for apparatus used in testing, others develop new modular mechanical systems or new ways of producing printed circuit boards. The sample is somewhat biased in its representation of this group in that three of the five people chosen are themselves leaders of small subgroups. However, they also do drafting and are not markedly different from their fellow draftsmen in their attitudes toward their work and toward the organization.

GT&E – laboratory technicians

Two departments at GT&E, the research lab and the engineering lab, are concerned with research and development. The engineering lab employs 321 people, 17 percent of whom are engineers, 62 percent of whom are technicians, and 21 percent of whom are blue collar workers. Over half the blue collar workers are concentrated in two units: the shop that builds prototypes and the copy shop where technical drawings are reproduced. The other sections each employ one or two blue collar workers who attend to certain physical aspects of lab work.

The research lab employs sixty-four people. Twenty-one of these (33%) are engineers. The others are all white collar technicians, with the exception of four blue collar workers. The research lab is really more concerned with development and engineering than with research. The projects underway there are related to new technologies and new kinds of equipment to be marketed in the near future or, in some cases, already on order. For example, at the time of the study various groups in the research lab were working on equipment for the Italian earth satellite Sirio. Our sample includes ten technicians from the research lab and fifteen from the engineering lab. They have been grouped together for the purposes of the data analysis.

The work done in the research lab differs from that done in the engineering lab only in that it is concerned with newer and/or more complex aspects of transmitting equipment. In the engineering lab, the emphasis is primarily on adaptation of already existing designs to the requirements of various customers and on development of new equipment that does not involve the use of new or very complex techniques. From the point of view of the technician, there is little difference between the work of the research lab and that of the engineering lab. In the research lab it is more common for a technician and an engineer to work together as a pair. However, the ratio of engineers to technicians is not so different in the two labs as might appear at first glance. Eliminating the blue collar workers from the figures, the percentage of engineers in the engineering lab goes up to 21 percent, bringing it much closer to the 35 percent of the research lab. In both labs, it is the practice for the young technician to work under either an engineer or a more senior technician, moving to a more autonomous position with age. It is, however, somewhat easier for the technician in the engineering lab to move to an autonomous position. In the research lab, the practice of giving each engineer a technician to work under him makes gaining autonomy more of a struggle for the technician.

Both labs are housed in the long three-story office block. The sections are in rooms opening off one side of the central corridor, from which they are partitioned by walls of transparent plastic. The engineers' desks are in rooms off the other side of the corridor, in offices that are also open to view.

A few examples will give an idea of the kinds of jobs done by technicians in the labs. One of the technicians who works in the engineering lab, has been at GT&E nine years, and has acquired a certain amount of autonomy, described his job as follows:

I do small projects, for example designing a transformer, designing a filter, designing an equalizer or a passive net, taking measures in general on whatever project you're doing, also doing the documentation for mass production. . . . They give me the electrical characteristics, they tell me, "I need a transformer with the following characteristics – make it for me!" I do a bit of figuring and lay it out – same thing for an equalizer or a filter. But there are some jobs, obviously, that I'm not capable of doing, and so sometimes the engineer gives you the figures and you just build it, you give it a concrete physical existence, you test it, you take all the measures, if it has to be improved you improve it, in short you try to make it work. (Besola)

Another technician working in the engineering lab, with twelve years' seniority (he has been at GT&E since he was sixteen), still finds himself doing a fairly circumscribed job. His description would fit most of the jobs in the research lab equally well.

The engineer designs video amplifiers, filters, all the stuff needed for this section of a radio bridge. The engineer does the theoretical project, which naturally is subject to error, to variation. . . . After building the theoretical project of the engineer, I have to check all these things – that is, the engineer passes me the data he has calculated, I build the project together with the blue collar worker, then I make all the measurements, checking for all the specifications the equipment has to meet, and usually the measurements are not within the parameters specified in the theoretical project. I try to work out these bugs, because obviously the theoretical project is never perfect. Then I show all the measurements to the designer, the engineer, and he tells me what I have to do to get around, to solve, to improve on his original project. (Cestaro)

Siemens – laboratory technicians

Approximately 100 people work in the development sections of the Special Systems Laboratory, the functional equivalents of the labs at GT&E. About half are engineers and other university graduates, and the other half are technicians. The sample includes eleven people who work in the development sections of the Lab.

Most of those in the development sections are working on the project which is the raison d'être of the Lab: the decentralized electronic switching system called Proteo. The heart of this system is a digital computer. The largest sections in the Lab are those concerned with the hardware and software of this system. There are also other groups working on other projects such as a video telephone, medical equipment, and smaller switching stations.

The technicians in the software section work on various computer programs. Small groups of two to four people, engineers and technicians, will work together on a program. All the stages from the drawing of the flowchart through debugging are done collaboratively. Because programming does not require sophisticated mathematical knowledge, engineers and technicians are on fairly equal terms. The software section is perceived to be, and is in fact, the most egalitarian in the Lab. It was only in this section, for example, that the decision was made to abolish all merit raises.

In the hardware sections (logical and analogical circuitry), there is a somewhat more evident division of labor between technicians and engineers. In some cases, the jobs of the technicians in these sections are similar to those of the technicians in the labs at GT&E: They build and test circuitry that the engineer has designed. However, unlike at GT&E, the technician is kept informed during the design phase and is encouraged to learn how his work is related to that of others. The technician is also encouraged to study so that he may take more and more responsibility. Often responsibility for one portion of a project will be delegated entirely to the technician, who thus learns to become more autonomous.

Attitudes toward job and organization

Our analysis begins with the attitudes toward work and toward the organization. These attitudes are the primary elements of any discussion of the work situation. As will become apparent, the job cannot be considered simply as a specific task but must, instead, be conceived of as a task carried out within an organizational context.

The dimensions of job satisfaction

The voluminous literature on job satisfaction shows that it cannot be treated as a unitary concept. Two reviews of the literature spaced seven years apart, those of Vroom and Locke,[2] have indicated identical dimensions, although Locke has added two dimensions to Vroom's original seven. The dimensions given by Vroom are (1) attitudes toward the company, (2) opportunities for promotion, (3) the content of the job, (4) supervision, (5) pay, (6) physical working conditions, and (7) coworkers. Locke added two dimensions, namely, fringe benefits and recognition for work done, neither of which is very important in our context. The interview guide included questions on all Vroom's seven dimensions with the exception of the physical conditions of work, which did not seem to be relevant for our cases. We shall be looking at all of these dimensions in the course of our analysis.

The new working class theorists attribute particular importance to the contents of the job and the relations with co-workers following therefrom. In the remaining pages of this chapter, we shall look in some detail at how the workers view their jobs.

As a first step, we need to take a closer look at the dimension that Vroom calls "job content." Many of the new working class hypotheses imply a distinction between attitudes toward the task itself and attitudes toward relevant aspects of the organization within which the task is carried out. For Mallet and Gorz, it is precisely because the worker is involved in his job that he comes into conflict with the organization. If this is so, attitudes toward the task itself should constitute one distinct dimension, whereas attitudes toward the organization of work should constitute another. Two factor analyses of the items regarding attitudes toward the work task and attitudes toward the organization show that this is indeed the case.

The first factor analysis (see Table 4.1) includes sixteen items from three different content areas: attitudes toward the task itself, toward the organization, and toward the supervisor. Three factors are easily interpretable, as they correspond to the three content areas. In the Varimax rotation, these three factors account for 46.1 percent of the variance. The most important factor is attitudes toward the task. It alone accounts for 17.9 percent of the total variance. The next factor, attitudes toward the supervisor, accounts for 14.6 percent of the variance. In addition to the three items regarding the supervisor, another three items load highly on this factor. Of these additional three, two ("Should employees have more say in decisions that concern them?" and "Can you give me an example of a decision on which your advice might have been asked but wasn't?") also deal with relations with superiors. The third ("Do you think it would be useful to do more groupwork?") is a more general question about the organization of work.

The third factor, which accounts for 13.6 percent of the variance, may clearly be labeled "attitudes toward the organization." These are all items that ask in various ways whether, in the worker's judgment, the organization permits him to do his job well.

A second factor analysis was carried out omitting the three items on the supervisor (see Appendix A). The results are very similar. The factor loadings from this second factor analysis were used to weight items in the scales discussed below.

In both of these factor analyses, attitudes toward the task emerge clearly as a dimension distinct from attitudes toward one's supervisor

Table 4.1. *Factor analysis of sixteen items concerning attitudes toward the task, the organization, and the supervisor.*

Variable description	Item no.	Principal components factor loadings						Communality
		1	2	3	4	5	6	
Is work interesting	1.11	-0.723	0.261	-0.045	0.175	0.256	-0.150	0.711
Possibility for learning on job	1.12	-0.573	0.481	-0.213	-0.121	-0.008	-0.151	0.642
Increase in knowledge required	1.20	-0.478	0.362	-0.253	0.369	-0.352	-0.116	0.698
Is your knowledge utilized	1.21	0.389	-0.615	-0.080	0.035	-0.010	-0.213	0.583
Orders changed without explanation	2.3(a)	0.442	0.245	-0.425	0.035	0.349	-0.272	0.633
Do things without knowing why	2.3(b)	0.519	-0.080	-0.462	-0.017	0.214	0.387	0.686
Is work repetitive	2.6	0.660	-0.389	0.105	-0.065	-0.313	-0.118	0.714
Does boss do job well	2.9	-0.570	-0.407	-0.135	0.062	0.415	0.031	0.686
More collaboration useful	1.16	0.441	0.252	0.166	0.611	0.020	0.041	0.683
Reaction to organizational problems	2.1	-0.197	-0.456	0.149	0.328	0.052	0.407	0.544
No contacts is problem	2.4	0.461	0.068	-0.393	0.558	-0.005	0.054	0.687
Work group does good job	2.5	-0.505	-0.318	0.493	0.257	-0.052	-0.074	0.674
Should boss follow more closely	2.10(a)	0.305	0.576	0.109	-0.205	-0.392	0.224	0.682
Should boss give more autonomy	2.10(b)	0.481	0.074	0.327	0.218	0.096	-0.570	0.726
Should employees have more say	2.12	0.191	0.475	0.479	0.188	0.256	0.319	0.695
Your advice unsought	2.13	0.418	0.290	0.338	-0.285	0.465	-0.018	0.671
Latent roots		3.693	2.238	1.451	1.258	1.078	0.996	10.715
% of variance explained		23.1	14.0	9.1	7.9	6.8	6.2	67.0

Table 4.1 (*cont.*)

Variable description	Item no.	Rotated factor loadings (varimax)			Communality
		1	2	3	
Is work interesting	1.11	-0.684	-0.198	0.292	0.593
Possibility for learning on job	1.12	-0.774	-0.070	0.019	0.605
Increase in knowledge required	1.20	-0.637	-0.128	-0.033	0.424
Is your knowledge utilized	1.21	0.670	-0.272	-0.115	0.536
Orders changed without explanation	2.3(a)	0.030	0.142	-0.644	0.436
Do things without knowing why	2.3(b)	0.296	-0.061	-0.631	0.489
Is work repetitive	2.6	0.744	0.115	-0.177	0.598
Does boss do job well	2.9	-0.141	-0.626	0.313	0.509
More collaboration useful	1.16	0.140	0.503	-0.187	0.307
Reaction to organizational problems	2.1	0.218	-0.319	0.346	0.268
No contacts is problem	2.4	0.172	0.050	-0.583	0.372
Work group does good job	2.5	-0.005	-0.184	0.752	0.599
Should boss follow more closely	2.10(a)	-0.162	0.597	-0.232	0.436
Should boss give more autonomy	2.10(b)	0.357	0.465	-0.024	0.344
Should employees have more say	2.12	-0.081	0.680	0.151	0.492
Your advice unsought	2.13	0.167	0.586	-0.037	0.373
Sum of squares		2.870	2.333	2.180	7.383
% of variance explained		17.9	14.6	13.6	46.1

and toward other aspects of the organization. We shall have a good deal more to say below on the relationship between attitudes toward the job itself and attitudes toward the organization.

Some comparisons with other samples

The responses of our sample to the questions on job satisfaction are similar to those of other comparable samples. Blauner, in his 1960 summary of previous research on job satisfaction, gives the proportion in various occupations who would choose the same kind of work if they were to begin their careers over again. The percentages are given in Table 4.2. The technicians from this sample fall between the skilled auto workers and the skilled printers and paper workers.

Table 4.3 shows the proportion in the different job categories in the sample who say they would choose the same type of work again. The draftsmen at Siemens, whose job is less technical than some of the others, are the least likely to say they would choose the same career again.

When pressed as to what they might do instead, many of those who say they would not choose the same work again say that they like the

Table 4.2. *Proportion in various occupations who would choose the same kind of work if beginning career again.*

Professional occupations	%	Working class occupations	%
Mathematicians	91	Skilled printers	52
Physicists	89	Paper workers	52
Biologists	89	Skilled autoworkers	41
Chemists	86	Skilled steelworkers	41
Lawyers	83	Textile workers	31
Journalists	82	Unskilled steelworkers	21
		Unskilled autoworkers	16
	New working class technicians	46[a]	

[a] Data from this study (%).
Source: Robert Blauner, "Work Satisfaction and Industrial Trends in Modern Society," in S. M. Lipset and R. Bendix, eds., *Class, Status, and Power*, 2nd ed. (New York: Free Press), p. 477.

Table 4.3. *Proportion in different job groups in the sample who would choose the same type of work again. (Jobs listed in order of stated interest.)*

Would choose same job again	GT&E sales	GT&E testing	GT&E draft-ing	Sie-mens draft-ing	GT&E devel-opment	Sie-mens testing	Sie-mens devel-opment	Total
Yes	55.6%[a] 5	57.9% 11	55.6% 5	11.1% 1	47.8% 11	33.3% 2	45.5% 5	46.5% 40
No – go further	11.1% 1	5.3% 1	22.2% 2	22.2% 2	13.0% 3	33.3% 2	27.3% 3	16.3% 14
No – other	33.3% 3	36.8% 7	22.2% 2	66.7% 6	39.1% 9	33.3% 2	27.3% 3	37.2% 32
Total	10.5% 9	22.1% 19	10.5% 9	10.5% 9	26.7% 23	7.0% 6	12.8% 11	100.0% 86

[a] Upper entries are percent of column totals; the numbers below are units.

field they are in but wish that they had continued their studies through the university level. If we add those who give this answer to those who give an unqualified "yes," the percentage of favorable responses rises to 62.8 percent. Only among the draftsmen at Siemens do a majority say that they would rather have done something entirely different with their lives.

In their answers to the question, "Would you say your work is very interesting, fairly interesting, not very interesting, or not at all interesting?" the technicians in our sample respond similarly to the 358 white collar workers in Crozier's sample of insurance companies.[3] However, the employees in our sample are somewhat more satisfied: 72 percent find their work at least fairly interesting, compared with 62 percent of Crozier's sample. This is hardly surprising when one considers that Crozier's sample consists primarily of various grades of clerical workers. Within our sample, those doing clerical work are the least satisfied.

These similarities in the responses of our sample and those of other samples from different times and places are encouraging in that they suggest that our sample is fairly representative of a larger universe.

Attitudes toward task and organization: two scales

Unlike the question on career choice, the item on the interest an individual finds in his work shows a great deal of variability from job to job. There are five items in the interview guide. All of them have to do with attitudes toward the task and show a relatively similar variation by job (see Table 4.4). These items constitute the "attitudes toward the task" factor emerging from the factor analyses described above. A scale we have called the "work discontent" (WKDISC) scale was formed from these questions, each one weighted by its factor loading. Details on the construction of this scale are to be found in Appendix A.

Ordering the jobs on the WKDISC scale, we find that the technicians in the commercial offices at GT&E are the most discontented group and the lab technicians at Siemens are the most satisfied, with the others ranging in between (Figure 4.1). There is a dramatic difference between the two extreme groups, with eight out of nine of those in the commercial offices at GT&E scoring above the median on the scale as compared to one out of eleven of the lab technicians at Siemens.

Those who work in the Special Systems Laboratory are in every case happier with the tasks assigned them than their counterparts doing the same type of work at GT&E. Similarly, comparing the two organizations as wholes, it is apparent that those who work in the Lab are considerably more satisfied with their jobs. The only group at GT&E which is more satisfied than even the most dissatisfied group in Siemens is that of the lab technicians.

This difference may be attributed partly to the different types of production of the two organizations and partly to organizational differences. For example, the job of the tester is really quite different in the two companies despite the fact that the label is the same. Many of those in testing at Siemens design equipment for testing or test prototypes besides doing routine testing of circuits. The difference between testers in the two companies is much greater than that between draftsmen or lab technicians, and it is the only one of the three comparisons for which the difference between means is statistically significant. Nevertheless, there are differences for the other job categories as well. This is not too surprising. A mass production job, or even a batch production job, will inevitably be less interesting than the job of building prototypes. The organizational policies and climate also affect both the

Table 4.4. *Variables from WKDISC scale by job group.*

Item	GT&E sales	GT&E testing	GT&E drafting	Siemens drafting	GT&E development	Siemens testing	Siemens development	Totals
Is your work interesting? % Very or fairly	55.6	52.6	70.0	66.7	75.0	100	100	71.6 (n = 88)
Do you have the chance to learn new things on the job? % Yes	44.4	55.6	40.0	66.7	87.5	100	100	71.3 (n = 87)
Do you think that the work you do now requires more knowledge than that which you did when you were first hired? % Yes	44.4	63.2	70.0	77.8	75.0	100	100	72.4 (n = 87)
Could your work be done by someone with less training than you have? % No or sometimes	55.5	42.1	40.0	50.0	87.5	66.7	63.7	60.9 (n = 87)
Is your work repetitive? % No or usually no	33.3	22.2	55.5	66.6	87.5	100	90.9	63.9 (n = 86)

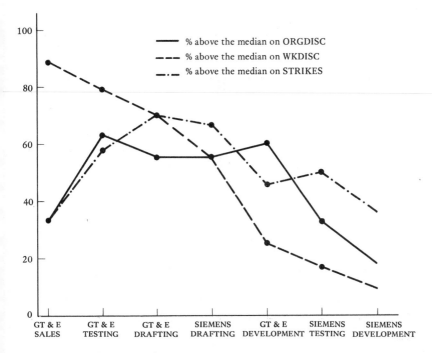

Figure 4.1. Plots of WKDISC, ORGDISC, and STRIKES by job group. (The lines joining the points are intended to make the figure more readable, not to suggest continuity.)

definition of jobs and the way in which these jobs, once defined, are experienced.

Within each factory, the technicians working in the labs are the most satisfied with their jobs. In the Special Systems Laboratory, the testers are nearly as satisfied as those working on development. The draftsmen are the most dissatisfied group in the Lab. Four out of the nine score above the median on the WKDISC scale.

At GT&E, the technicians who work in the labs are more satisfied than each of the other groups. They are followed by the draftsmen, the testers, and those working in the commercial offices, in that order.

We have referred to the scale in our discussion because the scale is more stable than the individual items. However, the same pattern is evident from the single items as from the WKDISC scale. The response to the question, "Is your work repetitive?" illustrates the differences in satisfaction between jobs: Among the testers at GT&E, 77.8 percent describe their work as repetitive; among technicians in the development sections of the Special Systems Lab, only 9.1 percent see their work as repetitive; and among the testers at the Lab, none see their work as repetitive (see Table 4.4). The variability on the other items is nearly as great. It is apparent that there are very substantial differences within the sample in attitudes toward the job.

Attitudes toward the organization show a pattern of variation quite different from that of attitudes toward the task itself. A scale measuring discontent with the organization (the ORGDISC scale) was constructed on the basis of the second factor analysis described above. The scale includes five items (see Table 4.5). For more information, the reader may turn to Appendix A.

Discontent with the organization as measured by this scale indicates an active and demanding stance vis-à-vis the organization. Those respondents who score high on the ORGDISC scale often convey a considerable amount of anger in their interviews. For this reason and for reasons of style, these respondents are sometimes referred to as having a militant attitude toward the organization. However, as we shall see in Chapter 6, the relationship between this attitude and strike participation is problematic.

Relationship between attitudes toward the task and attitudes toward the organization

The hypothesis stated and a first test. If the jobs are ordered from low to high according to their WKDISC scores and cross-tabulated with the dichotomized ORGDISC scale, a roughly curvilinear relationship appears (see Figure 4.1). This is also apparent from a glance at the variation of the single items by job (see Table 4.5). Those evincing the least frustration over organizational problems are those at the two extremes in their attitudes toward the task: the technicians in the commercial offices at GT&E, who are the most dissatisfied in their attitudes toward the task, and those in the development and testing sections in the Special Systems Lab, who are the most satisfied in their attitudes toward the task. Those who are most frustrated over organizational matters are the testers and lab technicians at GT&E. The draftsmen in both organizations are intermediate in their levels of discontent over organizational factors, although they are closer to the more discontented than

Table 4.5. *Variables from ORGDISC scales by job group.*

Item	GT&E sales	GT&E testing	GT&E drafting	Siemens drafting	GT&E develop-ment	Siemens testing	Siemens develop-ment	Totals
Do you sometimes receive instructions which are later changed or an-nulled without ex-planation? %Yes	22.2	31.6	30.0	33.3	33.3	16.7	0	26.1 (n = 88)
Would it be useful for you to do more group work? %Yes	11.1	55.6	66.7	37.5	59.1	40.0	9.1	43.9 (n = 82)
Is lack of contact with other sections a problem for you in your work? % Yes	22.2	31.6	20.0	33.3	8.7	0	0	17.2 (n = 87)
Do you think your work group manages to do a good job? % Fairly good or not so good[a]	66.7	94.4	77.8	77.8	86.3	83.4	72.7	82.1 (n = 84)
Do you ever have to do things without knowing what they are for? % Yes	33.3	40.0	42.1	55.6	54.2	33.3	18.2	42.0 (n = 88)

[a]Versus percent very good.

to the more satisfied groups. The differences between jobs, if not so great as on the WKDISC items, are substantial.

Despite the great differences in organizational structure between GT&E and the Special Systems Laboratory, the workers at GT&E are not consistently more dissatisfied than those at Siemens. The draftsmen are equally dissatisfied in both organizations. The testers and lab technicians at Siemens are considerably happier with the organization of their work than their counterparts at GT&E, but the employees of the GT&E commercial offices express as little dissatisfaction as the testers in Siemens. Before proceeding to look more closely at this puzzling state of affairs, a word must be said about the relationships between the single ORGDISC items and type of job.

Table 4.5 presents the responses to the ORGDISC items as they vary by job. The pattern of variation is not as consistent as for the WKDISC items. This is particularly evident in the case of the Siemens draftsmen. The lack of consistency suggests that attitudes toward the organization of work are not so unidimensional as attitudes toward the task. Aspects of the organization impinge in different ways on individuals doing different jobs.

The draftsmen at Siemens are the one group whose variability across items makes their rank problematic. Three of the items indicate that they are the most frustrated or one of the most frustrated groups. The other two items show them to be relatively satisfied, although not as satisfied as the GT&E sales or Siemens lab technicians. The standard deviation for the Siemens draftsmen on the ORGDISC scale is considerably higher than that for other groups. The relative unity of the ORGDISC factor is empirically derived from our sample. Although these items may constitute a single dimension for some jobs, this may be less true for others. Looking at the evidence in various ways (the means of the groups on the ORGDISC scale, the percentages above the median, and their average rank order positions on the five items), we might place the Siemens draftsmen slightly higher than the GT&E lab technicians. However these three groups are very close in their levels of discontent.

We present now the outline of a hypothesis to explain this pattern of variation of discontent with the organization by job. The hypothesis will be qualified and elaborated after we have looked at the jobs through the eyes of our respondents.

The groups that are lowest in their levels of dissatisfaction with the organization, the lab technicians and testers in Siemens and the employees of the commercial offices in GT&E, all work in situations in which there is a congruence between the type of work done and the organizational structure within which it takes place. The lab technicians and testers in Siemens do involving work in an organizational structure that encourages participation. The commercial office employees in GT&E do routine work in a hierarchical organization. The two most dissatisfied groups, the testers and lab technicians in GT&E, experience an incongruence between work and organizational structure because they do involving work in an organization that hinders their becoming involved. The draftsmen are intermediate on the work involvement as on other dimensions, but their work is closely controlled, making their mean ORGDISC scores relatively high in both plants. The effect of close control will be taken up again later in this chapter.

These relationships between task and organizational structure may be represented schematically as shown in Table 4.6. All the variables in the schema have been defined save one: the involving–not involving dimension along which we have categorized the jobs. A job is involving

Table 4.6. *Job type, organizational structure, and discontent with the organization.*

Work	Organizational structure	
	Participatory	Nonparticipatory
Involving	Siemens technical jobs (lab technicians and testers)	GT&E technical jobs (lab technicians and testers)
	Low on ORGDISC: mean = -.216	High on ORGDISC: mean = .075
	Siemens draftsmen	GT&E draftsmen
	High on ORGDISC: mean = .084	High on ORGDISC: mean = .071
Not involving		GT&E commercial offices
		Low on ORGDISC: mean = -.111

to the extent that it demands an investment of intellectual and/or physical energy on the part of the worker. Unfortunately there were no items in our interview guide to measure involvement. We have, therefore, relied on a global judgment based on the interviews and on common sense. In making this judgment we have been concerned only with gross differences between jobs.

The ordering might have been labeled technical–not technical as easily as involving–not involving. Jobs relating to the design, construction, and testing of electronic equipment have been grouped together as *involving* because they all require the application of knowledge about electronics to specific cases. The clerical jobs of the commercial offices clearly require a lower commitment of intellectual energy and were considered *not involving*. The jobs of the draftsmen fall somewhere in between the technical jobs and the clerical jobs on this dimension. Although we have no scale on which to place them precisely, they seem closer to those doing technical work than to the commercial offices employees in their involvement in work. The high ORGDISC scores of the draftsmen in both plants are due to the close control under which they work as well as to the effects of the variables in the schema. This point will be expanded upon further on in our discussion.

It will be seen that the lower left corner cell in Table 4.6 remains empty. None of the groups at Siemens do work as unsatisfying and un-involving as that of the commercial offices at GT&E. Nonetheless, the responses of that group at the Lab whose job is the least satisfying and involving, the draftsmen, tend to support the hypothesis of an inter-action effect between task and organizational structure. For, although the participatory structure of the Lab at Siemens leads to a substantial and significant reduction in discontent with the organization among those doing technical jobs as compared to those in analogous jobs at GT&E, for the draftsmen there is no such reduction. If anything, the draftsmen at Siemens seem somewhat more frustrated than their counterparts at GT&E. As we shall see below, they do not view the participatory structure as being particularly helpful to them. There is some indication that it has the effect of raising aspirations that cannot be satisfied.

Without data with which to fill in the empty cell, we can do no more than propose the hypothesis that those doing routine and uninvolving jobs in an organization in which they are encouraged to participate will be more discontent with the organization than those doing similar routine jobs in a hierarchical organization. Although the participatory organization clearly renders less discontent those employees who are in a position to benefit from this organization, namely the lab technicians and those doing technical work in general, its effect on those doing more routine jobs is unclear. We shall have more to say on this point later on in this chapter.

In order to test the hypothesis suggested by the schema, a *t* test was done comparing the mean of those groups low in discontent with the organization, that is, those doing technical work in the Special Systems Laboratory and those working in the commercial offices at GT&E, with the mean of the other groups. The difference is highly significant (.001, one-tailed).

The hypothesis illustrated. To gain a clearer understanding of how the interaction between task and organizational structure leads to this pattern of dissatisfaction, we turn back to our respondents' descriptions of their job situations. We begin with those groups at opposite extremes in their levels of satisfaction with the task, but uniformly low in their frustration with the organization: the lab technicians and testers at Siemens and the technicians in the commercial offices at GT&E.

The lab technicians at the Special Systems Laboratory are doing involving and interesting work in an organization that facilitates this work. The eleven respondents from this group are virtually unanimous in describing their work as very interesting.[4] Two employees explained that they are willing to make the sacrifice of living far from their homes only because of the particular satisfaction they get from their work. "I'm from Bologna. Every weekend I go back home, then come back up here during the week. . . . It's a sacrifice. I stay here because I found a job that I like, that satisfies me. . ." (Serano). One technician from Sicily says he would not return there, "even though the temptation would be great. Here I've found a job which I don't think I'll ever find anywhere else, to me it seems unique, maybe because I've never worked anywhere else, but anyway. . ." (Tigrotti). Another technician who attends the university at night remarked that he finds his job so absorbing that he ends up missing classes to stay at home and work.

The lab technicians in the Special Systems Laboratory are also very positive about the organization. One familiar complaint of lab technicians is that they are not given autonomy and responsibility. A quotation from one of the interviews gives an idea of the unusual situation in the Lab:

Then we came along, the four of us who had been in training together. Two of us were put in this group, that is, actually it was we who said, "we want to join that group because we feel suited to that kind of work," so we went there. . . . They had borrowed an engineer from another office and they told us, "Listen, go work with him and try to keep up with him." After a month he was recalled to his original office, so I was told, "Listen, we think you can go ahead with this on your own." They trusted me blindly, they left that job to me [the designing of part of a private telephone exchange]. I never thought it would be so difficult, so involving. I had to design the circuits . . . make choices, helped out by others, taking advantage of their experience, but still, I had to figure out by myself how to do research on the components that had to be used. They didn't have them in the lab so I had to do some research to find out what the market had to offer, which ones would be most appropriate for this circuit, I selected them myself . . . People reproached me good-naturedly about being too indecisive. If I had to make a choice, it took me ages. . . . They told me, "You don't need a nursemaid, you're old enough to decide on your own." (Mongillo)

The environment is supportive. People pass on information willingly and are not reluctant to spend time teaching their more junior colleagues:

During the training period, there was theoretical training for a couple of hours. The rest of the day was free. We looked through mimeos, reports, and then we could go and ask anybody for explanations, or review things we had learned, or go look at books. I asked about stuff left and right. The explanations were exhaustive. . . . (DelToro)

The initial period of formal training is often followed by a longer informal training period. However, unlike at GT&E, the technician is not permanently assigned to work for an engineer in a dependent position. "In the beginning I wasn't sure how to define the relationship. I always asked advice and he told me to be independent, he always pushed me to be independent. Obviously I ask advice when I need it, but I also try to be independent" (Tigrotti). There are no rigid role barriers between engineers and technicians. "When I began working here, even though I worked on the same stuff I work on now, I worked with an engineer who told me how to do everything, while now I work on the same stuff independently, so in a year and a half I've learned a hell of a lot" (Massa).

A kind of creative chaos results from the freedom to "do one's own thing." In answer to the question of whether he encountered any organizational problems in getting his work done, one technician said,

Speaking of organization within our group, we do other things besides the subject . . . the main work, there are lots of other little things to do, so sometimes, I don't know, we get kind of spread out, like one guy will go to a conference, another will study some English, another will do a little program for someone who came and asked him for it, so sometimes we have trouble figuring out where we're at. Then, I don't know, after a day or two of working scattered all over the place, it takes a while to get reorganized, to get back to working together . . . but only this kind of difficulty. (Serano)

Yet the autonomy that is encouraged does not take the form of competitive individualism. On the contrary, most work is done by groups and it is groups that are seen as deserving the credit for work well done. "There isn't that need to make it, that putting down of other people. That's why I said that the people here are pretty hot stuff" (Facciuto).

The situation of the Siemens testers is similar. They are as enthusiastic about the task itself as those in the development sections, but somewhat less enthusiastic about the organization they work in. As noted earlier, the testers do a variety of jobs. To the extent that they are assigned tasks in which their productivity is controlled, they chafe at the restrictions imposed on them. Hence their less positive attitude toward the organization.

In contrast to these two groups, those working in the commercial offices at GT&E do a routine paperwork job in an organizational structure that is, unfortunately, characteristic of Italian industry: hierarchical, rigid, and authoritarian. But, although the technicians in the commercial offices are lower in job satisfaction than any other group in the sample, they express very little discontent about the organization.

The work itself is boring. The young GT&E technician quoted at the beginning of this chapter, whose job consists of making up bills for replacement parts, says:

It might be an interesting job if they taught me the function of each part, but they don't. I'm a robot, in fact I've come to the point where I let the work pile up as much as possible and then whip it off as quickly as I can, in two or two and a half hours, really quickly. I do it whenever the hell I feel like it, I don't give a damn about anybody or anything, if it's a customer I like I send the stuff right away; if I don't like him I make him wait a month and a half. (Guerrieri)

The employees complain that they do not have any opportunities to use the technical knowledge they have learned in school or on previous jobs. When asked if his job required any technical knowledge about the equipment, one man answered,

The work I do could be done by somebody with less technical knowledge. . . . We do mainly paperwork. If I write something on paper, I know what it's about, but that's about the only advantage I have. Someone without the technical education could write the same thing, do the same work, but he wouldn't understand what he was doing. That is, it's only an advantage as far as my own moral satisfaction is concerned. (Vassallo)

Several people brought up this point spontaneously. One technician had expected that the job would not only permit him to learn but would also place him in personal contact with customers:

I'd like to do a technical job, where there's something to be learned. Where I am it's a bit too commercial, but then it's not even. . . we have to prepare estimates, but we don't get to talk to the customers much. It's not even that sales oriented. The boss talks, the boss decides, and we execute. . . . If there's some problem, the boss talks to the customer. . . . Besides, there isn't much that's technical about it. (Alessio)

Notwithstanding this high level of discontent with the job itself, these employees have few complaints about the organization. Their jobs are routine, and the division of labor is established by long practice. In answer to the question, "Can you give me an example of a decision that concerned you, on which you might have given an opinion but weren't consulted?" one technician said matter-of-factly, without bitterness, "So far I haven't ever had to decide anything to do with work on my own. If and when it happens, we'll see" (Taleggi). There are few organizational problems. "The organization is always the same. It doesn't change much. Once one has made out one's work schedule, maybe there are times you work more and times you work less, but once you know the work you have to do and have organized it a bit, whatever difficulties there were disappear" (Taleggi).

But the fact that routine and administrative practice have eliminated much of the uncertainty in these jobs does not in itself explain the absence of complaints. One might suppose, on the contrary, that the monotony and narrowness of the job would be associated with frustration and anger directed toward the organization. If this does not occur, it is because the employees feel themselves to be in such a weak position that they cannot rebel. The most common response is withdrawal and apathy. Two young technicians expressed themselves with the same formula: "I can't expect much, I've just begun working" (Taleggi, a young man who has been on the job one year); "It's tough to find a real technical job, to get specialized. They don't give us much to learn here, but you can't expect much more" (Alessio).

Very few of those in the commercial offices say that they ever have to do anything without really understanding what it is about (see Table 4.5), despite the fact that their entire work deals with equipment about which many of them know nothing. "One guy [in my office] who is an electrical *perito* like me has never *seen* a telephone switching station. He has to supply telephone materials without ever having seen a switching station! It's already a lot that in my case they sent me for a month [to a switching station] " (Alessio).

They claim to understand completely what they are doing, not because they are dishonest, but because understanding the function of the equipment is so far from their jobs as to make it seem irrelevant. Although many of these technicians would like to be able to learn more, to understand more, this aspiration is abstract, not related to their day-to-day work.

It is difficult to convey in a short quotation the evasiveness and ambiguity of the answers of these employees. The following exchange gives something of the flavor of the interviews.

Interviewer: As far as interestingness is concerned, would you say that your job is good, so-so, or not very good?

Taleggi: Let's say that I'm never satisfied. Naturally, to get to the ideal – I don't know, maybe one never gets to the ideal. That is, the job may be good from one point of view, but I don't know, from another point of view, it might be. . . for example, in my case the job would be fine, let's say I'm uncomfortable because I'm so far from home, so I lose a lot of time travelling. . .

Interviewer: But as far as interestingness, the job itself. . .?

Taleggi: Well, I haven't been working that long – a year – so I don't have that much experience, I don't know, one gets into the work more, into the details. . .

Interviewer: So then you're saying that for now it's not so interesting?

Taleggi: No, it's not that it's not interesting; maybe as time passes I'll become more interested as I get to know. . . as I get more experienced in the job, that is, as one gets to know a job, either one gets to appreciate it more or one gets more bored with it.

The fearfulness of these employees also manifested itself in the high rate of refusals to be interviewed. It was necessary to ask thirteen people to obtain nine interviews. This 31 percent refusal rate contrasts with the 16 percent refusal rate for the rest of GT&E. Whereas in the labs and the testing department, people would cluster around to ask for appointments, in the commercial offices it was difficult to convince the employees that the study was not secretly funded by management or, worse yet, by the union.

Why do these employees feel themselves to be in such a weak position that they must withdraw? On the one hand, there is the fact that they are easily replaceable – they do a job anyone could do after only a brief period of training. This objective lack of bargaining power vis-à-vis management is experienced subjectively as a sense of insecurity that leads the person to say, "I can't expect much." On the other hand, there is the character of the job itself, which, by failing to involve the worker in any meaningful way, does not arouse in him those aspirations that would inevitably bring him into conflict with the organization.

The lab technicians and testers at Siemens and the technicians in the commercial offices at GT&E are all relatively satisfied with the organization of their work. In both cases there is congruence between the organizational structure and the task. The organization of the Special Systems Laboratory allows the technicians in the development sections and the testers the autonomy and freedom they need to carry out well their rather openly defined jobs. The organization of the GT&E commercial offices does not allow for freedom, autonomy, self-development. But these things would be unheard-of luxuries in an office job. Instead of acting on their latent discontent, a discontent that is evident from their dissatisfaction with their tasks, the employees withdraw.

We consider next those doing technical work at GT&E, namely, the testers and lab technicians. Both groups express much frustration and dissatisfaction about the organization of their work.

The testers are the most dissatisfied of the seven job groups so far as the organization of their work is concerned. They are also dissatisfied with the task itself. Testing jobs were seen as repetitive by 77.7 percent of the testers interviewed. Many workers spoke of the pressures to "produce" (i.e., to test), preventing them from pursuing the technical questions that often arose. But the frustration of the testers arises less from the boredom inherent in the task itself than from the involvement demanded by the task and rejected by the organization. The anger at not being able to delve more deeply into the problems encountered on the job is one of the most striking themes in the testers' interviews. This contradiction leads to an aggressive stance. Testers express vigorously the desire for freedom to pursue technical problems, for the right to rotate jobs, and for working conditions that would give them the possibility to further their professional development:

Everything that is incompatible with production is suppressed. . . . For example, the piece of equipment itself may consist of several circuits that influence one another. Each one has a certain purpose, and sometimes to be able to follow all the circuits would require a certain education, an effort on the part of the employer, because he would have to give up some time that might have gone to production to enable you to understand the whole thing, or else maybe one day you could do one kind of circuit and the next day another kind. . . . Instead they give you one circuit, you learn that by heart, and you go on doing that one. . . . Maybe there's one guy in the entire group who really understands the whole piece of equipment. (Basti)

Often testers would speak of how they got carried away in trying to puzzle out the reason for some strange malfunction. A moment later they would again be talking about the repetitiousness of the task, the lack of possibilities for development:

If I could start all over again I'd go to university, but by now. . . . Electronics is complicated, and at the blue collar level there are so many things one would like to know, but one doesn't have the background, so one feels kind of bad. I might understand the basic outlines of how a given circuit works, but there's a whole interesting part if I were to design something. . . . That's the nice part of the work. Instead, the blue collar worker puts in the circuit board, "passes," or "doesn't pass." It's a rather boring job that doesn't give much satisfaction. . . . (Fiore)

Some minutes later, he sounds quite different:

Sometimes, even in a job one has been doing for a long time, one runs into situations that – like today, there were two repairs in a circuit which I've been doing for a while, and I still haven't managed to find out what's wrong. I lost an hour. The others I repaired easily, but these two. . . . (Fiore)

In many cases, an initial enthusiasm gives way to a sort of devil-may-care apathetic attitude, which is uniquely expressed in the Italian word *menefreghismo:*

I've been there for a year now [testing transmitters]. The first two or three months it was great, true, but then. . . the same drag, over and over. . . . There are about four screws to turn or not to turn. After a certain amount of time, five or six months, you understand the equipment, you've really gotten into it, you've run into so many repairs that you know it by heart. In those first months I did three or four transmitters a day. Now I do one at most. I can't stand it. I wake up in the morning and I think, "Oh! I have to go there!" It becomes more and more of a drag. If you're really into what you're doing the day flies. But here you count the minutes with an eyedropper. Now I do the work in two minutes, whereas before maybe I took an hour, but I enjoyed it. It's convenient for them, but not for us. (Pietracorta)

This attitude is furthered by the feeling that nobody gives a damn about the quality of the product. In answer to the question of whether he ever was irritated by organizational difficulties, one tester said, "If you let yourself get the least bit involved, you'll get mad. For example, it's two years now that they keep sending amplifiers through with the same mistakes, and nobody bothers about eliminating them" (Barboso).

The pressure to produce colors all relationships.

Basti: Lots of times when you go ask your superiors or someone more expert for an explanation, they don't explain anything. You go and ask them, "Look, I found this problem, what do I do?" They won't say more than, "Change that resistance," or "Change that transistor," without giving you all the reasoning that brings them to that conclusion. . . . So next time something similar happens I have to go right back and ask again.

Interviewer: But couldn't you ask your co-workers?

Basti: No, it's not allowed, at least the foreman wouldn't like it. He says, "Why should they waste time? That's what I'm here for."

The individualistic strategies of adaptation arising as a result of this pressure do not facilitate the achievement of the unit's objectives. From his first day at work the newly hired tester, often fresh out of school, finds that no one is going to go out of his way to teach him the tricks of the trade. On the contrary, these tricks are jealously guarded. The novice finds himself seated at a table in front of an unknown piece of equipment that he is to test. "The first day I came to work here I thought I was in Houston, or at Cape Kennedy, all these blinking lights, these little things. I was starting from zero. . . . They handed me this book in English. . ." (Corvino). The new tester is placed beside a more experienced worker who is to teach him the job. But the teacher is often unwilling. One young man who had been at the job for four years explained the situation to me.

I used to give out a lot of information. I would test the new circuits, I'd be the first to do them, and I'd see that there were solutions and I'd show all the tricks to the guys who didn't have much experience – only they would produce at a high rate. . . . They'd turn out circuit after circuit to try to stand out, so I decided not to show anything anymore. (Marchiando)

The shortage of testing instruments provides other occasions for conflict.

Lots of times what happens is this. I need an instrument, I don't have it so I go to my boss, who says, "Borrow it from Tom, Dick, or Harry," so I go ask them. "No, I need it," so back I go to the boss, to pester him some more. "That guy can't give it to me because he doesn't have it." I go to others, I make the rounds of the whole factory; two hours pass, I go to the boss and I say, "What do we do?" "Take that instrument over there, it will do," and I go ahead. . . . For me it doesn't matter if the instrument is big or small, the important thing is that I be able to do my work. Lots of times an instrument of mine will disappear. There is an endless shortage of instruments – they even stole mine, I don't know whether it's still in the plant or not, I can't find it. . . . Few people have all their stuff, their original stuff. They don't hand it out. Those people like me who do lend their material often, almost always never see it again. My foreman once bawled me out because I informed him that one of my instruments had disappeared. "How can it be that you let yourself get robbed all the time?! You're not supposed to lend your stuff around!" But I don't have that kind of spirit, 'cause if a guy comes over, a friend, and I say, "No, I won't give it to you," and he says, "Why not?!" I wouldn't know what to answer, I just give it to him. (Iovene)

The lab technicians at GT&E are also relatively dissatisfied with the organization. Although their specific complaints are partly different from those of the testers, the mechanism is the same: An involving job brings the technician into conflict with an organization that does not enable him to carry on his work in a satisfying way.

On the whole, the technicians in the labs find their work interesting. In satisfaction with the job itself they rank immediately behind those doing technical jobs in the Special Systems Laboratory. But their expressions of satisfaction are often qualified by remarks relating to the frustrations they encounter in trying to work in a rigid, hierarchical organization. Unlike in the Lab at Siemens, each work group has a permanent structure, and, within each group, each person is assigned a permanent role. Engineers and some senior technicians do all designing. Often the technician is reduced to carrying out orders from the engineer under whom he works with no understanding of what he is doing. Study is forbidden, even on matters related to the job.

The work is really interesting, but. . . especially in this job, you have to begin to do things by yourself to notice that it's really interesting. And since up to now I've always followed at the heels, that is, worked under someone else, the other person absorbs all the refinements, the details of the work, so that you're left with the mechanical parts, you're not left any of the essence, the interesting part. The mechanical part impoverishes you, makes you feel that it's not interesting. (Grandi)

Partly because of the friends who climb all over everyone around them, partly because of the superiors, they really haven't given me the chance to learn much. . . . Personally I'm a bit lazy when it comes to politics, but it seems to me that, at least so far as GT&E is concerned, the work is divided rather sharply between blue collar and white collar workers, and also among white collar workers themselves. . . . We had to design a system and make it work. In practice, one guy designed the whole thing. . . . The only part that was left to us three technicians was the measurements, the tests, the checking up. . . (Fanelli)

Subordinates do not feel free to search for information wherever it is to be found but, rather, feel that they can only go to their bosses. This impedes the horizontal flow of communications essential in the development of a complex project.

Unfortunately it has happened to me often [to have to do something without really understanding what it is about]. Just the other day I had to do this series of measurements. "You have to do this, this, and this." They don't tell you, "This is the base band group amplifier. Do you know where it goes in the system?" No, they don't tell you. "You don't worry about it, I'll take care of the rest." There you are with your head in the sand, trying to do something you don't know how to do. So you go ask someone else. When I went to ask someone else what it was for, where it fits in, my boss said, "You shouldn't have gone to ask, I am the boss, I'm supposed to handle that." Well, if I'm supposed to work with my head in the sand, that's fine with me. . . (Grandi)

Fifty-four percent of the lab technicians at GT&E agreed that they sometimes worked on pieces of equipment or circuits without knowing what these were to be used for or how they were related to other parts of the project. One technician who fought successfully for more autonomy described his experience:

I got into an argument because I didn't like working like a machine – that is, I was used to knowing what the hell it was I was doing. That guy made me do stuff in the dark, so we got into an argument, and I went to the boss and said, "Listen, I'm not learning anything with that guy, I'm not doing anything interesting. Do me the favor of moving me somewhere else, 'cause I'm not working with him anymore!" (Baratta)

Information is used as power. By not transmitting information downward, the superior is able to keep the subordinate in a dependent position. One of the technicians perceived this with remarkable clarity.

Everyone has tried to keep away from him, not to be under him. Since he is a technician with a lot of experience, he knows a lot, he has absorbed all the knowledge in the company. He knows everything, so it's easy for everyone to go ask him rather than going crazy reading papers, and he takes advantage of this, he uses it to dominate the place. (Pirotta)

It hardly needs to be pointed out that because the technician's pay and career depend on how he is evaluated by those above him, the upward flow of information about personnel is as important to him as the downward flow of technical information. The fact that the boss controls this flow of information means that the employee has no way of ensuring that he will be fairly evaluated. Clientele systems develop: The boss rewards those who serve him best with promotions or merit raises. The technician feels that he is constantly struggling, not only to enlarge his area of autonomy, but also to gain access to more interesting jobs. Many employees feel that the company is not only uninterested in their professional development, but that it has an active interest in keeping them where they are. "If you're good they leave you there because you're indispensable, so you'll never get ahead." (Del Buono)

The pressures of excessive work loads and impending deadlines create strains in many sections.

My work could be interesting, but we're going through a period in which we're rather short of personnel in the office, so there is a ton of work to be done in a great hurry, to the detriment of the work itself. If things worked as they are supposed to, the work would be much more interesting. (B. Malerba)

In two or three days some people are supposed to arrive to look at a certain piece of equipment, so the boss asked us yesterday if we could finish by Tuesday, which meant that people had to go to work today [Saturday] and maybe even Sunday. . . . Apparently the boss knew about this visit months ago. . . One does things gladly, because people in the same section have to help one another, but one helps out if it really is something unexpected. O.K., let's give up a Sunday for the company, even if it's not. . . But, in a situation in which the bosses don't care about you because you're at the bottom of the ladder, you're not very attached either. . . My boss never was interested in me. If I'm home sick one day, he doesn't even notice. . . . He's only interested in his papers and in the two cretins who dominate him. (Pirotta)

As in the testing department, here too the organizational climate often turns involvement into apathy. But here, as in the testing department, the protestations of not caring are voiced with an anger that is quite absent among the workers of the commercial offices.

Cooperation is difficult, not only because of ill will, but also because one tends, given the overall treatment to which one is subject, one tends to coast along and say, O.K., this job was assigned to this guy, let him worry about it and then give me what I need, from there on it's my business. . . . If it's no good, I'll tell him to fix it. If it's O.K., but the whole thing doesn't work and the problem is in my part, that's my business. . . . There's a generalized egoism which wrecks everything. Each one of us is afraid that he will have to answer for the mistakes of someone else. (Cassella)

As the quotations show, these employees are highly articulate and aware of the effects of the organization upon them. Given the organizational problems, it causes little wonder that so many of the lab technicians at GT&E, when asked, "Is your work interesting?" answer, "It would be interesting work, but it all depends on how it is carried on and governed. . ." (Moreau).

It will be noted that discontent with the organization has been considered as a subjective stance that may or may not correspond to objective conditions. In the case of the commercial offices, the lack of complaints about the organization was interpreted as withdrawal rather than as a reflection of the organizational reality. In the case of those doing technical work at GT&E, dissatisfaction with the organization was interpreted as an aggressive, militant attitude caused not by the organizational structure alone but by the organizational structure *together with* the type of work performed. The commitment with which the job is performed will determine the person's attitude toward the organization. The interviews suggest that the greater a person's involvement, the more likely he is to come into conflict with a rigid organization – a conflict arising from being frustrated by that organization in his effort to do a good job.

This interpretation rests on the assumption that the organizational structure in the commercial offices is not really significantly different from that in other parts of the factory. None of the information gathered by the author in a year of observation contradicts this assumption. Those working in the commercial offices are, if anything, more closely controlled than those working in the labs. Other research, for example that of Lawrence and Lorsch,[5] suggests that in most factories the research function is more loosely organized than the sales function. It seems justifiable, therefore, to conclude that attitudes toward the organization are the outcome of interactions between job and organization rather than accurate reflections of organizational structure.

The cases of the testers and lab technicians at GT&E exemplify one kind of incongruence between task and organization, that is, the combination of an involving task and a confining organization. The other possible type of incongruence is that which exists between a routine and uninvolving task and a participatory organization. The closest approximation to this situation in our sample is that of the draftsmen at Siemens.

The draftsmen in the Special Systems Laboratory are generally lukewarm in their appraisals of the task itself: The mean of the group on the WKDISC scale is very close to the sample mean. In our earlier description, we compared the work of the electrical draftsmen to solving puzzles. Although each new puzzle is different from the one before, there is a certain sameness to the task that makes it uninteresting to many people after the initial fascination has worn off.

Now I work on the printed circuits. Before I was in documentation, but after a year the work seemed a bit too boring, uninteresting, so I tried to switch and I switched. At the beginning the work I'm doing now seemed more interesting than the documentation, but as time passes I see I'm back where I started, that is, I'm losing interest. . . . Maybe it's the kind of work – you finish one job and there you are facing another one; it gets boring. I'd like a job in which one could get more interested in the work, in which you see something. . . . I mean, a job that would make me work more together with others. . . have a certain vision of the whole. . . (Chilocava)

The mechanical draftsmen also express an unenthusiastic approval of their jobs. The drafting work here gets monotonous as well.

It may be interesting the first year, the second, the third, but when one has been at it for four years. . . I can't understand how some people at Siemens do it for twenty years. The guy who gets a medal for having been at Siemens for twenty-five years – they shouldn't give him a medal, they should shoot him. (Chieppo)

It should be pointed out that, both among the mechanical draftsmen and among the electrical draftsmen, there are those who like their work. But, in contrast to the other workers in the Special Systems Laboratory, they show no real enthusiasm and, in some cases, there is an active dislike.

As already noted, the draftsmen in the Lab are considerably less positive than the lab technicians in their feeling about the organization. Because they work for the engineers and technicians in the development section and because their productivity can be measured fairly easily, they find themselves working under much closer control than the lab technicians. This control seems all the more constraining when compared to the freedom enjoyed by others in the Lab.

At least in another office I'd have the chance to improve, because in addition to the work, they – that is, for any given problem – they study it before going to work on it, whereas we don't have this possibility. We have a schedule and it must be met. There's nothing doing, the work doesn't change, it's not like you can say, "What I haven't done today maybe I'll do next week." That's the thing, there's pressure, everyone is in a hurry. I try, when the courses are posted, when there are meetings, lectures, I try to participate, to get mimeos. . . When I have a free moment I look at them, for example software. I got the mimeo for the software course, I'm beginning to read it. I'd like to get more involved, learn new things, but I don't have the time or even the chance to do it, because if they see you not doing anything, maybe you're reading a technical journal, they'll give you more work immediately. (Chilocava)

Like the draftsmen at GT&E, the Lab draftsmen are frustrated that their point of view is not taken into account by the lab technicians and engineers, who feel free to change the design repeatedly without consulting them.

I'm tying the noose around my own neck, because I get incredibly pissed off if there's some organizational difficulty. The organization is still very uncertain. We're trying to scale down the grandiose ideas of the designers who want the sun and the moon, who want everything done differently from everyone else, . . . 'cause we're not everyone's servant. They can't change everything every ten minutes just because they feel like it. (Chieppo)

There is also the more direct control by the supervisors. In keeping with the ethos of the Lab, this control is exercised with a velvet glove. The head of the electrical draftsmen's office claims that he would give the workers more freedom, but what would the higher-ups say?

Now that I'm going to school my boss lets me study. . . . If I take some reading material on electronics into the office, he doesn't tell me I can't read it unless there's an urgent job. He says that so far as he's concerned I could read all day, but if the higher-ups pass by and see me reading a book instead of working, they wouldn't like it, so he says to watch out for that, not to let myself be seen. (Iuteri)

In this same office, the boss attempted to put into operation an incentive system based on negative reinforcement.

The boss proposed that for each error we be fined 50 lire [8 cents] – that is, it wasn't a fine, it was to go toward a fund for a nice dinner at the end of the year. I said, "Look, a fund for any dinners is fine with me, but to have a 50 lire fine for each mistake is not justified in my opinion." I talked to some of the others, we went to the weekly meeting of the group, and got it removed. (Chilocava)

As the ending to this little episode shows, the velvet glove does, indeed, soften the atmosphere. The aspirations raised by the proximity of the development labs are in part satisfied by the organization. Discontent is also kept down through the policy of allowing people to move to other jobs if they so request, a policy made possible by the rapid growth of the Lab. If we compare the Siemens draftsmen to the GT&E draftsmen, it would appear that the net effect of the participatory superstructure is not significant. From the draftsman's point of view, the participatory institutions of the Lab are indeed simply a superstructure imposed upon a job situation basically similar to that of draftsmen working in more traditional organizations such as GT&E.

Consideration of the case of the draftsmen prompts a digression on control systems and an addition to the schema presented in Table 4.6. To the extent that the output of the individual worker can be, and is, controlled, he will resent that control and express greater dissatisfaction with the organization. Control of output and pressures for increased productivity alone go far toward constituting an authoritarian and hierarchical organizational environment. This is apparent in the case of the testers at GT&E as well as in that of the Siemens draftsmen. Largely because the productivity of the GT&E tester can be so closely measured and controlled, he is more frustrated than the lab technician working in a similar type of organization.

If a job is involving, if it demands positive action on the part of the employee, he will come into conflict with a rigid organization in the course of trying to do his job well. This kind of conflict may occur even if there is no direct control over individual productivity. It is the kind of conflict that is emphasized by Gorz and Mallet as typical of the new working class situations and which, in our sample, is exemplified by the GT&E lab technicians and testers.

But if a job does not demand the engagement and commitment of the worker, conflict will ensue because the control system must impose itself forcefully upon the worker. In this type of job the division of labor has transferred the control function, which was once internal to the individual, to an external agency, a "control system."[6] Paradoxically, it is precisely those jobs not demanding or permitting the involvement of the worker that require close and unpleasant control systems to ensure that the work gets done. This is the case for the draftsmen in our sample as well as the employees of the commercial offices. If people in these jobs express discontent with the organization, it is as much because of the control system as because of other characteristics of the organization. This feeling arises only from the negative features of the situation. It is reactive and defensive. In this it differs from the type of conflict brought about by involvement and commitment to the job. More often than not, the outcome is withdrawal rather than expression of discontent with the organization.

The proposition that close control leads to anger and resentment is hardly new. Much of the literature on job satisfaction can be summoned as supporting evidence. The assembly line is perhaps the most glaring example of close control. Assembly-line workers are clearly resentful of the lack of autonomy in their jobs. It is interesting to note that their pattern of collective action is characterized by withdrawal and apathy punctuated with sporadic outbursts rather than by sustained militancy.[7] This is what our schema would lead us to expect given the totally uninvolving quality of assembly-line work.

Taking the control system into account, we can add to our understanding of why the different job groups respond as they do to the items on the ORGDISC scale. The more closely a job is controlled, the more discontent the workers will be with the organization, regardless of how involving or satisfying the task in question. We have suggested that a participatory structure will have opposite effects upon workers doing involving work as compared to those doing uninvolving work. In the first situation, this type of structure will meet the workers' needs, whereas in the second it will raise aspirations that cannot be met without a radical redesigning of jobs. A control system, on the other hand, has a unidirectional effect, making people discontent insofar as it limits their autonomy. The absence of close control over productivity and performance, however, cannot in itself lead to a rise in aspirations.

Three propositions. We can summarize the discussion thus far and the schema presented in Table 4.6 as a series of propositions.

1. The more involving a person's job, the more active a stance he will take vis-à-vis the organization. If the organization is rigid and/or the control system places pressures on him that contrast with his desire to do a good job, discontent and a militant attitude will result. If, on the other hand, the organization encourages his participation and does not seek to control him unduly, he will be both committed and satisfied.

2. The more the organization encourages the individual to participate in decisions of all sorts, the more active a stance he will take vis-à-vis his work and the organization. If his job is monotonous, uninteresting, or too closely controlled, he will tend to express his discontent actively rather than to withdraw. If his job is involving and permits him sufficient autonomy, he will be satisfied and involved.

3. The more closely the worker is controlled, the more angry he will be in his attitude toward the organization.

The first two propositions point to circumstances under which the individual will take an active rather than a passive stance vis-à-vis the organization. Whether this active stance will lead to greater satisfaction or to a more combative attitude will depend on the person's situation with regard to the other factors. Unlike the first two variables, closer control leads to only one outcome, namely, greater resentment.

Our data provide convincing support for the first and the third propositions. The evidence in support of the second is not quite so strong. Evidence for the first proposition comes from two sets of comparisons. First, there are the comparisons between those doing technical jobs at

GT&E (testers and lab technicians) and those in the commercial offices. Both the testers and the employees of the commercial offices are very dissatisfied with the task itself. But whereas the testers are in continuous conflict with the organization, those in the commercial offices tend to withdraw. The major difference between the two groups is in the amount of commitment and involvement that their tasks demand.

The comparison between lab technicians and commercial office employees suggests the same thing. The lab technicians like their jobs better than do the employees of the commercial offices, but they are much more dissatisfied with the organization. Again, the major difference between the two groups is in the amount of commitment and involvement demanded.

The second set of comparisons in support of the first proposition is between those doing technical work at GT&E and those doing similar work at Siemens. These comparisons indicate that involvement can be channeled into enthusiasm or into discontent, depending on the organizational structure and the nature of the control system. The Siemens lab technicians and testers are enthusiastic, whereas the GT&E lab technicians are discontent and angry. The GT&E testers are even more discontent and angry, their situation being aggravated by the control system.

The third proposition is also supported by several comparisons. The testers at GT&E complain more about the organization than do the lab technicians primarily because they are more closely controlled. The draftsmen in both organizations are as discontent as they are largely because their output is controlled. This is most clearly evident in the case of the Siemens draftsmen who work in an otherwise participatory organization. The apathy of the commercial office employees can be explained by the fact that their productivity is not so closely controlled as is that of the testers and draftsmen, as well as by the fact that their work is so uninvolving.

The second proposition is the most difficult to support from our data. We have lamented before the fact that our sample does not include a group in the Special Systems Laboratory comparable to the GT&E commercial offices employees. The case of the Siemens draftsmen provides the closest approximation to a group doing routine uninvolving work in a participatory organization. We have attributed their high level of discontent with the organization primarily to the fact that they are closely controlled. Although this is certainly part of the explanation, it seems that their discontent is exacerbated by the participatory organizational structure. The Siemens draftsmen are as high as, or slightly higher than, the GT&E draftsmen in discontent with the organization, yet, their work is if anything less closely controlled. In addition, they work in an organization that in other respects allows a considerable amount of freedom. This participatory organizational structure reduces the discontent of those doing technical work very substantially. But the draftsmen remain high in their levels of discontent. The close control to which they are subject may, indeed, make many of the advantages of the participatory structure meaningless to them. Nevertheless, other advantages remain: the possibility of attending courses during work hours, the weekly meetings at which problems may be discussed, the right to study during work hours (a right that may be contested by the bosses, but that exists in principle), the possibility of changing one's job, and the generally freer atmosphere. For these reasons, one might expect the Siemens draftsmen to be somewhat lower in discontent with the organization than the GT&E draftsmen, but they are not. The fact that their level of discontent is as high as that of the GT&E draftsmen is indicative of their more active stance toward the organization.

On two items from the ORGDISC scale, "Do you ever have to do things without knowing what they are for?" and "Is lack of contact with other sections a problem for you in your work?" the Siemens draftsmen emerge as the most discontent group in the sample. Looking back at Table 4.5, we can see that the Siemens draftsmen are considerably more dissatisfied than the GT&E draftsmen on these two items. Taken together with the quotes presented earlier, these findings suggest that the participatory organization has raised the aspirations of these workers who feel that they have a right to expect a certain minimum amount of satisfaction from their work.

Further evidence for the second proposition comes from comparisons between those doing technical jobs at Siemens and those doing analogous jobs at GT&E. The lab technicians and testers at Siemens talk shop with friends after work more than do their counterparts at GT&E (61% vs. 32%), in fact more than any of the other job groups. They also read technical magazines more (45% vs. 26%) and are more likely to say they would be sorry to leave technical work for a managerial job (73% vs. 29%). These comparisons indicate that the lab technicians and testers at Siemens are more involved in their work and take a more active stance than their GT&E counterparts. This difference can be attributed primarily to the difference in organizational structure. The same differences do not hold for the draftsmen, perhaps because the questions are not relevant for jobs that are not, strictly speaking, technical.

Our conclusion must be that although our data provide some support for the second proposition it remains a hypothesis for future research.

Effects of the job on other aspects of work life

We go on to examine the effects of the job on other aspects of work life. For this purpose we define a job as a task performed within an organizational context.

Strike participation

A more detailed discussion of the antecedents of strike participation must be deferred to Chapter 6. Here we would only like to point out that the strike participation scale shows a pattern of variation by job very roughly parallel to that of the ORGDISC scale (see Figure 4.1). The two groups lowest in their levels of discontent with the organization, the employees in the GT&E commercial offices and those in the development sections at Siemens, emerge as the groups that strike least. The same *t* test done earlier using the ORGDISC scale was carried out using the strike participation scale. The jobs low in discontent with the organization, namely the technical jobs in the Special Systems Laboratory and the commercial office jobs at GT&E, were grouped together and compared with all the others. The *t* test was significant at the .068 level. This finding is suggestive if not statistically significant.

A glance at one of the single items in the strike participation scale gives some idea of the magnitude of the variation by job (Table 4.7). The differences are not great but are similar for all the items in the scale.

If strike participation and discontent with the organization show similar patterns of variation by job, the two should also be correlated at the individual level. In fact, the correlation between the strike participation scale and ORGDISC is low but significant ($r = .231$).

The obvious explanation for the correlation is that discontent with the organization leads to participation in strikes. What then requires explanation is not the fact that there is a correlation between ORGDISC

Table 4.7. *Approval of the strike weapon by job group. (Jobs listed in order of stated interest.)*

Is strike useful?	GT&E sales	GT&E testing	GT&E draft-ing	Sie-mens draft-ing	GT&E devel-opment	Sie-mens testing	Sie-mens devel-opment	Total
Yes	12.5%[a]	36.8%	55.6%	33.3%	36.0%	33.3%	9.1%	32.2%
	1	7	5	3	9	2	1	28
Yes, quali-fied	37.5%	42.1%	11.1%	66.7%	44.0%	33.3%	72.7%	44.8%
	3	8	1	6	11	2	8	39
No	37.5%	21.1%	33.3%	0%	20.0%	33.3%	18.2%	21.3%
	3	4	3	0	5	2	2	19
Don't know	12.5%	0%	0%	0%	0%	0%	0%	1.1%
	1	0	0	0	0	0	0	1
Total	9.2%	21.8%	10.3%	10.3%	28.7%	6.9%	12.6%	100.0%
	8	19	9	9	25	6	11	87

[a]The upper entries are percent of column totals; the numbers below are units.

and strike participation but, rather, the fact that this correlation is not larger. But there are also alternative explanations for the correlation. For example, it might be argued that both discontent with the organization and strike participation are determined by the employee's political attitudes. When we discuss strike participation in Chapter 6, we will see that this is not the case.

Relations with boss and co-workers

The workers were asked the question, "Do you think your boss does his job well?" The one group that stands out in its answers is the group of Siemens development section technicians, 91 percent of whom express satisfaction with the way in which their boss carries out his job. The employees of the GT&E commercial offices also seem relatively satisfied with their bosses (56 percent satisfied). The most dissatisfied group is that of the Siemens draftsmen, with only 25 percent satisfied. Those doing technical work at GT&E are also rather dissatisfied (39 percent satisfied). All of these responses may be explained analogously to the responses to the ORGDISC variables.

In general, the pattern of variation of this item is once again similar to that of the ORGDISC scale. The one group whose position is rather different on the items regarding the boss is the group of Siemens testers, only 33 percent of whom express satisfaction. Given that they work under closer control than do the technicians in the development sections, it is hardly surprising that they express less appreciation for their bosses.

As in the case of the ORGDISC scale, we note that the workers in the participatory organization are not all more satisfied than those in the more rigid organization. Again, the only group that benefits dramatically from the organizational structure of the Special Systems Laboratory is the group of lab technicians in the development sections.

As with strike participation, here too one might expect a correlation at the individual level. In fact, the correlation between satisfaction with one's boss and ORGDISC is .328.

The workers in our sample were asked whether they would say that they had friends among their co-workers and, if so, how many of these they saw socially after work hours. These items do not show a great deal of variation by job. However, one finding that emerges from both items is that the employees of the GT&E commercial offices tend to have few friends at work: 78 percent of these employees see none of their colleagues after work, as compared to 50 percent in the sample as a whole. These employees also tend to say that they have no friends at work or that they are equally friendly with everyone, rather than specifying how many friends they have and who they are. Apparently, the withdrawal from the work situation that we have noted as characteristic of this group pervades their relationships with co-workers as well. Work is seen as an unpleasant necessity from which one escapes as soon as one's duties are over.

Attitudes toward individual mobility

Three questions were asked to determine the individual's feelings about upward mobility within the organization: "Would you like to become a supervisor even if this meant leaving a technical job for an administrative job?" "Is it very important for you to improve your position in the company?" and "If you had to say what the most important characteristics of a job are, which would you choose as the most important?

And the second most important?" (In this last item "possibility of advancement" was listed as one characteristic.)

These items show some consistency in their variation by job. The employees of the GT&E commercial offices are consistently oriented toward individual mobility. Individualistic mobility strivings are another aspect of the nonsolidaristic approach to work in this office revealed by the low number of friendships. In an atmosphere in which there is little friendship among colleagues and where the work itself does not provide much sense of accomplishment, people are more likely to direct their energies into mobility projects and the alluring fantasy of escape into a higher sphere. If self-esteem cannot be derived from work, it can be obtained from external rewards instead. As one commercial office employee answered in response to the question of whether he would like to become a boss:

In a certain sense, yes, as a recognition of the work I do – I mean, since it's based on merit, at least officially, as long as you're a mere executor of orders you don't really get much satisfaction. If all the personnel were respected, O.K., I wouldn't care, but since that isn't the case. . . . (Alicea)

Alicea expresses the alienation of office work. It manifests itself in the lack of trust in co-workers as well as in upward mobility aspirations. The item on whether merit judgments should be made by peers rather than by the boss is correlated with all three of the upward mobility items (correlation coefficients between each of the three items and the peer-judgment item are .209, .289, and .241). Those who are unwilling to trust their peers are also oriented toward individual mobility. The GT&E commercial offices workers are among the most distrustful groups. Seventy-one percent of them are unwilling to trust their peers, as compared to the sample mean of 60 percent.

We have singled out the employees of the commercial offices in GT&E as the most career-oriented group in our sample. Although their average rank ordering on these four items does earn them this distinction, the GT&E lab technicians are not far behind. In general there is a notable difference between Siemens and GT&E on this dimension. All the work groups at Siemens are relatively uninterested in career possibilities, whereas those at GT&E, with the exception of the testers, are more interested in getting ahead. Yet it is probably easier to get ahead in the Lab than at GT&E. This seemingly paradoxical finding can be explained by the normative difference between GT&E and the Special Systems Laboratory. Among the white collar workers at GT&E, it is considered natural to want to get ahead. As one technician said, "Certainly yes [I would like to become a boss], obviously anyone would like to become a boss" (A. Malerba). But in the Lab at Siemens a solidaristic atmosphere prevails. The possibility of having power over others, of forcing them to work, is rejected, at least verbally. "I wouldn't like to become a boss, because I would have to behave like those who are bosses; otherwise my group wouldn't work well, that is, I'd have to make my subordinates slave, see to it that they produce as much as possible, and I wouldn't like to do that" (Iuteri).

Although this attitude is shared by many of the leftists in both organizations, at Siemens an anticompetitive attitude has become the quasi-official norm of the organization. The notion that merit raises should be awarded by the peer group rather than by the boss, which seems unworkable to 71 percent of the respondents at GT&E, has been turned into practice at the Special Systems Laboratory. The item on judgment by peers was, therefore, changed for the Siemens interviews so as to read, "Would you be in favor of abolishing merit raises?" Even after this modification of the question, the Siemens respondents emerge as much more solidary in their answers than the GT&E respondents (68% vs. 29%). (Responses favoring judgment by peers or abolition of merit raises are considered solidary.) Given that one of the groups at Siemens (the software group) had gone so far as actually to abolish merit raises, and other groups had discussed this step, the difference between the two organizations is readily understandable.

The one group at GT&E which is not career oriented is that of the testers. This is a working class environment. The testers are the only group in our GT&E sample in which there are a substantial number of blue collar workers. Studies of working classes in various countries have pointed out that the subculture is ambivalent at best in its attitude toward mobility. This seems to be the case for our sample as well. Those technicians classified as blue collar workers are less likely to say they would like to become bosses ($r = .262$). The testers are not, however, particularly trusting in their orientation toward their peers. Our earlier description of the organization of this section suggests why.[8]

Effects of the job on participation and involvement in other areas

Much of our argument thus far has been an attempt to show the importance of the task and the organizational structure in determining whether a person will take an active or a passive stance in his work life, and within those categories whether he will be angry, satisfied, or apathetic. But so far we have looked only at the effects of the job on strictly job-related attitudes: attitudes toward work and toward the organization, toward co-workers, bosses, mobility, and, very briefly, strike participation.

We now turn to look at the effects of the job on other areas of involvement and participation: higher-level participation in the company, after-hours involvement in work-related subjects, and political and civic participation.

We speak here of the *effects* of the job. Given that ours is a study done at one point in time, how can we be sure of the direction of causality? How can we be sure, in other words, that whatever relationships we may find are not the results of a process whereby certain kinds of people with certain patterns of leisure activity choose jobs that are congenial to them? Obviously, we cannot be sure, but such self-selection is unlikely to be important among our sample. The educational choices of all the technicians are similar, and, because of the oversupply of technicians, their ability to choose one specific type of technical job rather than another is severely limited.

The general hypothesis we shall be exploring states that participation or involvement in the workplace will lead to involvement in other areas of life as well. This hypothesis is one of a family that Harold Wilensky calls "spill-over hypotheses," according to which one's adjustment to life outside work is determined by one's adjustment to life at work.[9] The competing hypothesis, which he calls "compensatory," is formulated according to a hydraulic model: Those needs that are not satisfied at work will seek satisfaction elsewhere. The latter hypothesis does not explain the available evidence as convincingly as the former. Its inadequacy is particularly apparent in the area of participation. Research on participation in industrial settings, in voluntary associations, and in politics suggests that people with certain attributes tend to participate more across a variety of situations. Some of these attributes, most importantly the sense of competence, are largely the result of past participation. There is little evidence that lack of participation in one sphere increases participation in some other sphere. A version of the compensatory hypothesis has been used as an explanation for the intense participation of otherwise nonparticipant groups in revolutionary movements. But there is fairly general agreement that the spill-over hypothesis provides the better explanation for sustained participation in organizational settings.

Propositions 1 and 2 regarding attitudes toward the task and the organization are similar to the spill-over hypothesis. However, the postulated mechanisms whereby involvement in one area leads to involvement in another area are more direct in these two cases. The propositions link participation in specific areas to participation in other closely related areas rather than referring to a generalized tendency to participate.

Carole Pateman has also used the spill-over hypothesis to argue that true political democracy is impossible without industrial democracy, that people will not participate in the making of decisions remote from their day-to-day lives if they are not allowed to participate in those which most directly affect them.[10]

As we shall see, our data only provide slight support for the spill-over hypothesis. In fact, with a few exceptions, there is little consistent variation by job of participation and involvement in areas not directly related to the job.

Participation in decision making within the company

In the pilot interviews, technicians were asked whether they thought employees should have more say over company policy. They dismissed the possibility as unrealistic. It was obviously too fantastic to be contemplated. The question was therefore modified to a more general formulation: "Do you think the employees should have more say over decisions made in the company?" If queried as to what this meant, the interviewer would add that the question referred to decisions regarding the subject's work. This item was followed by a more specific one: "Can you give me an example of a decision on a matter on which you might usefully have given an opinion but weren't consulted?"

According to the spill-over hypothesis, we might expect those doing more involving work to be more desirous of additional decision-making power. Similarly, we would expect those in the more participatory organization to desire more say than those in the nonparticipatory organization. These expectations are not borne out on either item. In fact, contrary to these expectations, the lab technicians at Siemens are the least desirous of more participation. They feel that they already have enough say over the decisions that affect them. The measure of participation that they have been granted does not seem to have whetted their appetites.[11]

In their views of the official mechanisms for participation, the employees of the Special Systems Laboratory are divided and ambivalent. Tallying their answers to the question, "Do you think the company does all it can for its employees, makes some effort, or does as little as possible?" one would conclude once again that there is little difference between Siemens and GT&E on this subject.[12] The entire sample is dubious of the companies' intentions. However, among the Siemens employees there is a depth of feeling about the organization as an entity that is lacking at GT&E. The Special Systems Laboratory is an object toward which workers orient themselves and about which they take stands; GT&E is not such an object.

Many of the Siemens technicians compared the Special Systems Laboratory favorably with other organizations and spontaneously expressed appreciation for the climate they found there.

I don't think you'd be able to find another lab in Italy with a climate like this. That's my opinion. I repeat, this is my first job, but from what I've heard other people say, it seems to me that this little bit of freedom is more than plenty compared to lots of other companies. (Preti)

But, although these technicians are generally pleased with the freedom allowed them in their daily work, they deny the existence of any real participatory democracy in the Lab. The limits of participation are clearly perceived.

The power that is delegated isn't really that much, because the decision-making power stays in the hands of the decision makers. Yes, there is the appearance, there is the policy of giving the impression that the others have some say. . . . It's like the guy who believes in the heroism of war, maybe he loses but he believes in the heroism of making war. But if one thinks about it a minute, one says, "Why should I go? Why are they sending me to war?" Here it's the same thing. Why do we have all these discussions? What value do they have? We spend half the day discussing this or that, but what weight does our discussion carry in the final decision? (Ferraiolo)

In a certain sense I believe in the spirit of the Lab – I believe in it in the sense that, even if it's not as good as it would like to be, people live better, work better, even though I know it's sometimes a mystification. . . .

[He explains how, in a recent incident, the head of the Lab mobilized the entire Lab in support of his position against the top management of the company.] I think in that case, as in others, the heads of the Lab, who had certain interests, showed great political skills in determining the will of the base. . . .

But the fact that there is the possibility of expressing oneself in assemblies is in itself very important, because if there's something I don't like going on and I say it publicly, a repressive reaction becomes impossible. (Massa)

Both of these employees believe they have enough say in matters related to their work despite the limitations they see:

From the technical point of view, it seems to me that everyone in the Lab has as much say as possible in the sense that everything a person says is considered not because it was said by that person but for its content. From the political point of view, things are a bit different. . . (Massa)

Desire to participate in decisions within the Lab that can be broadly defined as political is not great.

As long as it's a question of changing one form, we can do it, but if something larger is involved, it's not up to me to say, it's up to whoever has a complete view of the whole piece; we don't have anything to do with it, we don't go to that level. (Fratantonio)

There is little evidence of spill-over here.

Involvement in work-related subjects

Two questions were asked to ascertain how interested the person was in electronics (or mechanics if he was a mechanical draftsman). The spillover hypothesis fares better here. Those doing technical work at Siemens are more likely than any of the others in the sample to talk about electronics with friends after work. They are also more likely to read technical magazines outside work (see discussion of evidence for the second proposition earlier in this chapter). However, it is only in the extreme case of the technicians doing involving work in a participatory organization that the spill-over effect occurs. Those doing technical work at GT&E are not more likely to talk about electronics after work or to read technical magazines than are those not doing technical work. Nor do the draftsmen at the Special Systems Laboratory show greater interest in electronics or mechanics than do the GT&E draftsmen.

Organizational memberships and other uses of free time

Sixty-seven percent of the technicians in our sample belong to no formal organizations at all. (Union membership is excluded from this count.[13] Sixteen percent belong to recreational or sports organizations. Only 17 percent belong to cultural or political organizations. There is no evident relationship between job and organizational membership. In none of the job groups does the fraction belonging to political or cultural organizations go over 24 percent. If we include sports and recreational associations, then no more than 44 percent of any job group belong to formal organizations. These numbers are too small and the variance is too slight to conclude very much beyond the observation that the men in our sample tend not to join formal organizations. The affluent manual workers in the British sample of Goldthorpe, Lockwood, et al. were more likely to belong to formal organizations than are the technicians in our sample.[14] This low level of organizational involvement is only one aspect of a lack of communal ties that we shall explore further in Chapter 5.

The employees of the GT&E commercial offices and the draftsmen at Siemens engage in fewer leisure-time activities than do the other groups. When asked how they spend their free time, they tend to mention the catch-all phrase, "seeing family and friends," instead of noting specific activities. This finding adds one more perspective to the view of the commercial office employees as withdrawn and inactive. Aside from this, the variation by job does not support the spill-over hypothesis; nor, in fact, is it easily interpretable.

One very important use of free time is night school. Thirty percent of the sample were attending night school, either at the secondary level or at the university level. Technicians at all levels are very aware of the barrier to upward mobility that exists for those not in possession of the requisite degrees. Night school provides a way to get ahead without violating the solidaristic norms of the peer group.

Particularly high percentages of the Siemens lab technicians and the GT&E testers are in school (64% and 42%, respectively). The lab technicians at Siemens all have technicians' diplomas. Those who go to night school are studying physics or mathematics at the university level. We have already noted that their interest in electronics extends beyond the workplace. Given the kind of work they do and the environment in which they work, it is not too surprising that a majority should feel motivated to continue their studies.

Many of the testers at GT&E do not yet have the technician's diploma. They have usually completed at least the equivalent of junior high school and two years of professional school, leaving them three more years of technical high school to attain the diploma. They and the draftsmen are the least educated groups in the sample. But unlike the draftsmen, the GT&E testers work in an area in which they can apply directly the knowledge of electronics they gain in school, and in which the technician's diploma is a ticket to instant upward mobility.

To sum up, our data provide some slight support for the spill-over hypothesis in the cases of the extreme groups for which organizational structure and task reinforce one another, that is, for those doing the most involving jobs in the participatory environment and for those doing the most uninvolving jobs in the authoritarian environment. The hypothesis is at least partly supported in the areas of outside interests, free time activities, and night school attendance. It is not supported in the areas of desire for more participation within the company and membership in other organizations outside work. The data suggest that life at work and life outside work are relatively independent within the range of variation in our sample.

Prior orientations to work

Just as the job may have effects on life outside of work, so the converse is true as well. Action theorists such as Silverman, Goldthorpe and Lockwood, and Ingham have argued that workers' orientations prior to entering the work situation will have much influence on their reactions to that situation.[15] The action approach stresses that the individual is not a passive object in an objectively defined situation: He is an active agent in a situation he himself defines. The individual's cognitive definition of the situation, not the situation alone, will determine his response.

The simple hypothesis following from this argument is that prior orientations to work influence reactions to the job situation. In order to measure orientation to work, we included an item from Goldthorpe, Lockwood, et al.'s affluent worker study. We asked the technicians what to them are the most important characteristics to look for in a job and how they would rate their present job on these characteristics. Aspects most frequently mentioned were interest, high pay, friends, and career possibilities. For each aspect, a dummy variable was created grouping together those who said it was important as against those who said it was not. This produced four dummy variables, one for each aspect.

If orientations to work are, indeed, formed outside the immediate work situation, they should be highly correlated with the technicians' backgrounds and with features of their situations outside of work. The data show that some orientations are influenced by background and even more by the immediate family situation, whereas others are less strongly influenced.

Attitudes toward pay are most strongly affected by such factors. Those who see pay as one of the two most important characteristics in a job are more likely to be married than single (r = .272) and to be married with children rather than married without children (r = .316). They are also likely to be older (r = .231) and not to be attending night school (r = .234). As might be expected, the immediate family situation plays a large role in determining the importance accorded to pay. Other background variables do not, however, seem particularly important.

The value placed on having an interesting job is also affected by family situation, although less strongly and in an opposite direction. Those who attribute importance to interest tend to be childless (r = .257). The desire for an interesting job gives way to a greater awareness of remuneration as the fantasies of youth yield to family responsibilities. The only distinguishing characteristic of the backgrounds of those who value interest is that they are slightly more likely to have gone to an upper-track junior high school (r = .223). As in the case of pay, the desire for an interesting and varied job is not strongly tied to background, although it is tied to immediate family situation.

Concern with finding friends at work is not correlated with family situation, but it is correlated with two background variables. Those to whom friendship at work is important are more likely to have gone to a lower-track junior high school (r = .306) and to have grown up in the North (r = .270). An ex post facto explanation for these relationships is easy to find. Immigrants from the South have already been forced to decide that friends are less important than having a job. And the lower-track junior high school socializes students to be less concerned with career possibilities or intrinsic intellectual interest in a job.

Interest in career opportunities is the only one of the four dummy variables not significantly correlated with any background or family situation variables.

The backgrounds of the technicians do not explain a great deal about their orientations to work. Background does influence whether or not friends are considered important, but it does not affect other orientations much. The immediate family situation has greater impact. It affects two orientations – the values given to pay and to interest.

To the extent that orientations to work are correlated with characteristics of the work situation, it can be argued that they do not exist prior to this situation but are, instead, consequences of it. This supposition will be stronger if, as with the technicians in our sample, choice plays little role in the selection of a job. Orientations to work are influenced to varying extents by the job situation.

The orientation to pay, most strongly related to nonwork variables, is not affected by the work situation. The orientation to interest is only tied to the job situation by one link: Those in the lower job categories care less about having an interesting job than do those in the higher categories ($r = .326$). On the other hand, the orientation to career is more highly dependent on the job and the atmosphere of the plant. The effects of the job on attitudes toward career were discussed previously in this chapter and will be taken up again in Chapter 6. Finally, how strongly friendship is valued is also affected by the work situation. Technicians who have experienced some mobility at work and who are better paid are less interested in friendship as an aspect of life at work ($r = .229$ and $r = .224$, respectively).

In sum, factors both inside and outside the work situation have an impact upon orientations to work. Which of these influences is more important is not a question that can be answered in a general manner, as some orientations are influenced primarily by outside factors, others primarily by the job, and still others by both. The fact that orientations to work are partly formed outside the work situation in no way implies that technology or other aspects of that situation do not have independent effects on such orientations.

What are the consequences of different orientations to work? Orientation to work has immediate, direct effects on other attitudes and behaviors and, in certain cases, it has contingent, interactive effects, improving our ability to explain an attitude or behavior only in conjunction with another variable.

Two of the orientations affect strike participation – one immediately and one contingently. Technicians to whom career opportunities are important tend not to strike ($r = -.316$). Career orientation has an immediate effect on strike participation independent of whether or not career opportunities are perceived to exist. The hypothesis that those who accord importance to career opportunities will be militant if they perceive no chances for promotion is not supported. The desire to get ahead indicates an identification with the hierarchy and a rejection of a collective strategy. Among those who see career opportunities to be few, the hope may perhaps remain that they will be the lucky ones. In general, however, the men who attribute importance to career are also optimistic about getting ahead. We will have more to say on strike participation and career ambitions in Chapter 6.

An emphasis on the importance of pay is contingently related to strike participation. Technicians to whom pay is important are not more likely to strike than those to whom it is not. But those who are dissatisfied with their pay are more likely to strike than those who are satisfied ($r = .238$) and this tendency is accentuated in those to whom pay is important. A new variable was created to gauge the increase in explanatory power obtained by taking into account orientation toward pay. Those who are highly dissatisfied with their pay and consider pay to be important were coded 1, those who are very dissatisfied but do not consider pay to be important were coded 2, and so on, up to those, coded 5, who consider pay to be important and are completely satisfied. The correlation between the new variable and strike participation rises to .290.

Thus, knowing the value a person places upon pay improves our ability to explain strike participation even though the valuing of pay is not itself related to strike participation. This type of indirect effect is precisely what the action hypothesis would predict, for it shows how a given orientation can have opposite consequences as it is brought into different work situations.

The other two orientations, those toward an interesting job and toward having friends on the job, have no strong effects on work-related attitudes or behaviors.

It is no more possible to generalize about the consequences of orientations to work than about their causes. We have, however, found two cases in which orientations help to explain the important phenomenon of strike participation, thereby lending support to the action hypothesis.

In some instances, judgments about the work situation are as strongly linked to background and family situation as are orientations to work. For example, the men who have children are not only less likely to say that interest is an important aspect of a job, but they are also more likely to say that their own job is interesting ($r = .309$). It might be thought that those who do not place great value upon interest in a job are less exacting in judging this aspect of the job. But the correlation between the value placed upon interest and the judgment of this aspect of the job is close to zero. The judgment is directly linked to family situation just as the orientation is. Similar results are obtained for judgments about pay.

In practice, then, family situation and background variables sometimes affect attitudes to work directly as well as interactively with orientations to work. The neat analytic distinction between prior orientation, determined by family situation and background, and judgment of an actual situation, determined by prior orientation and by the objective characteristics of the situation, is not always maintained. This comes as no surprise to the social psychologist, who knows that judgments are influenced by reference groups, aspiration levels, and many other factors.

For some purposes, such as the analysis of the relationships among orientation to pay, judgment about fairness of pay, and strike participation presented above, it is useful to treat orientation to a situation and judgment of that situation as independent and unrelated elements interacting to produce an outcome. But for others, orientation and judgment must be viewed as related parts of attitude clusters affected by factors outside the work situation and by the work situation itself. For example, those who consider pay to be important are characterized by a retreat from involvement in the technical elements of the job, a generally individualistic approach to work, and an interest in getting ahead. This individualistic syndrome probably develops in large part prior to the work situation, but attitudes toward career are also affected by the job. In this instance, it is much more difficult to disentangle the relative importance of prior orientation and of the job.

The effects of nonwork variables may be direct or mediated through reactions to the work situation, broad or specific, and more or less significant in various cases. It is clear, however, that such effects exist and that sometimes they are important. In this respect, the action theorists have made industrial sociologists more aware of a factor heretofore underemphasized.

Although proponents of action theory often use the technological determinist position as a straw man, nothing in our data indicates that the two approaches are incompatible. Reactions to the job and the organization are accentuated or diminished by prior orientations, but not qualitatively changed. Orientations may have independent effects on strike participation, absenteeism, or turnover. But there is no reason to expect, nor would the technological determinist claim, that an orientation toward pay, for example, would be determined by technological or organizational factors. Rather than attempting to prove that one or the other approach is correct, researchers would do better to ask what factors are most important in explaining a particular phenomenon. In Chapter 6, we will ask this question regarding strike participation.

The stress on prior orientations is not the only, nor even perhaps the most significant, contribution of the action approach. The major corrective in action theory lies in its view of man as an active, thinking, rational being rather than a merely passive, expressive, emotional one. From a rationalist perspective, it is clear that the work situation restricts the number of strategies available to an actor. This explains, in part, the similarities in behavior and attitudes within work groups and the differences between work groups. David Silverman, whose book on *The Theory of Organisations* is perhaps the most comprehensive statement of the action theory approach to organizations, implicitly recognizes this when he praises the work of Crozier and others who work with a model of groups pursuing rational strategies deriving from their organizational situations. (However, he notes the limits of strategic analysis in that it does not deal with possible variations in the actors' definitions of the same situation.[16]) As our earlier analysis showed, strategies can often be derived from the immediate situation with little reference to prior orientations.

Even in considering the immediate situation, an emphasis on rational action must not lead to a disregard of the effects of socialization. In its eagerness to substitute an instrumental, cognitive view of man for an expressive, emotional one, action theory creates an artificial separation between socialization, presumed to have occurred at some earlier stage, and rational action based on values acquired at this earlier stage but occurring in the present. Although Silverman, for example, gives lip service to "a view of social reality as socially constructed, socially sustained, and socially changed," in fact no attention is given to the processes whereby values and definitions of the situation are changed.[17] Socialization is relegated to the past. In the present there is only rational action. Yet there is abundant evidence that socialization does not cease with childhood or even with adolescence. The effects of work on personality are well documented, particularly in the forthcoming longitudinal study by Kohn and Schooler.[18] Were action theorists to look more closely at the processes whereby definitions of situations are created and maintained, they might find themselves having to deviate from the position that all orientations, being freely arrived at, are equally valid.

A less one-sided perspective on human behavior would see man as active within his environment and at the same time subject to its influences. In the realm of cognition, such a view has been propounded by Piaget for well over thirty-five years and is expressed in his twin concepts of "assimilation" and "accommodation."[19] *Assimilation* is the cognitive structuring of data from the environment to fit it into the person's existing intellectual organization; *accommodation* is the changing of the intellectual structure as it adapts to handle new data. These two processes occur simultaneously in the cognitive development of the person.

Piagetian concepts are directly relevant in understanding the formation of a cognitive structure, such as the images of the class hierarchy discussed in the next chapter. By analogy, they are relevant to other forms of behavior as well. A job, for example, socializes in certain respects those who perform it; but an individual holding a job also follows rational strategies based on his immediate situation and on preexisting values. Which of these will be the more powerful explanatory factor will depend on the particular case and the type of behavior to be explained.

Summary

In this chapter we have looked at the effects of organizational structure and task on a number of dependent variables related to work life and life outside work. We have also discussed the effects of prior orientations on behavior at work. The findings may be summarized as follows.

1. Discontent with the organization and attitudes toward the supervisor are the resultants of interactions between task and organizational structure. Those in incongruent situations, in which either the task or the organizational structure is involving or encouraging of participation while the other is confining, tend to be dissatisfied with the organization and with supervisors. Those in congruent situations, in which the organizational structure and the task are both confining or both involving and participatory tend to be apathetic or satisfied, respectively, but not actively dissatisfied. Strike participation shows the same pattern of variation as attitudes toward the organization and the supervisor, but less strongly.

An important aspect of organizational structure is the control system. Close control leads in all cases to greater anger and discontent with the organization.

The lab technicians at Siemens and the employees of the commercial offices at GT&E, the two groups in the most congruent situations, are similarly low in discontent with the organization, discontent with supervisors, and strike participation compared to the other groups in the sample.

2. An additive model seems to explain the relationship between task and organizational structure, on the one hand, and relationships with co-workers, attitudes toward mobility, involvement in work-related subjects, night-school attendance, and use of free time, on the other. To the extent that the job affects these variables, it is primarily in the congruent cases, that is, those in which task and organizational structure are both confining or both involving. The GT&E commercial offices employees tend to have fewer friends at work, to be more interested in individual mobility, and to have fewer specific leisure-time activities than the other groups. The Siemens lab technicians are less interested in individual mobility, more involved in work-related subjects, and more likely to be going to night school than are the other groups. Along these dimensions, the employees of the GT&E commercial offices and those of the Siemens development sections are likely to be at opposite ends. There is some slight support for the spill-over hypothesis in these findings.

3. Social origins and immediate family situation affect both orientations to work and judgments about the work situation. The men who are married and have children are more concerned about pay and less concerned about the intrinsic interest of the job. They are also more negative in their judgments about pay and more positive in their judgments about interest.

The work situation has an influence too, and in some cases even a predominant one, on orientations to work. For example, interest in career possibilities is aroused or dampened by the job and the plant environment.

Turning to the consequences of orientations to work, technicians who are interested in getting ahead in the company are less likely to strike. Interest in pay accentuates the tendency to participate in strikes among those who feel that their pay is unfairly low.

These findings give some slight support to the contention of the action theorists that prior orientations to work influence reactions to the job situation. But they also point to two limitations of action theory. First, the theory tends to underemphasize the fact that rational strategies emerge in work groups regardless of individual differences in orientations to work and that these strategies are systematically related to job and organization. Second, the action approach is limited in that it does not take into account the fact that the work situation is not only the setting for rational behavior, but it also socializes personality. Despite these shortcomings, action theory is useful in calling attention to the rational, goal-oriented aspect of human behavior. Our analysis of discontent with the organization relies on a similar model of behavior.

5. Life outside work and images of the class structure

If Marx attached fundamental importance to the work role, it was not only because of the amount of time a person spends at work, but also because he saw this role as determining all others. In the late nineteenth century, the income differential between the manual and the nonmanual worker, between the proletarian and the petit bourgeois, was only one manifestation, and perhaps not the most important one, of the chasm between the two classes. Even the lowest grades of clerks, whose salaries were comparable to those of skilled craftsmen, were able to set themselves apart, to avoid the contaminating association with manual labor.

From top to bottom clerks associate with clerks and artisans with artisans – but comparatively seldom with each other. A clerk lives an entirely different life from an artisan – marries a different kind of wife – has different ideas, different possibilities, and different limitations. A clerk differs from an artisan in the claims each make on society, no less than in the claims society makes on them. It is not by any means only a question of clothes, of the wearing or not wearing of a white shirt every day, but of differences which invade every department of life, and at every turn affect the family budget. More undoubtedly is expected from the clerk than the artisan, but the clerk's money goes further and is on the whole much better spent.[1]

The kind of work someone does no longer carries with it an ascribed status to the same extent. In this limited sense, Dahrendorf was correct when he said that lines of cleavage that were once precisely overlapping are so no longer.[2] If people's ways of life off the job can vary independently of their work situations and if we can no longer assume as basic the manual–nonmanual dichotomy, which was so salient a feature of traditional working class images of society, then we must go beyond the study of the work situation in order to understand the political role of any group. Because the technicians of the new working class straddle the blue collar–white collar line, their perceptions of their class situation are all the more important.

The arguments of the new working class theorists are primarily concerned with the work situation. It is here, they contend, that the new working class is different. Our analysis too is centered on the work situation. But whatever judgment we may come to concerning the militancy of technicians struggling for greater control over their working lives still leaves open the question of the political significance of this militancy. Workers may be militant without being revolutionary. The term "revolutionary" is itself subject to more than one interpretation. One weak point in the argument of the new working class theorists is in fact their leap from the work situation to the political situation with no mention of life outside work.

In the first part of this chapter we shall describe the nonworking lives of the technicians in our sample. Unfortunately, our data in this area are not as extensive as we might have liked. The second part of the chapter discusses in some detail our respondents' perceptions of the class structure of the society in which they live. Images of the class structure integrate and make intelligible many of the findings on class-related behavior. From them we can learn how the technicians in our sample see their own jobs, their status, and their future in relation to those of other groups.

Patterns of life outside the workplace

Some of the characteristics of our sample make their nonworking lives rather unlike those of a cross section of the population. Forty-eight percent of them are less than twenty-five years old, and only 30 percent are over thirty. This lopsided age distribution is not unusual in the rapidly growing Italian electronics industry or, indeed, in all of those advanced-technology industries that employ large numbers of technicians in research and development organizations.

A second characteristic of our sample that has important effects on their nonworking lives is that only a minority (45%) grew up in the Milan area. Twenty-one percent come from other areas in Northern Italy, 14 percent from Central Italy, and 15 percent from the South.

Because of their youth, many of the technicians in the sample are single (51%). If they are single and among the many who do not come from the Milan area, they must live either with co-workers (9 of the 44 who are unmarried) or by themselves, renting a room in an apartment or in one of the dormitories that exist for workers and students from other regions or even renting a small apartment of their own (11/44). Those who come from the Milan area live with their parents.

The variables of marital status and origins together define the life styles of the technicians in our sample.

The single men

Among the single men, those who still live with their parents in the place where they grew up lead different lives from those who came to Milan to work leaving family and friends behind. About one-half of the twenty-three young men who live with their parents spend at least some of their free time with friends they have known for several years, often since childhood.[3] There is usually a hangout in the neighborhood, a café or a church-sponsored recreation facility, where the peer group gathers in the evenings after dinner.

Sometimes these groups break up as their members get married, or move away, or simply develop different interests. But a few people still maintain friendships begun in childhood, even after they have been married for many years. Eleven of the forty-three married men mention that they still keep up with old friends. Ten of these eleven grew up in the province of Milan and nine of them still live in the same areas they grew up in. Nearly always, these friendships are between husbands rather than between families. The café remains the center for this kind of social activity. "Usually in the evenings I go to the café, drink my coffee, talk to my friends about sports or politics, then, after an hour, an hour and a half, I go home to my wife" (Fanelli).

The value placed upon old friendships is in many cases remarkable. A few people who were raised in distant parts of the country have school friends working in the same factory, with whom they continue to maintain a special relationship. It is through these relationships as well as through relatives or other sources that people in the South find out about particular jobs, apply for them, and come north. Several respondents distinguished between these childhood friendships and the more superficial friendships formed later on. Asked if he had friends among his workmates, one draftsman answered:

I'm friends with everyone and with no one. . . . I happened to meet them, but I might just as well have met others. . . . We have done things together sometimes, I don't know, gone out to eat or drink something together, or to have fun, but not regularly. I believe in true friendship. The friends who are important to me are my childhood friends. The others are casual relationships in the sense that what I do with you today I could also do with someone else. . . . I only see these childhood friends rarely now, one of them I haven't seen in a year, but that doesn't change our relationship. (Colasanto)

Despite their emotional importance to some people, less than one-third of the sample (26/88) mention old friends as being among the people they see most often, and not all of those mentioned as old friends are childhood friends. Physical immobility would seem to be a precondition for the maintenance of these relationships, a precondition usually not met by the men in our sample, and one that may be expected to be met less as the region develops further.

If the pattern of social life of the single technicians who grew up in the area centers around a long-standing peer group, the leisure hours of those who grew up elsewhere must obviously be spent differently. Some of them consider their residence in Milan to be temporary, and bracket their working days between weekends and holidays spent "at home." Six of the twenty-one single technicians not from the Milan area go home often. Two commute weekly over distances of 180 and 300 miles, respectively. They both have girl friends in their home towns.

But, whether or not they view Milan as their adoptive home, these young men spend at least five days a week there and usually more than that. Most of them live near the factories in which they work.

Many of those who work at GT&E live in Cassina dé Pecchi or in Cernusco sul Naviglio, the two towns closest to the plant. These towns have been transformed from farming villages to suburbs in the last decade. In Cassina, for example, the new main square is surrounded by high-rise apartment buildings, while fields are still farmed only 200 yards away. These high-rise apartments are filled with workers from GT&E and other local factories that have moved out from Milan in search of less cramped quarters and a more docile and abundant labor force. It is in these buildings that many of the workers live, particularly those who moved from their previous homes upon coming to work at GT&E, and for whom the major criterion in choosing a place to live was proximity to work.

Under these circumstances they can hardly avoid contact with others who work at GT&E. The young workers eat together in the same restaurants every day and fight their loneliness and homesickness by keeping one another company in the evenings. Some form close friendships. For others these relationships are casual. No one seems highly committed to the life of a bachelor in Cassina dé Pecchi. Sometimes friendships are formed between people who work in the same section and who both live near the plant. More usually, the leisure-time friendship networks are formed along other lines. People who come from the same town or who take their meals together at the same place every night are likely to become friends.

There is little to do in the village. The ratio of single men to single women in Cassina is highly unfavorable to the men, adding to the barrackslike atmosphere. Although downtown Milan is less than one-half hour away, the commuter train runs infrequently at night. Favored activities are strolling, going to the movies, and television watching.

The Siemens Special Systems Laboratory is also out in the countryside, about five miles to the west of the city in the new Siemens complex at Castelletto. The plant is in the process of being transferred from the old site in Milan, and many functions still remain there. Because of the recency of the move, because the village nearest to the Castelletto plant is not within walking distance, and because it does not yet possess its complement of high-rise apartment buildings, most of the single technicians from the Lab who do not live with their parents live near the old Siemens plant in Milan. In this established neighborhood, the Siemens workers are spread thin and are not as visible as are the GT&E workers in Cassina. A few live in dormitorylike hotels and a few rent rooms. The center of their social life is the restaurant where they find dinner and a bit of conversation. Some feel lonely and isolated. One young man seemed on the verge of a nervous breakdown:

Since I've been in Milan I've really had a breakdown, because I'm alone here, you go out and you don't meet anyone, that is you meet various people but it's different, meeting people is one thing and having friends is another. . . . Now I've become a bit apathetic, let's say indifferent to life outside, because in the Lab, the Lab is the only place I feel at ease. . . The doctor gave me two weeks off for a nervous breakdown, I calmed down some because I went home, but the nervousness is still there, I'm always nervous, whereas before I was always calm. . . . Despite this, even if I were to find a job at home I wouldn't go now. I'd be tempted but I prefer to stay, because I like the climate [at work]. (Tigrotti)

This *extreme* isolation is the exception rather than the rule. The others in this situation find ways to satisfy the need for contacts with others by making friends with people who live in the dormitory-hotels or who eat in the same restaurants. The workers of the Lab also have more planned contacts with workmates than do the workers at GT&E. It was pointed out in Chapter 4 that the Siemens technicians do not see much more of one another off the job than do the GT&E technicians. But whereas 31 percent of the GT&E sample live within two miles of the factory and, hence, are virtually thrown together with other GT&E workers, this is not the case for the employees of the Special Systems Laboratory. An expenditure of energy is usually required of them if they are to meet, and they are often willing to make this expenditure. In fact, 58 percent of the employees of the Lab see at least one colleague regularly after work, compared to only 47 percent of GT&E employees sampled.

From what we have written so far, one might think that the single technicians do little else but hang around with their friends. To counter this impression, we hasten to point out that 44 percent are enrolled in night school. Not all of those enrolled in night school are single, but the majority are (20/26 = 77%). Fourteen percent of the married men are also going to night school, bringing the total to twenty-six people, 29 percent of the entire sample.

Going to night school involves a major commitment of time and energy over a period of several years. One-half of those in school are working toward the technician's degree. Classes are held five nights a week and all day Saturday. The program takes three years of full-time study to complete, and five years in night school. At the university level, attendance is not required, and it is possible to pace oneself by taking a greater or lesser number of exams according to how prepared one feels. Nonetheless, if one is serious about obtaining a degree, the time commitment is once again enormous. Only a few subjects are taught at night. The one chosen by nearly all those in our sample who are attending the university is physics. The physics course takes four years full time and seven or eight years at night.

During the school year, close to one-third of the men in our sample think of little else but work and school seven days a week. School dominates all their "free" time. Their friends are mostly people from the same plant who are also in school. When they are not studying together they are at the movies together.

I've passed two exams. I can make it, but it's rough, it involves a total commitment. You have to give up all other commitments, you have to dedicate yourself to work and school, and that's it. I get off work in the evening and go straight to the university. We stay until 9:30 or so, depending on the course. We form evening study groups. By the time I get home it's about 9:30, 10 o'clock. I eat in a hurry because going to sleep on a full stomach isn't very. . . so I eat and then go right to sleep. (Terri)

That so many of the men in the sample should be willing to go through this experience is truly a remarkable fact. It evidences the high aspirations of these young men and their awareness that only by obtaining a degree will they be able to break through to new possibilities for promotion. The same technician just quoted explains this quite clearly while also expressing his ambivalence about careerism:

One is forced by the existing bourgeois society to go to night school, because even if one is opposed to this society, practically, at least in my case I must admit that I don't live by my principles, because, on the one hand, contemporary society seems to have lots of things that need changing, but, on the other hand, I conform, I go to the university, because I want to learn more. . . I go to the university because I feel that I am limited from the outside. . . . In the society as it exists today, depending on one's degree one is blocked, one's career is limited. It's not that one wants to be careerist, it's not that one wants to get God knows where, but at least one wants to be acknowledged, to be recognized, and one knows that without a degree one can get to a certain point and then that's it, you aren't worth anything beyond that. (Terri)

School provides a secure avenue of mobility, one which does not require one to violate the solidaristic norms of the peer group by behaving in a careerist way.

Attitudes toward mobility are discussed further in the next chapter, where we look at those variables which are functions of both the work situation and the situation outside work.

The married men

With marriage, life changes for the men in the sample. Our findings on the social lives of the married couples show a pattern of privatization similar to that described by Goldthorpe, Lockwood, et al. as characteristic of the affluent manual workers in their sample. Social life centers around the relatively isolated nuclear family. Most leisure time is spent at home. The role segregation between husband and wife is no longer as extreme as in traditional working class communities. With the exception of those people who continue to live in the neighborhoods in which they had grown up and who still see childhood friends, most of the friendships are between couples.

The married men tend to see friends less than do the single men, and to see relatives more. In fact, whereas only 9 percent of the single men say that the people they see most frequently are relatives, 59 percent of the married men give this answer. In a way, this result is an artifact. The relatives most often mentioned are parents and parents-in-law, people our respondents saw every day before being married without having to "visit." But there is also evidence that the amount of time spent with friends decreases sharply. Fifteen of the forty-three married men (35%) say they see no friends at all. And the married men who *do* see friends see them considerably less often than do the unmarried men. Thirty-five percent of this group see friends less than once a week, while only 8 percent of the unmarried men see friends this rarely. Having children reduces still further the amount of time spent with friends.

We do not have detailed data on which relatives our respondents see socially and how often. But the evidence suggests that relatives do not fill the gap left by friends as leisure-time companions.

One measure of the degree of privatization is the respondents' own spontaneous comments when asked how they spend their free time. Seventeen of the forty-three husbands specifically mention that they spend most of their free time with their wives and, if they have any, with their children. Some of these couples do not have relatives in the vicinity. "Here in Milan I don't even know my neighbors, we don't have any contacts, we don't know anyone, except for my sister – she comes to visit now and again" (Besola). Of these seventeen couples, five see no one at all, neither relatives nor friends. In all but one of these cases the husband is not from Milan. Seven more couples say that they see relatives more often than they see friends, but that they spend most of their time at home with their immediate families. The remaining five of the seventeen see friends occasionally but spend most of their leisure time alone together. The men generally express satisfaction with this life style.

I'm very attached to my family and my home, so when I get home from work I enjoy moving that picture because I don't like it where it is, or doing little jobs here and there, or else studying, looking at magazines, cultural or technical magazines. (Brunelli)

I usually stay at home, talk about this or that, about how the day went, with my wife, because working out of town I'm out all day long. I prefer to pass the evenings with my wife. If I were to go out in the evenings it wouldn't be very nice for her. (Boninsegna)

Another measure of privatization comes from statements on how often friends and relatives are seen. This question was asked specifically for friends but not for relatives. Fortunately, most respondents also provided the necessary information on how often they see relatives in answering the questions on use of free time and amount of time spent with friends. In most cases this enabled us to judge whether or not they see relatives very frequently, that is, several times a week. Only 35 percent of the married couples clearly see relatives frequently. For 18 percent we do not have sufficient information. Forty-six percent of the married couples see relatives once a week or less. Evidently a very substantial number of couples have only loose ties with relatives.[4]

We have noted that the married men do not see friends very often. But do those who do not see friends much make up for this by seeing relatives more often? Apparently not. Seeing relatives and seeing friends tend to go together rather than to exclude one another. Those who often see relatives live in the communities where they have grown up, communities where they have friends as well as relatives.[5]

About eleven of the married men seem particularly well-integrated into the communities in which they live. They see relatives and friends frequently and, in many cases, participate in some kind of structured activity in the community that brings them into contact with others.

Summarizing the findings on the married couples, twenty-one couples may be said to lead privatized lives, either by virtue of their own comments on their use of leisure time or because of the rarity with which they see friends and relatives. This is virtually half of the married couples in our sample. At least eleven of the married men may be said to be highly integrated into their communities. Eleven more are neither privatized nor highly integrated so far as we can judge. These data indicate a considerable degree of privatization among the married men.

*Participation in formal organizations and
other structured leisure activities*

Before drawing any conclusions about our sample as a whole, we must take into account the respondents' participation in formal organizations and other more or less structured activities.

We noted in Chapter 4 that the technicians in our sample are not joiners: only 33 percent (29/88) of them belong to some formal organization outside the workplace. A substantial portion of the sample (35%) does, however, belong to one or another of the three unions that compete for membership. Counting union membership, the proportion belonging to an organization goes up to 58 percent. Being entirely voluntary, union membership is of considerable significance as an indicator of commitment to the goals of the labor movement. However, membership does not in itself imply a commitment to union activities. For most people, this commitment ends with the end of the workday. Those who do spend time on union work are usually members of one or another of the political parties. In the case of this sample, we can safely say that we will not be underestimating activity in formal organizations if we omit union membership from consideration.

Ten people (11% of the sample) belong to political organizations (parties, cooperatives), and seven of them are very active in these organizations. This is a comparatively large number for a sample of this size. Membership in other kinds of organizations is so infrequent, however, that the overall level of participation is lower in this sample than in Goldthorpe and Lockwood's sample of affluent manual workers. In fact, 48 percent of their manual worker sample are members of some organization, as are 67 percent of their white collar comparison group.[6]

Given the relatively small number of men in formal organizations and the diversity of these organizations, it is difficult to ask questions regarding the determinants of organizational membership. Comparing those who are not members of any organization with those who are, it is not evident that the backgrounds of individuals or their present situations substantially affect membership in organizations. Whether raised in the Milan area or in the South, whether having graduated from secondary school or not, whether married or single, makes little difference so far as membership in organizations is concerned.[7] The one exception is union membership, which is discussed further in Chapter 6.

In answer to the general question about use of free time, 59 percent of the sample cite no major activities beyond seeing family and/or friends. Only 16 percent mention studying. This figure is so low because some of the interviews were carried out during the summer months when school is not in session. Five percent devote a considerable portion of their free time to political activities, and 3 percent have a second job.

Seven percent mention a work-related hobby, such as building electronic equipment at home, as a major free-time activity. In answer to other questions, 29 percent say they read technical magazines outside of work, and 36 percent say they talk about electronics with friends after work. For some people such discussions with friends are in the context of their night-school studies, but for others this is not the case.

There is obviously a high degree of involvement in electronics, the subject matter of the technicians' work.

Ten percent mention other kinds of outside activities: playing musical instruments, participating in a photographic club, working with the families of convicts, etc.

What these figures do not reveal is that there are a very small number of people who are highly active and involved in numerous organizations. For example, one technician, twenty-two years old and single, is active in his political party, is on the Tax Commission of the small town where he lives and grew up, sees many friends every day, and plays in a rock band – activities sufficient for any professional curriculum vitae.

Turning to the determinants of structured leisure-time activity, we find that married men with children tend slightly more often to say that they spend free time with family and friends rather than in some specific pursuit. In answers to other questions, they also emerge as reading less, reading technical magazines at home less (although they read technical magazines at work more, probably in compensation), and talking less about electronics with friends.

Education does not have the expected effect on organizational membership and use of free time. The men in the sample do not vary much in their levels of education. However, within the range of variation of the sample, the results are rather surprising. In comparison with those who have already completed secondary school, those who have not completed secondary school are slightly more likely to be members of organizations (political, union, and others) and are more likely to use their leisure time in some specific pursuit. More of those without secondary school degrees are engaged in every category of structured free-time activity except electronics hobbies. The reasons for this reversal of the usual effects of education are unclear.[8]

An occupational community?

It is by now a commonplace that class consciousness develops out of a sense of community and that a sense of community, in turn, derives from an actual experience of community. Printers, dockworkers, railroad men, miners – all those occupations in which workers tend to form occupational communities – have had a special importance in the labor movements of many countries. Blauner has defined the occupational community in terms of three characteristics: (1) Workers in their off hours socialize more with persons in their own line of work than with a cross section of occupational types; (2) workers talk shop in their off hours; and (3) the occupation itself is the reference group for the members of the community – its standards of behavior, its system of status and rank, guide conduct.[9]

Blauner points out that occupational communities rarely exist among urban factory workers. David Lockwood, in his article on "Sources of Variation in Working Class Images of Society," has sketched an ideal type of what he calls the "proletarian traditional" worker. This type includes not only the members of Blauner's occupational community but also extends to other workers living in stable, working class communities who have much interaction with workmates and kin.[10] Lockwood also outlines two other types of worker: the "deferential traditional" and the "privatized." The two traditional types, the proletarian and the deferential, are immediately recognizable from other writings. The third type, the privatized worker, emerges from Goldthorpe, Lockwood, et al.'s own study of affluent manual workers. Each of these three types is defined by a particular relationship to various aspects of the work situation and the community situation, and each is associated with a particular image of the class structure.

For the proletarian traditional worker, "work associations also carry over into leisure activities. . . . Workmates are normally leisure time companions, often neighbors, and not infrequently kinsmen. The existence of such close-knit cliques of friends, workmates, neighbors, and relatives is the hallmark of the traditional working class community."[11] This kind of working class subculture has been described by Bott, Gans, Hoggart, and others. According to the prevailing subcultural view, the class structure is divided into two classes, namely, "us," the workers, and "them," the bosses and managers. These classes are considered to be in opposition to one another, the defining criterion of class being power rather than status or money.

The deferential worker is likely to live in a small town or rural area and to have little occasion to form strong attachments to workers in similar situations. His relationship to his employer is personal and particularistic. In the community, "the boundaries of the several status groups making up the local system are maintained by various means of social acceptance and rejection in both formal and informal association."[12] The image of society that arises in this situation is of a hierarchy of prestige and status groups, "in which each 'knows his place' and recognizes the status prerogatives of those above and below him."[13] This is the sort of imagery described by W. Lloyd Warner in his many studies of stratification in small U.S. cities.

The privatized worker differs from the two traditional types in that he is not highly integrated into the society, nor does he have a strong sense of group membership. He works in a mass-production industry. His job is repetitive and lacking in autonomy. It is a way to make a living and nothing more. There are no strong attachments to workmates:

Such "alienated" workers do not form cohesive groups inside the factory, and they are not prone to form occupational communities outside the factory. . . The dominant relationship is the cash-nexus. But, although he is "alienated" labour, he is unlikely to possess a strongly developed class consciousness because his involvement in work is too low to allow for strong feelings of any kind except perhaps the desire to escape from it altogether.[14]

The privatized worker lives with other manual workers in neighborhoods that tend to be fairly recent. "Unrelated by the ascriptive ties of kinship, long-standing neighborliness and shared work experiences, and lacking also the facility for readily creating middle class patterns of sociability, workers on the housing estates tend to live a socially isolated, home-centered existence."[15] In this environment, people can judge one another only on the basis of externals such as possessions. These workers have what Lockwood calls a "pecuniary model of society," according to which individuals are distinguished from one another only by the magnitude of their incomes. Society is viewed as composed of "an amorphous aggregate of individuals" rather than of actual groups, be they classes or strata.

In delineating these types, Lockwood seeks to show how the community structure and the work situation determine different life styles and different models of the class structure. The types and the accompanying typology of class imagery are conceptual tools intended to "help to specify the conditions affecting the direction of working class politics."[16] To each type corresponds a political position and a political style. The proletarian traditionalist is the class conscious worker who in England will be the staunch Labor supporter and in Italy and France the no less staunch supporter of the Marxist parties. The deferential traditionalist is the working class Tory. The politics of the privatized worker are described by Goldthorpe, Lockwood, et al. as "instrumental collectivism." With this term they describe his pragmatic, nonideological attitude toward his union and toward the Labor Party. According to Goldthorpe, Lockwood, et al., the privatized worker does not develop this attitude as a result of his work situation, but rather he brings it into the work environment from outside.[17]

Despite the importance of the notion of occupational community, the types described by Lockwood are characterized mainly by the structures of the communities in which they live rather than by the nature of their work situations.[18] The major difference between the proletarian traditionalist and the privatized worker lies in their different community situations and in the different attitudes they bring to work rather than in the job itself. In *The Affluent Worker*, Goldthorpe, Lockwood, et al. describe privatization as a pattern of social life outside work, a pattern that revolves around the home and the conjugal family. It is, they argue, the consequence of an instrumental orientation to work that leads the worker to abandon the traditional solidary community in search of a higher standard of living.

Following Lockwood's article on class imagery, further research has sought to locate the proletarian and deferential workers in reality.[19] The results of this research lead to qualifications of Lockwood's ideal types. Cousins and Brown summarize these qualifications in their study of Tyneside shipbuilders, often cited as archetypal "proletarian traditional" workers: "Our argument . . . is both that the social situation of workers in a traditional industry and their images of society are more varied than has been allowed for; and that the links between social context and social consciousness are looser than has been suggested."[20]

Keeping these qualifications in mind, we can retain Lockwood's types as benchmarks with which to compare the technicians in our sample. Later, in our discussion of class imagery, we will make some more precise comparisons between our sample and others.

As with many of the other groups that have been objects of empirical research, the workers in our sample will not be fitted neatly into a typology. Some lead privatized lives, their social contacts extending only occasionally beyond the nuclear family; others are integrated into larger networks and see friends and/or relatives every day.

The single technicians, having no other source of companionship to fall back on, have a greater number of extrafamilial ties than do the married men. Each person interviewed was asked to name the two friends with whom he spent the most time. Among the single technicians, 38 percent of those chosen were people from the same factory.

Those single men who do not spend most of their leisure time with colleagues participate in long-standing peer groups or see old friends. Many
of these friends are school friends who do similar jobs in other plants. If
we add those 26 percent who do similar jobs elsewhere to those 38 percent who are from the same workplace, we get a total of 63 percent of
friendships with people in the same occupation. More than half of the
single men (52%) also talk shop with friends outside of work. (The comparable figure for the married men is only 24%.) According to these
data, the single men as a group meet two of Blauner's criteria for occupational community: (1) Workers socialize more with people in their
own line of work than with a cross section of occupational types; and
(2) workers talk shop in their off hours.

But if this is an occupational community, it is not an intense one
such as is found among the manual workers of Blauner's examples. It
is founded more upon convenience and upon the fact of being thrown
into association together than upon shared hardships and dangers. It
is a temporary network, especially for those living away from home.
The patterns of mutuality, the reciprocal obligations, the ritualistic
quality Lockwood points out as typical of traditional working class
communities, all of these are absent. This community does not meet
Blauner's third criterion: The occupation is not the reference group
from which members of the community derive standards of behavior,
systems of rank and status, or values guiding conduct.

The lives of the married men approximate those of Lockwood's privatized type. The elements of occupational community are present to a
much lesser extent than among the single men. Only 22 percent of the
friends they see most often are colleagues, and half of these are seen
only rarely. Only 24 percent talk shop with friends. We have pointed
out that less than half of the married couples state that they see kin on
a daily basis and that half the couples may be said to lead privatized
lives.

The occupational community, such as it is, is a transitional phase to
a more privatized life. Only in those cases in which men have remained
in the locales where they grew up do they continue to maintain close
ties with old friends and relatives. In most cases the ties to colleagues
are casual and are not maintained after marriage.

Geographical mobility is the major cause of the decline of traditional
life patterns. If either the husband or the wife is not from the area, he

or she will not have kin or old friends with whom to associate, and will fall back upon the spouse to satisfy needs for companionship. This, in turn, makes it difficult for the spouse to maintain his or her obligations to the network. Ten miles' distance, one-half hour of traveling time in an urban area, is sufficient to disrupt the traditional networks.

Goldthorpe, Lockwood, et al. point out that the men in their small, white collar, comparison sample lead lives no less privatized than those of their affluent manual workers. "They too are not involved in any very intensive social round of visits, mutual entertainment and other shared activities with a wide circle of friends, such as might be observed in the case, say, of couples of higher managerial or professional status."[21] They offer this as evidence of a "normative convergence" between white collar and blue collar workers – "one focal point of this being an overriding concern with the economic fortunes and social relationships of the conjugal unit."[22] We see this convergence as the coincidental by-product of a breakdown of traditional communities together with a lack of very strong involvement, such as professional involvements, which might bring together people with common interests spread over a wider geographical area. The number of people in our sample who mention friendships developed through common interests despite distance was very small.

Images of the class structure

Many authors have sought to tie people's images of the class structure to their actual life situations. In addition to the intrinsic interest in these images, they have been considered to be important in that they are closely associated with political attitudes and voting. Views of the class structure are seen as intervening variables between life situations and political attitudes and behaviors.

The basic issues underlying the discussion of class imagery, including Lockwood's article summarized in the preceding section, are the question of the conditions under which people view the stratification system in terms of differences in power, in status, or in money[23] and the question of the consequences of these different views. The three dimensions of power, status, and money correspond to Lockwood's three types of worker: the proletarian traditional, the deferential traditional, and the privatized.

We begin with a description of class images among the men in our sample, and then proceed to discuss the determinants and consequences of class imagery.

A descriptive analysis of class imagery

The class models of our sample are in many ways similar to those of Goldthorpe and Lockwood's privatized workers. Lockwood described the privatized worker as having a pecuniary model of society. In a later paper, John Goldthorpe provides a more detailed description of this model:

> The general tendency is for membership to be claimed in a class, often seen as newly formed, which takes in a wide range of all wage and salary earners – and is, therefore, describable as (literally) the working class – and which, even if not actually ranked in an intermediate position, is still felt to be made up of persons with "middling" economic standards. . . . This class is then invariably distinguished from some higher class, or classes, whose economic superiority is believed to be such as to put their members in a qualitatively different situation; and sometimes, too, from a lower class of deprived, undeserving, or disadvantaged persons, which tends similarly to be accorded a "special" character.[24]

The new working class technicians in our sample also tend to have an image of a large central class within which distinctions are seen as determined primarily by money. However, this image coexists with that of a power elite that exercises some form of political and economic control. The highest class, which Goldthorpe and Lockwood's privatized workers perceive to be in a qualitatively different position in the realm of consumption, is seen by our respondents to be in a qualitatively different position in the realm of power as well. Although the class images of our sample show some remarkable similarities to those of the Goldthorpe–Lockwood sample, the persistence of power imagery among the Italian technicians leads us to substantially different conclusions from those arrived at by Goldthorpe and Lockwood.

Given the parallels between the Goldthorpe–Lockwood study and our own, it was thought that direct comparisons would be interesting. Some effort was made to ensure that our data on class imagery would be comparable to theirs. The method of data collection was similar, and information was gathered on those aspects of class imagery mentioned by Goldthorpe, Lockwood, et al. in their Appendix on "The collection and analysis of data on respondents' images of class."[25] The following points were covered in our interviews: (1) the number and names of social classes distinguished by the respondent; (2) the composition of classes; (3) the determinants of class position; (4) the respondent's position; (5) the respondent's assessment of the likelihood of social mobility; (6) the respondent's opinion as to the inevitability of class differences.

A typology of images of the class structure was then worked out from the data. The question we asked ourselves in developing these types was, What classes does the respondent mention in his description of the class structure? It is noteworthy that the respondents' models fitted easily into a few types. Somewhat arbitrarily we decided to distinguish six types. Only 15 percent of the cases were too idiosyncratic to fit into one of the six categories. Another 9 percent of the sample said they did not know what classes existed or denied the existence of classes altogether.

The six types are presented graphically in Figure 5.1 along with the number of respondents categorized under each type. It must be admitted at the outset that a division into six types rather than into four or seven is somewhat arbitrary. We have distinguished these particular six models with an eye to those differences between models that have important implications for the person's view of his place in society. Thus, the fact that some people added a peripheral class to their three-class scheme, as did some of those with type V schemes, was not considered an important alteration, whereas the fact that someone expanded the working class to include white collar occupations, such as perhaps his own, was considered significant, and was used as the distinguishing criterion between types V and VI. The types should not be construed as the only six models that can be extracted from the data. Nonetheless, as we shall argue later, each type represents a logically consistent structure meaningful to the respondents who adhere to it. The types are described below.

Type I. Ten people (11%) see the social order as a continuum from rich to poor. The number of classes specified varies. But because classes are not seen as real social groups with distinct boundaries, the number of classes distinguished is not important. Within a large middle range there are no meaningful cutting points between classes. If the very rich and the very poor are differentiated from the ordinary people, it is only because of their consumption possibilities.

Two examples will illustrate this model; in both, money is viewed as

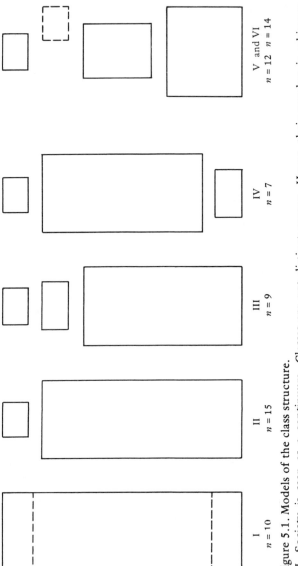

Figure 5.1. Models of the class structure.

I   Society is seen as a continuum. Classes are not distinct groups. Hence, their number is arbitrary. "Rich," "average," and "poor" are common terms.

II Dichotomous images.

III Three classes: a large lower class plus two higher classes.

IV Three classes: a large central class plus small classes on top and bottom.

V   Three classes: the two lower ones, called "working" and "middle," plus one higher class. Sometimes a fourth class such as "petite bourgeoisie" is added.

VI Same as V, except that the dividing line between middle and working classes does not fall on the manual–nonmanual line. (In all but one case, this line is drawn above the manual–nonmanual line.)

the underlying dimension. The first respondent, Cestaro, mentions four classes.

Interviewer: What classes exist in society?

Cestaro: Not the nobility, because by now it has been eliminated, even though there are still some nostalgics who feel that they are nobility... but if someone makes 150 million [250,000 dollars] he feels socially more evolved than someone who makes 50 million, and someone who makes 50 million feels more evolved than someone who makes 10. It's a hierarchy based on income, even though there are people who make a lot of money and are very democratic and don't consider themselves socially higher up.

Interviewer: So how many classes do you think there are and what would you call them?

Cestaro: It's hard to say. I couldn't give a definition. In practice each person feels like a class unto himself. As I said before, someone who makes a lot feels as if he were in a different society, but it's hard to know what to call it or how to classify it.

Interviewer: How many classes would you say there were?

Cestaro: It's hard to say how many.

Interviewer: Well, approximately...

Cestaro: On the order of three or four. There's the class of the elect, that is, people who earn disproportionately much, like industrialists, university "barons" [i.e., big name professors], or some doctors, stuff like that, the kind of people who can buy themselves yachts, that's one social class. Then we go down to the class of the professionals, which includes more people. There are some professionals who make an awful lot, and others who can be considered a part of the third class, the class of the white collar employees, because unfortunately the white collar workers consider themselves as a class. And the last social class is that of the workers. So I'd say four altogether, as an average, starting from the blue collar workers and going up to the industrialists.

Interviewer: What is it that puts someone in one class or another, that distinguishes the classes?

Cestaro: Money and that's it, because if an industrialist were to go broke, be left penniless he would fall immediately into the working class, he wouldn't be an industrialist anymore. That is, it's not blue blood and all the rest, it's how much someone earns that counts. Even the poor pilgrim who wins the lottery goes up to the higher social class. He's become a big shot, because he has money...

Boninsegna, the second respondent, mentions only three classes.

Interviewer: How many classes are there?

Boninsegna: Three: the upper class, the rich, who have their own spots...

Interviewer: Who have their own spots?

Boninsegna: Who have their own clubs for themselves. Not that they have people in front of the door to stop others from going in, but they keep them out in their own way. For example, you go into one of these places to have coffee and it costs like two or three thousand lire [three to five dollars], so they exclude some people right away, so the place will only attract certain people.

Then there are people in the class, let's call it the normal class, who lead normal lives. Then unfortunately there are people who live in shanties. This is the third class, the very poor.

Interviewer: What distinguishes these classes?

Boninsegna: I think the main thing that distinguishes them is money.

The first respondent is unwilling to name any classes, and only after some prodding does he name four. The second respondent is more typical of the group in that he names three classes, among them a large central class he calls the "normal class," and which others call the "less rich," "those who are doing medium well," etc. Six of the ten men in this group mention three classes. One respondent calls his central class "the middle class," another, "the working class." For the technicians who hold this model of the class structure, the distinction between working class and middle class is not very important. They tend to see working class and middle class as two names for the same central grouping or to see only the upper part of the middle class or the lower part of the working class as outside the central class. In three cases, the respondents describe themselves as being in the middle class and then as being in the working class or vice versa.

All those in this group place themselves in a large central class. When pressed to say whether they would call themselves middle class or working class, there is often some hesitation. Six of the ten say middle class and four say working class, the deciding factor usually being the respondent's own political sympathies. As we shall see later on, leftists tend to identify as working class and others to identify as middle class.

This type of class model is identical to that described by Goldthorpe, Lockwood, et al. as typical of the privatized worker. They too note the emphasis on consumption possibilities and the designation of a large central class called indifferently middle class or working class.

Type II. Fifteen people (17%) have dichotomous images of the class structure. This view contrasts with the view of society as a continuum in that the terms used invariably suggest a polar opposition between the two classes. The higher class is pictured as being small, and is opposed to a large class including most of the population. The dichotomous view is best exemplified by those who see society as divided into exploiters and the exploited, as does the respondent quoted here.

Interviewer: What classes are there?

Bruno: There is. . . we can call it. . . the class of the "haves," those who have at least. . . who own most of the goods in Italy, and the others, the "have-nots." Now the problem is. . . that is, the struggle we must fight. . . the problem is to reduce this thing.

Interviewer: Who do you consider to be in the class of the haves?

Bruno: In practice, those who control. . . the big monopolies. . . I don't know, industrialists, merchants, people like that.

Interviewer: And the others? Would you say then that dependent workers are all in one class?

Bruno: All dependent workers. . . in practice, the exploited. . . exploiters and exploited. . . from the merchant to the guy who rents out his land for cultivation. . . the big entrepreneurs. . . divided into two categories, those who don't want to let go their grip and those who want a little bit more.

Another respondent, Cafiero, expressed this same view as follows.

Interviewer: How many classes would you say there are?

Cafiero: How many? I don't know the number. I know that the population is divided into many classes – maybe not as blatantly as in the Middle Ages, vassals, etc., but maybe there are more.

Interviewer: Let's try to list them as you see them. What classes are there according to you?

Cafiero: Well, the society is divided into the working class, which is exploited, and the class of owners, then, . . . well, I think these are the two main classes. Then, obviously, the working class can be further broken down, that is, a part that has attained a certain ease and another that is still exploited. . . in much worse conditions.

Interviewer: What do you mean by working class?

Cafiero: By working class I mean just that, those people who work, that is, the people, just the people, the majority of the population.. . . all those who work and who are exploited by the others.

In the first case the notion of class struggle is made quite explicit. In the second example, we can see how secondary distinctions come to be made within the large lower class. Given that the opposition between the two major groupings is seen as primary, the question of where to accommodate the middle class often perplexes those who hold to a dichotomic image. Unlike the classical working class dichotomy which lumps white collar workers together with the ruling class, these technicians, most of whom are themselves white collar workers, take cognizance of the great spread in the stratification hierarchy. One respondent describes the society as divided into capitalists and proletarians, and then adds a third class, "a reactionary class," which is not clearly defined. This technician, Chilocava, who finds himself moving to the left in the political spectrum because of his experiences at work, is unable to arrive at an unequivocal statement as to the position of the middle class in the stratification system.

Interviewer: Where would you put the white collar workers? Do you think they are a separate class or not?

Chilocava: It's hard to say that they are part of the higher class – or part of the lower class – that is, it's hard to say that they are on one side or the other. Certainly the white collar worker who makes 200 thousand lire a month [$320], maybe he feels exploited too, but he feels less exploited than the worker who says, "I'm fighting for a more just society, a society that looks more to my interests," while there's the white collar worker who says, who doesn't give a good goddam, because he says, "Why should I bother? The system is fine for me, I have 200 thousand lire a month and I could even have more." I don't know in which class to put them.

Interviewer: I don't know. Maybe somewhere in between?

Chilocava: Yes, in between. Anyway there can be white collar workers who make 200 or 300 thousand lire a month and they are still unhappy with their lives – they too are fighting against the affluent society, capitalist society, etc., because in one way or another they feel exploited as does the blue collar worker, or maybe they have ideals that go beyond career and pay.

For two of the respondents the recognition of the range of inequality in the system together with an emphasis on money as the basis of distinction results in dichotomous images that approach the image of society as a money continuum. These respondents see society as divided into "those with money and those without," "the rich and the miserable." Although the two classes are seen as being in opposition to one another, money is the major criterion of class membership.

Most commonly, however, the dichotomous model of society is associated with the notion of power differences as the determining criterion. In fact, ten of the fifteen people with dichotomous images use terminology indicating a power difference between the two classes, for example, "those who give orders and those who work," "the exploiters and the exploited." As just noted, two people give the classes names that indicate money differences. Even here, however, the oppositional relationship suggests more than just a difference in the realm of consumption. In the other three cases, the dimension underlying the oppositional relationship is unclear.

When asked explicitly what it is that distinguishes the classes, six of the fifteen men in this group answer "power" or "relationship to the means of production." This proportion seems greater when we note that only ten people in the whole sample mention power or relationship to the means of production as the underlying dimension of the stratification system. Yet 34 percent of the sample name "the bosses" as the highest class in their model, and another 19 percent name "the managerial class," or "the industrialists."

There seems to be a tendency to cite money as the basis of stratification no matter what model of the class structure one holds. Five of the fifteen people with dichotomous images and 54 percent of the whole sample say that money is what distinguishes the classes, even though only 11 percent of the sample have images that correspond to such an assumption. Money is certainly the most obvious symbol of class differences. But the fact that money is seen as the distinguishing criterion does not necessarily mean that the person sees the society as a money continuum. Money is not used only for consumption. Someone who says that money is the principal dimension underlying class differences may have in mind the ability to buy and control stocks, land, etc. In fact, because money is a generalized medium, the answer "money" must be interpreted in the context of the total image of the class structure.

Three people with dichotomous images mention behavior, personal characteristics, or life style as underlying criteria. This answer is also frequent throughout the sample: 24 percent give answers falling into this category.

Why is it that so few people in the sample, and less than half even of those who view the stratification system as divided between two opposing classes, explicitly mention power as an underlying dimension? Our hypothesis is that there is a pervasive unwillingness to think explicitly in terms of power relationships. The view of consensus as positive and conflict as negative is so strongly rooted in all of us that even when Marxist terminology is accepted as a part of everyday language, or when life experiences are such as to create a view of society as divided into conflicting groups, the idea of social groups in conflict with one another is expressed implicitly rather than openly.

All of those with dichotomous models place themselves in the lower of the two classes named. When pressed to say whether they are in the middle class or in the working class, eleven of the fifteen say working class. However they are often unwilling to acknowledge the distinction. Many, such as Chilocava, describe the working class as all those who work for a salary or wage. These respondents simply deny the existence of a middle class. Others, such as Facciuto, admit that according to conventional usage they belong to the middle class, but reject any identification with this negatively evaluated group:

Interviewer: If you had to say you belonged to the middle class or to the working class, which would you choose?

Facciuto: Listen, I feel as if I belonged to the working class, because even though I'm at the white collar level so far as my employment category is concerned, I'm still a dependent worker, and as such I think the salary difference between me and a skilled worker is pretty small, and also so far as standard of living, so I don't think there's any difference between me and a blue collar worker.

We shall find similar efforts to avoid middle class identification among respondents holding other models of the class structure as well.

The view of society as divided into two opposing classes is the image described by many authors as typical of the working class. The dichotomous image held by the men in our sample differs from the classical dichotomous image only in that the line between the two classes is always drawn well above the manual–nonmanual line, so as to include all dependent workers within the lower class. Dichotomous imagery is considerably more frequent in our sample than in the "affluent worker" sample (17% of our respondents hold this view vs. 4% in the Goldthorpe et al. sample).

Types III and IV. At first blush it might seem that no two views of the class structure could be more different than the view of society as a money continuum and the dichotomous image. These images are, indeed, radically different, both in form and in the underlying world views that they suggest. Yet, among the men in our sample, the two images also have one important feature in common: They both posit the existence of a large central grouping within which there are no class differences. The men with dichotomous images place the dividing line very high in the social structure, so that a small group is opposed to the rest of society. Those who view society as a continuum obviously see no sharp breaks at all.

Types III and IV may be seen as in some sense intermediate between the view of society as a continuum and the dichotomous view. We find once more the large central class. Distinct groups are also seen as existing on the top and, in the case of type IV, on the bottom as well. Unlike in the money model, their distinctiveness is not seen to reside only in their greater or lesser wealth. However, these models are also unlike the dichotomous images in that three, and sometimes four, classes are specified, and they are not described in terms of polar opposites such as exploiters and exploited or rich and poor.

We turn now to the differences between types III and IV. The type III image sees society as composed of a large central class of dependent workers, some sort of elite, and one, or sometimes two, classes in between. The intermediate class is called "the petite bourgeoisie" or "the class of the professionals." Sometimes both are mentioned as separate entities. The type IV image also posits three classes, but here a large middle class is seen as bounded at the top by an elite and at the bottom by the very poor.

Nine people in the sample (10%) hold type III images, and seven people (8%) hold type IV images. The following is an example of the type III image.

Interviewer: How many classes would you say there were?

Corti: How many? Well, I guess I'd say at least three.

Interviewer: Which are those?

Corti: The bosses, the free professionals, let's call them that, and the workers – three major classes.

Interviewer: By workers you mean all dependent workers, or who?

Corti: Well, the free professionals, there are the lawyers, the doctors, those engineers who have their own companies, accountants. The class of the bosses obviously includes all those who own some commercial or industrial activity or something like that. Then, in the realm of work, one can divide it into two groups: those who *really* work, and the directors and managers, call them what you will, who are comparable to the free professionals in that their work relationship is more like that of a free professional than like that of a worker.

Interviewer: And who would you put among the workers? In GT&E, for example, all the way from the engineer to the blue collar worker?

Corti: Well, there's obviously some difference, but whether you would call them completely separate classes. . . I have the impression that this difference is decreasing, because the position of the engineer is declining, degrees are becoming less important, that is, the blue collar worker and the engineer are both working people. The engineer is no longer a white fly [because of his white coat] among so many workers. . . . They aren't all managers or bosses, they're working people. They have different jobs than do the blue collar workers, but I can't call this a class, it's a different kind of work, just like an administrative job is different from a technical job.

Interviewer: Which class would you put yourself in?

Corti: In the class of the workers.

Interviewer: And if you had to say "middle class" or "working class?"

Corti: What do you mean by middle class?

Interviewer: If you had to choose between these two. . .?

Corti: Obviously in the distinctions I drew this middle class doesn't exist, so the question is already answered. . . . I see the working class and the middle class as more or less at the same level. I'm talking about GT&E now, not about other factories. . . I have friends who are blue collar workers who are better friends than those who are not, than those who are top management (not that I have any friends who are top management, but anyway. . .), anyway, as I said before, I'm not one to hold to these distinctions. . . . Unfortunately for us, first we classify ourselves, "I'm an engineer, you're a blue collar worker, I'm a white collar worker," etc., so we think we're different, but if we kept our eyes open we'd notice that we're all in the same cauldron, and these distinctions which we create are taken advantage of by others who turn them into reality.

The type IV image is illustrated by the following response.

Interviewer: What classes are there?

Guarnieri: What do you want to know about? The enormous differences there are? There is a middle class, a poor class, but I don't believe in its existence much, and then there's an elite class that is beyond our scope. There is a poor class, in fact they say that unemployment is increasing, but, on the other hand, you also see ads in the papers looking for workers, especially in Milan. It is part of the Italian character to want to be like this [unemployed], especially in the South. In Milan you can see that people keep pretty busy, working, etc. In the South, and even in Rome, it's the opposite. There are wooden houses, shanties. I've been there often. It's an ugly thing, but naturally these people have a TV, a car, and maybe even an apartment in a housing project. But they rent it out and go back to living in the shanty. . . . We're pretty twisted as far as mentality goes.

Interviewer: And above the poor class?

Guarnieri: There's a middle class, which consists of the majority of the population.

Interviewer: That is the blue collar workers, etc.?

Guarnieri: Yes. I consider myself to be in this category. Those who have a job already have something. In fact, among the poor I should add the old-age pensioners. Unfortunately there is no social security. This is sorely missed in Italy. . .

Both those with type III images and those with type IV images place themselves in the central class. When asked to choose between a working class identification and a middle class identification, four of the sixteen people in these two groups refuse, insisting that the class of dependent workers cannot be divided along the blue collar–white collar line. Several others can only be persuaded to make a choice after considerable insistence, or make a choice while maintaining that the middle class and working class are really the same thing. We encounter again the unwillingness to acknowledge the meaningfulness of the manual–nonmanual distinction, even among those who identify as middle class.

Those with type IV images, who see a class of very poor people below their own, tend to call their central class "the middle class" (4/7), whereas those with type III images are likely to label their central class "the class of dependent workers" (3/9), or "those who work" (3/9). Only one of the type IV technicians calls his central class "the proletariat," or "the working class," whereas three of the type III technicians use these terms. This suggests that, unlike those holding type III images, those with type IV images see themselves as relatively privileged.

It is curious that only ten people in the entire sample (the seven with type IV images plus three of those with unclassifiable images) mention the existence of a lumpenproletariat, a class of the very poor. Even among these ten, the lumpenproletariat is sometimes added as an afterthought, or its existence is denied in the same breath with which it is affirmed (see the above response by Guarnieri). Those who notice the poor do so only in support of their own claim to middle class status.

The fact of seeing three classes rather than two is associated with a nonconflictual view of the relationships between these classes. At least this is true when one of the classes is a large central class, as is the case with types III and IV. We turn now to consider the "conventional" images, which see society as divided into a working class, a middle class, and some sort of elite. Here, as we shall see, positing the existence of three classes does not necessarily imply a nonconflictual view of society.

Types V and VI. Twelve people in the sample (13%) hold type V images, and fourteen people (16%) hold type VI images. Both types are characterized by two large classes, generally labeled "middle" and "working," plus one or two higher classes labeled in various ways. People adhering to the two types differ in their perceptions of where the boundary between the middle and working classes falls. Those we have classified as type V follow the conventional usage in drawing the boundary at the blue collar–white collar line, whereas those we have called type VI extend the boundaries of the working class above this line so as to include themselves. The type VI image is often associated with a negative view of the middle class and a correspondingly positive view of the working class.

In the type VI models, the line between middle class and working class is moved up precisely to avoid the necessity of identifying oneself as middle class. Ten of the fourteen respondents in this group identify themselves as working class. Conversely, most of those with type V models (9/12) place themselves in the middle class. These self-placements follow logically from the models held by the two groups of respondents.

An example of each type follows: Vassallo illustrates type V, whereas Baratta gives a type VI response. It will be noted that the type VI model defines a larger working class and a commensurately smaller middle class.

Interviewer: What classes would you say there are?
Vassallo: There's the managerial class. Then there's us, the middle class, that is technicians and normal white collar workers, and then there's the working class.

Interviewer: How many classes would you say there are?
Baratta: I feel that I am. . . I'm working. . . that is, white collar, but I still consider myself as part of the working class. . . I'm one of those people who isn't disgusted by eating chicken with one's hands, and who doesn't mind saying "prick" when necessary. That's what I'm trying to say. I'd say there certainly is this category, then there's a middle category, the one of the *periti* [those with technician's degrees] – but not all of them, some *periti* – which is in between the worker and the professional, the engineer or the person who's high up. I'd say three classes. . .

Many respondents in both groups V and VI see the difference between the middle and working classes as one of outlook and attitude. Thirteen of the twenty-six people explicitly mention some such characteristic as one of the dimensions underlying the stratification system. Among the type VI respondents, those who view attitudes as an underlying dimension tend to describe the middle class outlook in negative terms, as the quote from Baratta illustrates. A few respondents make criticisms that are implicitly or explicitly political, referring to the middle class as "those who feel superior," "the rotten apple," or "the fence-sitters."

An analysis of the labels of the two main classes in these models is not very revealing: "middle" and "working" recur over and over again. The terms used to describe the highest class vary, however, and give some further suggestion as to the respondents' views of the basis of the system in addition to that gained from the direct question on this point. Almost half (5/12) of the respondents holding type V images and more than half (8/14) of those holding type VI images call the highest class "the bosses." The term suggests the idea of a power elite. Besides those who use this term, with its Marxist connotations, many respondents use terms such as "the managerial class" or "the industrialists" (6/12 of the type V respondents and 2/14 of the type VI respondents). These terms might suggest an occupational grouping or a power elite, and it is difficult to tell which connotation the respondent has in mind. In total, then, 50 percent of the respondents in these two groups call the highest class by a name clearly indicating an underlying power dimension, and a further 31 percent call the highest class by a name possibly indicating a power dimension.

A few respondents explicitly point out that the criterion which distinguishes the middle class from the working class is not the same as that which sets off the highest class from the others.

Interviewer: What is the underlying criterion that distinguishes the classes?
Costantini: I'd say above all his education, except when you're talking about being a capitalist, then it's a question of birth, it's a different matter, you don't have to study for that.

Despite his vaguely Marxist conception of the highest class, Costantini is not a political leftist.

When asked explicitly, "What is it that determines a man's class position, that is, what distinguishes the classes?" most of the respondents in these groups cite money and/or personal attributes such as culture, education, and status. Money is given as the primary underlying dimension by twelve of the twenty-six respondents in these two groups. Seven say personal attributes are most important. Three people mention power or relation to the means of production as the most important factors.

Type V models of the class structure are conventional in the sense that the definitions of the major classes in the schema correspond to those used by sociologists, journalists, and other social commentators. In placing themselves in the middle class in this schema, these respondents are following the conventional definition of their class position. Unlike some of the other models, the type V class structure does not suggest certain political attitudes, or certain views on social mobility, or, indeed, particular personal positions on any matter.

By contrast, in the type VI models there is a distortion of conventional usage so as to render the respondent's working class identification consistent with his white collar position. As we shall see later, type VI images are associated with leftist political attitudes.

Respondents answering "Don't know," or "There are no classes." Eight people (9% of the sample) either deny the existence of classes or say they don't know how many classes there are. Both responses evince feelings of anxiety aroused by the very idea of stratification.

Those who deny the existence of classes project ideas of hierarchy onto others. Classes are seen as existing only in other people's minds.

By denying their reality, they can be wished away. This appears clearly in the following example.

Interviewer: One often hears talk of social classes. Do you think there are social classes in Italy?

Faiella: According to me they are all equal. If I have to call someone a cretin, I call him a cretin even if he is a *perito* [i.e., has a technician's degree] . It's all a question of knowing how to live. . . . Classes. . . look, I'll give you an example. I had three or four friends – so far as culture and money went, they were less than nothing. They hit on the right kind of work – now they have Alfa Romeos, they can afford nice clothes, etc. They have made themselves into "class." They hang out with Milan high society, but so far as I'm concerned they're still ignoramuses, illiterates. If there are people who value them, they must be the same way, because for me classes don't exist.

Interviewer: So if you had to say you belonged to the working class or to the middle class, what would you say?

Faiella: Class of pricks. [interruption] You ask me, "Where do you put yourself?" On the one hand, I'm presumptuous, I'd like to put myself up, because my intelligence, let's just say it's there, it's not above average, but it's not below either. There's some initiative there, I've proven it, it's not like I've only done this job, I've done lots of jobs, and always well. I've taken other initiatives – interests such as also cultural. . . and I've always satisfied myself. So where can I place myself? I can place myself somewhere where I live well, honestly, in peace. . . . So for me there is no class, there is only knowing how to live. . .

The hostility evoked by the idea of class is evident; but so also is the self-doubt and the defensiveness. Faiella attacks those who have "made it" within the system. He denies the legitimacy of the system itself. Yet he returns to question his own intelligence and achievements. Uncertain whether to blame himself or the system for his failure, he is confused.

Two others of the eight people in this group are similar to Faiella in that they are so filled with hostility directed toward the hierarchy that they either deny its existence (two cases) or cannot articulate any coherent picture beyond invective (one case, coded as "don't know").

Five people say they don't know how many classes there are or cannot verbalize a coherent picture of the class structure. They are vague rather than resentful. The feeling that class distinctions are an unpleasant matter best not reflected upon remains.

As we shall see in looking at variables associated with class imagery, these people are not simply a residual category. On the contrary, they stand out as one of the most identifiable groups.

Images of the middle of the stratification hierarchy and class identification. Several points emerge from the exposition thus far. We deal first with our respondents' views of the middle range of the stratification system and then with their views of the top of this system.

There is a notable similarity between the workers in our sample and those in the Goldthorpe–Lockwood sample in their conceptualization of a large central class. Sixty-seven percent of the respondents' images include a large central class comprising all or most dependent workers. Only 17 percent of the sample draw a class boundary corresponding to the manual–nonmanual line.

The data on class identification show that all but three of the fifty-nine respondents who see a large central class place themselves within this class. Furthermore, many respondents explicitly deny the importance of the manual–nonmanual distinction. When pressed to choose between a working class and a middle class identification, six respondents refuse, insisting that they belong to the single class of dependent workers; another four respondents consent to choose one of the labels while maintaining that the two classes are really the same; and six more respondents change the name of the central class from middle to working class or vice versa as they talk. Numerous respondents also point to the declining importance of the blue collar–white collar line over the years.

These data suggest that many of the technicians in our sample see themselves as belonging to a class that fits the description previously quoted from Goldthorpe, "a class, often seen as newly formed, which takes in a wide range of all wage and salary earners. . . ." In this, our findings and those of Goldthorpe, Lockwood, et al. differ from those of previous studies, in which a large central class was not found so frequently. The manual–nonmanual line was more frequently mentioned as a divider between classes or strata. As these findings have been adequately summarized elsewhere, they need not be reviewed again here.[26]

The view of society that includes a large central class may be increasingly typical of occupational groups close to or straddling the manual–nonmanual line. A privatized social life no doubt contributes to this view. But, in the case of our sample, a more important consideration is that the manual–nonmanual distinction is irrelevant in their daily working lives.

In positing the existence of a large central class, the respondent is expanding the group to which he sees himself as belonging so as to include within it the bulk of the population. Goldthorpe has pointed out that this tendency, dubbed "the expansion effect" by Oeser and Hammond, contrasts with the tendency observed by W. Lloyd Warner for people to draw finer lines of distinction close to their own position.[27] Goldthorpe sees the expansion effect as the logical concomitant of the image of society as a money continuum. The drawing of fine lines of distinction around and particularly below one's own position is seen as a consequence of a view of society in terms of status.

This interpretation is not supported by our data. Whether one sees money or status characteristics as the principal dimension underlying the stratification system is not, as we shall see shortly, related to whether or not one's class image includes a large central class.

If the technicians no longer give overriding importance to the manual–nonmanual distinction, it might be thought that it matters little whether they call the large central class the working class or the middle class. Goldthorpe argues that this is the case with the British affluent manual workers he studied. Here too, our findings are somewhat different. Among the men in our sample, the name given to the large central class, and the answer given to the forced-choice class identification question ("If you had to say you belonged to the middle class or to the working class, which would you choose?") are both related to other aspects of class imagery. As was pointed out above, type VI respondents create a large central class in their images by expanding the boundaries of the working class so as to include themselves within it. Those with dichotomous images are also likely to identify themselves as working class. In contrast, those whose models include another class below the one in which they place themselves (i.e., most respondents whose images correspond to types I, IV, and V, and some in the "other" category) are more likely to identify as middle class.[28] We shall see below that class identification is related to political views as well as to class imagery.

When forced to choose between working class and middle class identifications, the frequency of working class choices among the men in our sample is remarkable. Forty-nine percent of those who answer the forced-choice question (forty-one respondents) place themselves in the working class. Of those who are objectively in the white collar category, 45 percent identify as working class. In contrast, the spontaneous self-placements show a much lower percentage of working class identifications. The respondents recognize that the large central class in which they place themselves does not coincide with either the middle class or the working class as these terms are most commonly used. When forced to choose, however, their ideological preferences and their outlooks on society incline them to identify themselves as working class rather than as middle class.

There is no contradiction between the unwillingness to recognize the importance of the manual–nonmanual line, or even the insistence that working class and middle class are one and the same, and the preference for one or the other term on the forced-choice question. A person may quite consistently insist that the two classes are no longer distinct, but in choosing a label he will, nonetheless, be guided by the connotations of the two terms.

The proportion of working class identifiers among this group of new working class respondents is higher than that found in comparable lower middle class groups. Richard Centers, for example, reports that 34 percent of the white collar workers in this sample identified as working class on a forced-choice question.[29] One study of Italy, done by Joseph Lopreato, is reported in Lopreato and Hazelrigg.[30] The data are based on a national survey of 1,569 interviewees conducted in 1963–4. Many of the questions on class imagery are comparable to those asked here. Lopreato found that 39 percent of the petite bourgeoisie identified as working class. In their discussion of class identification, Lopreato and Hazelrigg point out that their sample is similar to other European samples in showing a greater propensity toward working class rather than middle class self-placements compared to U.S. samples.[31] But the 45 percent working class identification among the objectively petit bourgeois technicians of our sample shows an even greater tendency toward working class identification than among Lopreato's national cross section of the Italian petite bourgeoisie.

Summarizing our respondents' views of the middle range of the stratification system, the new working class technicians are similar to the British affluent manual workers in describing one large central class. The basis of the system in these models is not always seen as money, however. Using a strict definition, only 11 percent of our sample have money models. But a much larger number (59%) posit a large central class. This central class may be called middle class, working class, or class of dependent workers, and the choice of terms does make a difference, despite the respondents' frequent insistence that the two are the same.

The tendency to see a large central class is based on the technician's position, straddling the blue collar–white collar line. His work combines the manual and the intellectual and makes him disinclined to perceive a sharp boundary. Background variables are also important in determining class imagery. We discuss these in the section on the correlates of class imagery below.

Images of the top of the stratification hierarchy. Although the new working class technicians are similar to the British affluent manual workers in their views of the middle ranges of the stratification system, they are strikingly different in their views of the top of this system. Power imagery, so rare in the Goldthorpe–Lockwood sample, is very common in our own.

There are three ways in which to look at the importance of power in the class imagery of our sample. First, one can look at the prevalence of dichotomous images and power models. But, although dichotomous images are the most clearly expressive of a conflict view of society, other images are also compatible with an emphasis on power inequalities. Another way of weighing the relative importance of power in class imagery is to examine the answers to a specific question on the dimensions underlying the stratification system. Finally, the terms used in describing the top of the system may be analyzed. We compare our sample, in each of these ways, first to the Goldthorpe–Lockwood sample and then to samples from other studies.

Only 4 percent of the Goldthorpe–Lockwood sample had power models of society. According to an identical definition, 15 percent of our sample have power models of society.[32] According to the slightly broader definition used in this study, 17 percent of our sample fall into this category.

When asked explicitly to name the basis of the stratification system, only 2 people out of the 229 (less than 1%) in the "affluent worker" sample mentioned power differences. Eight of our respondents (10%) mention power or interests as underlying dimensions.

Although these are notable differences, the percentages are small in both samples. It is in looking at the terminology used to describe the classes that more substantial differences emerge. As noted earlier, 34 percent of the sample name the bosses as the highest class in their model. This term clearly indicates a power difference. Another 19 percent call the highest class the managerial class or the industrialists. Here again there is the suggestion of a power difference. By contrast, the use of any occupational or power terminology was uncommon in the Gold-thorpe–Lockwood sample.[33]

The occurrence of imagery and terminology suggestive of inequalities along a power dimension is very much greater in our sample than in the Goldthorpe–Lockwood sample. But how do the men in these two samples compare in this respect with those from other samples? This is not an easy question to answer, given the differences in coding and categorizing of data in different studies. A reanalysis of data from the major studies might be helpful, but serious problems of linguistic equivalence arise when one attempts to make cross-national comparisons. For example, the terms "the bosses" or "the managers" (*i dirigenti*) are common terms of reference for social groupings in Italian and in French, but not in English. It is fair to argue that this is in itself a significant fact. Nonetheless, it renders a more precise comparison of class imagery difficult.

Despite these difficulties, a few very general points can be made. The Goldthorpe–Lockwood sample seems to be unusual in the infrequency of dichotomous images based on criteria other than money. Following the same definition of a power model used by Goldthorpe and Lockwood, according to which 4 percent of their sample fit into this category, comparable percentages were derived from the published data of a few other studies. These percentages, presented in Table 5.1, show that the Goldthorpe–Lockwood sample has a particularly low frequency of this type of imagery. It might be pointed out in passing that the figures for the Italian samples show a remarkable similarity despite the different types of populations from which they are drawn. We consider the results of these Italian samples in more detail below.

Table 5.2 presents data produced in answer to specific questions asked in several studies on the dimensions underlying the stratification system. The considerable degree of fluctuation between studies is due to differences in the form of the question and the coding of the answers as well as to differences in the class imagery of the groups involved. The coding categories for the subjective dimensions of stratification vary greatly; hence, we have an omnibus category in Table 5.2, including behavior, personal characteristics, social background, and acceptance (or "snobbishness") under one heading. Other dimensions, either more "objective" or more easily defined, appear in all the studies, allowing greater comparability. These include income, occupation, education, and power.

Table 5.1. *Percent dichotomous images, excluding economic dichotomies, in various samples.*

Source	% Dichotomies	Source	% Dichotomies
Oeser and Hammond Melbourne 1954	11	Lopreato Italy 1964	15
Kahl and Davis Cambridge, Mass. 1955	10[a]	Cousins and Brown Tyneside, England 1968–70	14
Willener Lausanne 1957	20	Low-Beer Milan 1970	15
Pagani Milan 1960	17	Hiller Melbourne 1971	6
Goldthorpe, Lockwood, et al. Luton, England 1963	4		

[a]Includes economic dichotomies.
Sources: Oeser and Hammond (1954), Table 101, p. 273; Kahl and Davis (1955), p. 324; Willener (1957), p. 159; Pagani (1960), p. 107; Goldthorpe, Lockwood, et al. (1969), p. 150; Lopreato and Hazelrigg, (1972), Table VII:3, p. 167; Cousins (1975) and Brown, (1975), Table 4.6, p. 69; Hiller (1975a), Table 1, p. 14. For complete reference data, see the References at the end of this book.

In making comparisons, the reader must bear in mind that some studies present more than one response per person, so that percentages may total over 100.

One important difference in the form of the questions is that whereas some studies (Willener, Goldthorpe and Lockwood, Low-Beer, and Kahl and Davis) ask the respondent to name the major factor determining class position, others (Lopreato, Oeser and Hammond, and Pagani) ask the respondent how *he* goes about judging class position – a considerably different matter. Because income is not immediately perceptible, fewer people mention money in answer to questions of the second type. In short, only rough comparisons between studies are possible.

Power is rarely mentioned as a major criterion in any of the samples. The 9 percent found in this study is the highest percentage of any of the studies in the table. However, despite this relatively greater emphasis on power, money is not mentioned much less often than in other studies, including the Goldthorpe–Lockwood study. It seems to this author that Goldthorpe, Lockwood, et al. are on somewhat shaky ground when they argue that their sample's answers to this question indicate a clearly greater emphasis on money than is to be found in other samples. (However, when responses to this question are considered together with the type of terminology used, their case for the predominance of money models appears more convincing.)

The specific dimensional question is not very useful in understanding the class imagery of our respondents. It was remarked earlier that the emphasis on money seems to be compatible with all images of the class structure, including images positing well-defined groups with sharp boundaries. Technicians adhering to all models of the class structure frequently say that money constitutes the major differentiating criterion. With the exception of the type I (money continuum) respondents, all of whom obviously see money as the underlying dimension, the percentages naming money within each type vary from 40 percent to 67 percent. In the "affluent worker" sample, the fact of considering money as the major criterion of class was found to be closely related to other aspects of class imagery (location of class boundaries, relative size of classes, etc.) and told more about the respondents' model than, for example, his self-placement or the number of classes he mentioned. This is not the case in our sample.

We consider next the terminology used to describe the highest class. Five of the studies reviewed presented sufficient information to make possible rough comparisons on this aspect of class imagery.[34] Thirty-three percent of the terms used by Willener's respondents refer to an upper *class* (e.g., capitalists, managerial class), whereas 58 percent refer to an upper *stratum* (suggesting prestige, money, education, etc.). The Goldthorpe article on "Images of Class" provides a breakdown in terms of type of terminology used in the whole image, rather than just for the highest class. Occupational terminology is given by only 4 percent of the sample, and power terminology does not even occur as a category. Thirty-three percent used "mixed" terminology, but we are told that

Table 5.2. *Dimensions seen as underlying the stratification system in various samples.*

Source	Income (%)	Behavior[a] (%)	Occupa-tion (%)	Educa-tion (%)	Morals (%)	Power, author-ity (%)	Prestige, position, or status (%)
Oeser and Hammond Melbourne 1954[b]	26	43	18	36	—	6	9
Kahl and Davis Cambridge, Mass. 1955	61 (Includes life style)	—	8	—	9	—	—
Willener Lausanne 1957	35	24	28	9	—	6	—
Haer Tallahassee, Fla. 1957[b]	51	41	7	15	5	—	17
Pagani Milan 1960	20	60	3	10	—	—	—
Goldthorpe, Lockwood, et al. Luton, England 1963	56	11 (Includes life style)	10	—	—	4	—

Lopreato Italy 1964	9	41	23	5	—	3	—
Low-Beer Milan 1970	53	10	5	18	—	9	—
Cousins and Brown Tyneside, England 1968–70[b]	84	110	21	26	—	—	26
Hiller Melbourne 1971[b]	66	36	27	15	—	4	7

[a]This category includes behavior, personal characteristics, social background, and acceptance.

[b]These studies count more than one answer per respondent.

Sources: Oeser and Hammond (1954), Table 108, p. 284. "How important are the following factors in deciding to which class a person belongs?" Kahl and Davis (1955), p. 324. "In what ways are people in other classes different from people in your class?" Willener (1957), p. 168. "In general, what is it which leads you to place someone in one class or another?" Haer (1957), p. 118. "Criteria used to distinguish the behavior of people in the several classes." Pagani (1960), p. 123. "How do you think one recognizes the people as belonging to the various classes?" Goldthorpe (1970), Table 2. "The major factor determining the class position of individuals and groups." Lopreato and Hazelrigg (1972), Table VIII:1, p. 191. "To decide whether a given person belongs to your class, what single factor do you have to consider most?" Cousins and Brown (1975), Table 4.7, p. 70. "Criteria used to distinguish between classes." Hiller (1975), Table 6, p. 266. "Perceived determinants of class." For complete reference data, see References at the end of this book.

not many of these mixtures involve the use of occupational categories. The third study is Haer's. He mentions economic, prestige, racial, and "conventional" (i.e., upper, middle, lower) terminologies but makes no mention at all of power terms. It is safe to assume that power references were virtually if not totally nonexistent in his sample. Hiller finds 3 percent of his Australian sample using power terms (e.g., capitalists, bosses) and a further 3 percent using occupational terms. Finally, Cousins and Brown find that 46 percent of Tyneside shipyard workers call the elite group (or one of the elite groups) bosses.

Only this last study of "proletarian traditional" workers is in the same range as the technicians in our sample. Fifty-three percent of the technicians use either a power term or an occupational term with power connotations, providing convincing evidence for their relatively great emphasis on power.

The Lopreato study of an Italian sample should be mentioned even though the data are not presented in such a fashion as to make it directly comparable with our own on this point. Lopreato and Hazelrigg, in their discussion of class imagery, develop a series of types analogous to those developed above. At least three of these types include the notion of a power elite. These constitute 14 percent of the sample. To these must be added an unknown percentage of responses classified under the headings of "polychotomous images" and "residual images." If we assume that the proportion of people including a power elite in their images is the same in these two categories as in the rest of the sample, we can estimate this unknown percentage to be 4 percent. This brings the total percentage of those who see a power elite up to 18 percent.[35]

This is a much smaller percentage than that found in the present study. Part of the discrepancy can be explained by the observed pattern of variation by social class within the Lopreato sample. The three types of imagery including a power elite are more prevalent among skilled workers and above than they are among semiskilled workers and below (between 28% and 30% of all images in the four higher groups; between 22% and 23% in the three lower groups).[36] Our sample is comparable in class position to the higher groups.

Another part of the discrepancy is owing to the fact that over one-third of Lopreato's sample (40%) either had no class model or did not formulate a class image until confronted by a rather directive probe.

Taking as a base those of Lopreato's interviewees who are classified as petit bourgeois or as skilled workers (the levels corresponding to our sample) and who had models of the class structure, an estimated 36 percent posit the existence of a power elite. The comparable figure for our sample (excluding those without any image of the class structure) is 59 percent. It is not clear why Lopreato's sample should show a somewhat lesser emphasis on power than our own. However, the subjects in both samples perceive a power elite more frequently than those in the samples from other countries.[37]

We have argued that the present study finds substantially greater use of power imagery than the Goldthorpe–Lockwood study. Data from the Lopreato study also show a considerable use of power imagery, suggesting that Italians may be more prone to perceive a power elite than are British or U.S. citizens.

The comparison between the Lopreato data and our own does not show a decline in the frequency of dichotomous imagery or in the frequency with which a power elite is mentioned among the new working class group. If anything, the contrary is true: The technicians in our own sample put a greater emphasis on power differences than does a cross section of the population. It was previously noted that in the Lopreato sample the higher classes mention a power elite more frequently than do the lower classes. This is in itself an interesting fact in light of data from other countries that show power imagery to be more concentrated at the lower levels of the class structure.[38] When a view of society stressing the existence of power inequalities is so diffused throughout the population, it becomes difficult to argue that these views will decline as standards of living rise.

A methodological note. The final point emerging from the typology of class imagery developed in this chapter is a methodological one. Many authors have considered the various aspects of class images independently of one another. For example, Lopreato and Hazelrigg,[39] in their otherwise excellent review of this literature, discuss each of five dimensions of class imagery separately. This leads them into speculations regarding the number of classes mentioned (Why do so many studies find trichotomous models outnumbering dichotomous, tetrachotomous, or other views?) or the placement of self in the class structure (How many people identify as middle class, how many as working class, etc.?). But such questions are not meaningful unless they are placed in the context of a whole image, an overall gestalt, in the respondent's mind. Trichotomous schemes may be very different from one another, depending on the relative sizes and boundaries of the three classes. Categorizing them together is not very useful. Similarly, a self-identification as working class means something quite different if the working class is seen as consisting of all those who work than if it is seen as consisting only of manual workers. Again, categorizing together all those who identify as working class would be misleading. In arguing that class images must be considered as wholes, we are arguing that they have a logical consistency. If the parts did not make up a coherent whole, the researcher would after all do better to look at these images as agglomerations of separate dimensions.

The degree of consistency of class imagery is an empirical question. Throughout our exposition of types of models we sought to point out the logical relationships among the various elements. We pointed out, for example, that those respondents who see the dividing line between working class and middle class as being above the manual–nonmanual line generally identify as working class, those respondents who see only two classes describe the relationship between them as an oppositional one, and those who label their classes in terms suggesting greater or lesser income or wealth also say that money is the primary dimension underlying the stratification system. The types we have singled out are logically consistent structures, meaningful to the individuals who hold them.

Behind the consistency of class imagery one may observe, as John Goldthorpe says, the individual attempting to make sense of his experience.[40] A person's current image of the class structure is the product of an interaction between that person, with his ideology and his need for consistency, and the constantly changing environment. As cognitive structures, images of the stratification hierarchy provide convincing support for the Piagetian idea of cognition as an active process: "Cognition (as most clearly reflected in thinking) means putting things together or relating events, and this relating is an active process, not a passive connecting of events through external association and repetition."[41]

The correlates of class imagery

The preceding section dealt with the content and frequency of the various types of class imagery. This section deals with the correlates of this imagery.

Two initial caveats must be considered. First, contentions such as the one that our interviewees tend to see a large central class more frequently than do other groups obviously cannot be tested by analysis of variations *within* our sample. Our hypotheses in this section can deal only with variables on which there is variation among technicians.

Second, the number of instances of any one type of image is so small that it is impossible to carry out any but the simplest kind of analysis. No attempt is made to disentangle the causal links between the numerous background variables and the class models. Even the results presented must be taken as suggestive rather than conclusive. However, their credibility is substantially improved by their consistency.

We discuss primarily the groups whose class imagery is related to other variables in a consistent fashion. These groups are those whose models are most clearly associated with a specific interpretation of their social world: The men who see society as a dichotomy, those who see it as a money continuum, and those who deny the existence of class or who cannot articulate a coherent image. We also look into the relationship between class identification and other variables. Our procedure is first to examine how each of a series of variables is related to class imagery, and then to characterize briefly the groups singled out for special attention. Class imagery is related to two kinds of variables, namely, background variables and attitudinal variables. Many of the particular attitudinal variables discussed are important in the prediction of strike participation, the subject of the following chapter.

Associations between class image and selected variables. Political position is a key variable associated with class images. The relationships between class models and political position come as no surprise after the descriptive accounts. Two-thirds of the men with dichotomous images are leftists. (*Leftist* is defined as feeling closest to the Italian Socialist Party or further left; *center/rightist* is defined as feeling closest to the Social Democratic Party or further right. More is said on this division in Chapter 6.) People who stretch the borders of the working class to include themselves also tend to be leftists (71% leftists); those who have no class image or who deny the existence of classes tend to be in the political center or on the right (75% center/rightists). These findings are in conformity with our expectations and with the findings of other researchers.

It is interesting to note that technicians who see society as a money continuum are not more conservative or radical than the sample as a whole. This seems to support Goldthorpe and Lockwood's contention that the money model of society is essentially an apolitical one. We find, as have many other investigators, that middle class identifiers are more conservative than working class identifiers. The relationship is particularly apparent in the answers to the forced-choice question. Seventy-four percent of the working class identifiers are leftists, whereas only 29 percent of the middle class identifiers are leftists. In spontaneous self-placement, working class identification is also associated with a leftist position, but middle class identification is not associated with a center/rightist position. This is readily understandable. For a member of a white collar group (85% of the sample are white collar) to identify as working class has political meaning; but for a member of the same group to identify as middle class is less meaningful. The men who do not spontaneously place themselves in any class tend to be center/rightists.

Political position is a key variable in that it, like class imagery, is related both to background variables and to other attitudinal variables. If class imagery is an attempt to interpret one's world, and political attitudes are an expression of that same interpretation, it is not surprising that they should be similarly related to other variables.

Father's class position and father's political position are both related to class imagery. Seventy percent of those respondents with money models are sons of white collar workers or small businessmen, as compared with 42 percent of the sample as a whole. Technicians who have no class image (i.e., those who cannot articulate a coherent image and those who deny the existence of classes) tend to be of working class origins (75% as compared with 49% in the sample as a whole). Turning to father's political position, we note that the men with no class image and those with money models tend to come from families whose heads were center/rightists, whereas those with dichotomous images tend to come from leftist families.[42]

It might be thought that these relationships are mediated through the respondent's political position, that is, that father's occupation and father's political position affect the person's own political position, which is, in turn, related to his class imagery. Only a few paragraphs earlier we foreswore any attempt to disentangle such causal links. Suffice it to say that further analysis indicates that this is apparently not the case. Father's occupation and father's political position seem to be independently related to class imagery insofar as can be judged given the very small number of cases involved.

A number of attitudinal items concerning mobility aspirations and attitudes toward peers are related to class imagery. The men with money models tend more often than the sample as a whole to list career opportunities as one of the two most important characteristics of a job (30% vs. 17%), to say that it is important to them to improve their position in the firm (100% vs. 75%), and to say that they would like to become a boss (70% vs. 51%). Respondents with dichotomous images are less likely than the sample as a whole to list career opportunities as an important feature of a job (0% vs. 17%). Respondents without class images tend to cite career as one of the two most important characteristics of a job more often than the sample as a whole (37% vs. 17%) but do not express the desire to become bosses.

When asked if merit raises should be decided by colleagues, or, in the case of the Siemens workers, if merit raises should be abolished, technicians with dichotomous images are more likely to answer affirmatively, whereas those with money models or without any class image tend not to be solidaristic in their answers. The men with dichotomous images say they see more co-workers outside of work than do those with other images. The men who have no class images see very few co-workers outside of work. (All comparisons are relative to the sample mean.)

Characterizations of men with money models, dichotomous models, and no models. The respondents with money models of society tend to come from white collar families. They are individualistic in their outlooks, and less trusting of their colleagues than the sample as a whole. They are not unwilling to admit to aspirations for promotion within the plant even though such promotion is generally perceived to be at the expense of close ties to co-workers.

The men with dichotomous images come more frequently than expected from leftist families and tend to be leftists themselves. In contrast to those with money models, they are solidaristic in their orientations. They are more trusting of their peers and see them more outside of work. They express little interest in mobility within the organization.

These attitudes reflect in part value differences between the working class and the middle class. Those who have a money model of society are more likely to come from middle class backgrounds and to be from center/rightist families. Those with dichotomous images, although mirroring the sample as a whole in their class origins, are more likely to come from leftist families.

Those who have no class image are led by the contradictions in their backgrounds to be unwilling to entertain the idea of social inequality. They come predominantly from working class families, yet their fathers are more likely than average to have been center/rightist. Blue collar workers are 15 percent of the sample and 50 percent of this group. Seven of the eight men do not have technician's degrees. In their own political positions they are center/rightists. Conservatives of working class origin or downwardly mobile from the middle class, it is clear why they feel personally threatened by the stratification hierarchy.

In their attitudes toward peers and mobility, this group is highly individualistic. They tend to be isolates, and to show little willingness to trust their colleagues. They are slightly more likely than average to mention career as important, but when asked whether they would like to become a boss they say no. Their desire for middle class status is in contrast with their relatively low level of achievement. Insecure in status, unable to use class solidarity to support a faltering sense of self-esteem, they deny or repress the existence of classes.

Further remarks on the correlates of class imagery. We have presented a picture of consistent support for the hypothesis that a given class image, or the lack of any image, is associated with an outlook on life – solidaristic or individualistic. In the interests of completeness, one unconfirmed hypothesis should also be mentioned. The only available behavioral measure of mobility aspirations is attendance at night school. It was hypothesized that the men whose class models imply a more solidaristic outlook would be less likely to be in school, whereas those with money models would be more likely to be in school. This turns out not to be the case. Class imagery is not related in any clear way to nightschool attendance.

The absence of any relationship does not invalidate our argument that the technicians with money models are more individualistic in outlook and that the men with dichotomous images are more solidaristic. It was pointed out earlier, in the section on the single men, that mobility within the firm is seen by the respondents as a reward for apple-polishing more than for excellence. To these men, upward mobility within the firm implies a whole-hearted commitment to a competitive way of life and an accompanying willingness to treat one's colleagues as means to the end of promotion. But by going to night school, it is possible to have one's cake and eat it too. Upward mobility through education does not require struggle in the social Darwinist jungle of the factory.

Variables concerning mobility aspirations and attitudes toward colleagues are associated with class identification as well as with class models. Middle class identifiers are more likely than working class identifiers to mention career possibilities as important characteristics of a job and to say that they would like to become a boss. They are less likely than are working class identifiers to trust peers to make judgments about merit raises and less favorable toward the idea of working in groups.

To summarize, this discussion of class imagery has stressed three major points. The first is that the technicians in our sample tend to see a large central class. The second is that a surprising number of them call this class the "working class" rather than the "middle class." The third point is that they tend to describe the highest class as a power elite. Going beyond a descriptive account, variations in class imagery were related to political attitudes, mobility aspirations, and attitudes toward peers. Solidaristic and individualistic outlooks were found to be related to dichotomous and money models, respectively.

Conclusions

The underlying question throughout this chapter has been, What are the implications of life styles and class images for political and trade-union action? A fuller answer to this question must await our analysis in Chapter 6 of the data on strike participation and attitudes toward mobility. At this point, we pause only to weigh on one side of the balance those factors in the technician's life outside work which might lead him toward increasing class consciousness and, on the other side, those factors which might impede the growth of consciousness.

One of the possible impediments to the development of consciousness is the privatization of the lives of the married couples. Such life patterns are the consequence of enforced mobility in search of jobs. Among upper middle class professionals, isolation from the surrounding community is often compensated by social contacts generated through common interests. This is rarely the case among the new working class technicians. Nevertheless, they cannot be said to have "chosen" a privatized life style. In this respect, they are different from the workers in the Goldthorpe–Lockwood sample who have opted for a higher standard of living in preference to the solidarity and poverty of the more traditional working class community. The technicians' choice is made much earlier, and on different terms, when they first decide to continue their secondary education. Once they have completed their training, geographical mobility is forced on them if they are to find jobs utilizing their skills.

Under these circumstances, it is not clear that privatization must lead to a decline in radical leftist politics. On the contrary, political activity might be a way to gain a missing solidarity, both through involvement in a movement and by the furtherance of concrete measures to cushion the impact of mobility on social life.

The life situation of the single men is closer to that of the traditional occupational community. Such communities create solidary ties. It would be a mistake to downplay the importance of this type of community on the grounds that it is, in fact, temporary for each of the individuals concerned. These communities, although temporary from the perspective of the individual, are likely to continue to socialize new members. The electronics industry and other advanced sectors are expanding rapidly, and this expansion occurs primarily through the hiring of young technicians fresh out of school. The presence of substantial numbers of young, single technicians is likely to remain an important factor as new recruits take the places of those who settle down to privatized married lives. Furthermore, the effect of the temporary occupational community is not limited to the group of single men who participate in it at any one moment, large though this group may be. The socializing experience undergone during this period may have long-term effects in spite of the privatization of married life.

These life patterns neither exclude nor imply the inevitability of class conscious collective action. They suggest the possibility of organization for collective ends but tell us little about the possible direction of such action. To draw further conclusions, the life patterns must be considered along with the technician's image of the stratification system and his own place in this system.

A predominant feature of this image of society is a large central class, within which there is a range of inequality, but no sharp boundaries. The lack of integration into a stable community, the privatized life styles of some of the men, and the irrelevance of traditional class distinctions at the workplace all contribute to this view.

Within the large central class, the technician typically places himself somewhere in the middle. Anticipating data on perceptions of mobility opportunities presented in the next chapter, we can say that he is fairly optimistic in his view of possibilities for mobility in the society. (In answer to the question, "Do you think anyone with intelligence and the will to work can get ahead in Italy, or do you think one needs pull?" 30 percent said that one could get ahead without pull and 35 percent said that it would be difficult but not impossible to get ahead without pull. In answer to an analogous question on mobility within the firm, there was considerably less optimism.) The very existence of a large central class constitutes a challenge to individual mobility strivings, a challenge accepted by the large number of technicians in night school.

Very few of those interviewed see another social class beneath their own. Although they may see themselves as being in the middle of the central class, this class is usually not itself seen as central in the sense of being between two classes. It encompasses all from the lowest ranks through the middle and upper-middle ranks. The idea of being in the lowest class evidences the solidarity of the technician with the working class which emerges in other ways as well (see Chapters 6 and 7).

The top of the stratification system tends to be seen as a power elite, disjunct from the other class or classes. Individual mobility is seen as possible up to, but not into, this power elite. Whether the technician adopts the skeptic's position that there will always be a power elite or whether he associates the existence of a power elite with the capitalist system, the elite is seen as an interest group opposed to the people.

There is some evidence that Italians are more prone to power elite imagery than people in other European countries or North America. One might say that they are more cynical, more suspicious, more sophisticated, or more realistic, according to one's value biases. Be this as it may, our data on a young group in an advanced sector do not indicate that such imagery is on the wane. If anything, they suggest the opposite.

The life patterns and class imagery we have described imply two possible strategies for improving one's position. The first is the strategy of individual mobility within the large central class. The second is the collective struggle to improve the position of one's class vis-à-vis the power elite. With substantial support for the collective strategy, an individual who chooses this strategy need not abandon the route of individual mobility within the firm. If strikers are numerous enough, management can no longer discriminate against them. At present, the two strategies are still mutually exclusive within the firm. This is shown in the next chapter. But the technician is not forced to choose between the collective route and the individual route outside the firm, which is through education.

To say that the technician may choose a collective route to improve his position is not equivalent to saying that he is revolutionary in the conventional sense of the term. But if to be revolutionary means to be the champion of "revolutionary reform" in André Gorz's sense, the new working class argument becomes more compelling. These issues will be taken up again in Chapter 7.

6. Militancy, class consciousness, and the determinants of strike participation

Analytical sociology of the sort we have been doing requires us to divide a man's life into categories. It cannot consider at one moment the totality of a man's life. We have chosen to divide the lives of the men in our sample into halves: life at work and life outside work. But these are merely convenient categories in the organization of our exposition. We must now try to put Humpty Dumpty together again, focusing on those relationships which bridge the two halves.

This work began with the problem of trying to explain the new militancy of technicians. The reader may be wondering why nothing has been said so far about our interviewees' participation in strikes. Strike participation is affected by factors in a person's background, in his work life, and in his life outside the workplace. It can only be understood by taking all of these factors into account.

This chapter is devoted to an analysis of the determinants of strike participation. The method used is multiple regression. In the course of exploring this question, other attitudes and behaviors, also related to both work and nonwork aspects of the technicians' lives, will be discussed as independent variables in the regression equations. The most important of these jointly determined variables concern mobility aspirations.

Before embarking on the exploration of the determinants of strike participation, it is necessary to define more precisely the concepts of class consciousness, militancy, and strike participation, and the indicators of each.

Militancy, class consciousness, and strike participation: definitions and operationalizations

"Class consciousness. . . refers to a state of mind in which the individual identifies with a given class to the point of adopting its interests as his

173

own and engaging in concerted action within that class against the interests of another."[1] This definition makes clear that class consciousness does not exist apart from struggle for class interests. It follows that class consciousness cannot be measured only by asking people their opinions on various matters. Neither can it be measured only by the observation of behavior. Both measures are needed. For this reason, it is rarely measured.

Although class consciousness is very difficult to measure, class solidarity can be measured more easily. *Class solidarity* may be defined as that aspect of class consciousness which is measurable by talking to people, asking them about their class identifications and their perceptions of their class interests. Class solidarity as defined here has often been the subject of sociological inquiry. Nearly as often, it has been erroneously equated with class consciousness.[2]

An important question, raised but not settled by the definition of class consciousness quoted, is, How are class interests to be determined? There are two answers. Some Marxist authors claim the ability to determine the objective interests of each class. The viewpoint of the proletariat, expressed in Marxism, is the only valid one. This position derives from Lukács and seems consistent with Marx's own position. Marx states:

It is not a matter of knowing what this or that proletarian, or even the proletariat as a whole, *conceives* as its aims at any particular moment. It is a question of knowing what the proletariat *is*, and what it must historically accomplish in accordance with its *nature*. Its aim and its historical activity are ordained for it, in a tangible and irrevocable way, by its own situation as well as by the whole organization of present-day civil society.[3]

Non-Marxist sociologists have tended to define class interests empirically. In this view, class interests are determined by analyzing the actions of the members of that class or, subjectively, by asking the individual about his own perceptions of his class interests. The problem of "false consciousness" is thereby defined away. Lopreato and Hazelrigg, for example, take the position that class solidarity is the feeling of unity with, and closeness to, the class with which one identifies, regardless of whether or not the person's self-placement coincides with his objective class position.

The definition adopted here is closer to the Marxist one. We do not insist on our omniscience regarding the objective interests of classes. It is simply our aim to compare the actions of our respondents and their subjectively held positions with the Marxist interpretation of their objective interests. For Marx, class interests were determined by the person's relation to the means of production. To say that a person is or is not class conscious (or class solidary) is to say that he does or does not see his interests to be as Marx saw them and acts accordingly. Following this usage, the class conscious technician, being in the same relation to the means of production as other dependent workers, must identify his interests with those of the working class. He may recognize his objectively middle class position, but, if so, he will assert that the interests of the working class and the middle class are the same.

Class solidarity is measured by a single item: "To which political party do you feel closest?" Although other items relevant to class solidarity are available, political position is the best summary item. Given the wide range of parties in the Italian political spectrum, this question permits the respondent to locate himself with some precision on a continuum from left to right. On the left, there are three Marxist parties and numerous so-called extraparliamentary groups. Ordered from the most radical to the least radical, they are the extraparliamentary groups, the Socialist Party of Proletarian Unity (PSIUP – now defunct), the Italian Communist Party (PCI), and the Italian Socialist Party (PSI). This last has participated in coalition governments since 1963. In the center there are also three parties, each with its distinctive traditions and flavorings: the Social Democratic Party (PSDI), the Republican Party (PRI), and the Christian Democrats (DC). The Liberal Party (PLI) and the MSI, the neofascist party, comprise the right.

Militancy is defined as the willingness to take action in the furtherance of one's interests. Here, however, interests are defined empirically as being those expressed by the individual, either in words or through his actions. Whereas class consciousness and class solidarity are defined relative to one particular interpretation of class interests, militancy may or may not be directed toward goals compatible with the Marxist analysis of the class interests of an individual in a given class situation. For example, the Chilean copper miner, who earns well above the wages paid to other workers in comparable jobs in other sectors, and who strikes for higher wages from a socialist government, may be very militant, but he is not class solidary, and even less is he class conscious. Or, to take an example closer to our subject, the white collar worker who strikes to maintain existing differences in wages or working conditions between himself and blue collar workers is militant but not class conscious. Full class consciousness presupposes action and, hence, it presupposes militancy, but the reverse is not true. Militancy does not necessarily imply class consciousness.

At first glance, militancy seems easier to operationalize than class consciousness. Because class consciousness involves a long-term goal beyond any single action, it is necessary to know the meaning of the action for the person in addition to observing the action itself. In the case of militancy, action itself is the critical determinant. Observations of frequency and quality of individual strike participation might seem to provide sufficient data to operationalize the concept.

However, some qualifications must be made concerning strike participation as an indicator of militancy. Not everyone who participates in strikes is militant. A person may be pressured into striking. He may be unwilling or unable to break through a picket line. Or, more commonly, he may strike simply because the unions, or the workers' council, have called a strike. This hardly makes him militant. It is with this possibility in mind that we note the importance of the quality as well as the frequency of strike participation.

In Italy, to participate in a strike is usually to support the position of the unions or of other groups seen as standing for political positions on a wide range of issues. A person may participate prompted by feelings of solidarity or agreement with the general political goals of the trade unions without being militant at all in regard to the matters under dispute or in his attitude toward the organization against which he is striking. Such people are class solidary, but not fully class conscious. Conversely, a person who is inclined to be militant, but who finds himself in disagreement with union policies on larger political issues, may well decide not to strike even though he supports the demands of the unions. Instead, he may express his militancy in other ways, perhaps individually rather than through the union.

It seems, then, that a person need not be militant to participate in strikes and that a person can be inclined toward militancy yet not participate in strikes. The concept that seemed relatively easy to operationalize appears more complex upon closer scrutiny. Militancy cannot simply be equated with strike participation.

In contrast to class consciousness, militancy is more specifically issue-oriented. The militancy of workers is generally seen as arising out of the work situation. But participation in an on-going strike, although conditioned by organizational variables, need not be motivated by discontent with the organization, the job itself, or the paycheck. At the level of the aggregate, striking workers are militant workers by definition. For example, it can be assumed that a company-level struggle for demands drawn up by the workers' council is in some way related to these demands. At the individual level, however, strike participation is not, as we shall see, synonymous with militancy on workplace issues.

Strike participation itself is a rather concrete concept. Still, here too the problem of operationalization is not a trivial one. Unfortunately, it was not possible to obtain observational data on individual participation in strikes. Some aggregate level data for GT&E were presented in Chapter 3. For further analysis, we must rely on the respondents' own statements as to whether or not they participated. This compounds the problem of interpretation raised earlier.

How is declared participation in strikes related to actual participation? Comparing the figures on actual participation obtained from GT&E company files with the data from our interviews, we can judge the validity of this measure. In Chapter 3 distinctions were made among strikes over collective bargaining issues, or "contract strikes," strikes for specific political reforms, and demonstrative political strikes. In general, the interview answers seem to overestimate participation in the two types of political strikes and to underestimate participation in contract strikes.

Forty-four percent of the white collar workers interviewed at GT&E say that they *always* strike. The company's data show that the level of participation in the strikes for the 1971 company-level contract was about 75% percent of the white collar employees, while the participation in political strikes was much more unstable, touching lows of 3 to 4 percent in October 1970, and a high of 73 percent in the strike for more public housing on April 7, 1971.

A specific question was asked in the interviews regarding participation in this last strike, and 58 percent of the GT&E white collar workers interviewed said that they struck on April 7. In this case, the sample actually underestimated strike participation. Many people may have stayed home that day because there was no public transportation rather than out of conviction. Later, when asked, they may not have remembered the specific strike referred to and answered according to what they would have done on principle. This would account for the underestimation in this instance.

More usually, the interview data overestimate participation in political strikes. The majority of white collar workers do not participate. Those who are not in agreement with such strikes have no difficulty in abstaining from them. However, those who do adhere to the aims of these strikes may not be willing to make themselves conspicuous by participating. This would be true particularly in the cases of certain supervisors and persons who work in positions that make striking difficult for them, but who sympathize with leftist parties and feel solidary with the working class. Embarrassed at not having struck in support of goals with which they agree, they say they participated although they did not.

The situation is reversed in the case of contract strikes. The majority participates, and the nonparticipant is the deviant. Some of those who say they would not strike for certain demands are, nonetheless, loath to break through picket lines or to remain in the almost empty buildings when all the others have walked out.

What all this boils down to is that declared strike participation is influenced by the individual's political position even more than is actual participation. If people's decisions to strike or not to strike are affected by their attitudes toward the unions and the Marxist parties, their statements about these decisions are even more affected by these attitudes.

The investigator's impression was that respondents were not reticent or unwilling to admit strike participation. During the course of the interview the interviewer would make his own position apparent if this seemed necessary to counter any lingering suspicions that the research might be sponsored by management.

It would be damaging to our argument were there evidence that the interview responses grossly overestimate strike participation. Given that this is not the case, we shall accept declared strike participation as a valid, if not unproblematic, measure of actual strike participation. Throughout the following discussion we shall use the term *strike participation* to mean declared strike participation, unless otherwise specified.

In our original formulation of the research project, strike participation was thought of as a form of militancy that might or might not coincide with class solidarity. In other words, it was thought that some people might be leftists but not always participate in strikes, whereas others might be active participants in strikes without being leftists. But political attitudes affect strike participation more than had been hypothesized.

In fact, strike participation is so closely related to political attitudes that a factor analysis including seventeen items related to strike participation and political attitudes does not show these to be two separate factors. Questions regarding all three types of strikes load highly on the first factor, which explains 36 percent of the total variance. The item asking which political party the person feels closest to also loads highly on this factor. The next factor is not interpretable, and only explains 8.6 percent of the total variance.

The findings suggest that it is not meaningful to distinguish between participation in different kinds of strikes. It was, therefore, decided to treat strike participation as a single factor, whose relationship to other evidence of militancy and to political party sympathies would be a matter to explore.

This factor analysis and the accompanying correlation matrix were used to construct a six-item strike participation scale (for additional details, see Appendix A). The items included deal with participation in all three kinds of strikes (contract strikes, strikes for reforms, and demonstrative strikes). This scale is used as the dependent variable throughout our discussion on strike participation. The results would not, however, be very different were single items used instead of the scale.

This discussion of the problems encountered in operationalizing the concepts of militancy and strike participation foreshadows the results of the analyses presented below. Militancy as we have defined it is not the major predictor of strike participation, partly because declared strike participation is so closely linked to political attitudes and attitudes toward the unions and partly because participation in contract strikes is so widespread that only those who are very much opposed to striking refuse to participate. These findings lead us to question the role of immediate issues in the recent strikes. But first, let us examine the data.

The determinants of strike participation

We now present three regression equations, all with strike participation as the dependent variable. The variables are entered into the stepwise regression in order according to the highest partial correlation between the dependent variable and the independent variables, controlling for independent variables already entered into the equation. The first equation includes only objective variables, that is, background and structural variables. Attitudinal variables are added in the second one; union membership is added in the third. The complete correlation matrix is given in Appendix B.

Background and structural variables

Before bringing attitudinal variables into the prediction equation, we looked to see how much variance in strike participation could be explained by "objective" factors. All background and structural variables correlated with strike participation (and some not correlated) were included in the stepwise regression, but only two emerged with significant beta weights (see Table 6.1). Together they explain 24.0 percent of the variance. The total variance explained by all the variables entered in this regression is 34.7 percent.

The two items with significant beta weights are background variables. We will discuss these next. The third variable entered into the equation following these two is pay, which is also discussed below.

Grandfathers' class positions. Gino Germani's finding that grandfather's occupation was an important predictor of upward mobility in an Argentine sample induced the author to include the questions on grandfathers' occupations. Germani found that those who had white collar grandfathers were more likely to rise across the manual–nonmanual line. In our sample too, grandfathers' class position proves to be important. This variable alone explains 11.9 percent of the variance in strike participation.

The class of the interviewees' grandparents is coded similarly to their own class of origin. There are only four categories: peasantry, blue collar working class, lower middle class (independent or dependent), and upper middle class. The variable in the regression equation represents the sum of the grandparents' class positions. If a respondent had two upper middle class grandparents he would score 8; if both his grandparents were farmers he would score 2. The lower the person's score, the more likely he is to strike ($r = .346$).

It may seem curious that grandfathers' class positions are relatively highly correlated with strike participation, whereas father's class position is not ($r = .107$). We shall see later that grandfathers' class positions are also correlated significantly with respondent's political position ($r = -.276$) whereas father's class position is not ($r = -.077$). These findings indicate the strength and persistence of familial values over generations.

Table 6.1. *Regression of strike participation scale on background and structural variables.*

Variable description	Item no.	Coefficient	Standard error of coefficient	Standardized coefficient	t test	DF[a]	Significance	Unique variance
Sum of grandfathers' occupations	7.14	0.1560	0.042	0.334	3.69	82	under .001	.108
Where grew up: Milan/elsewhere	7.12	0.5419	0.146	0.344	3.72	82	under .001	.110
Pay now	4.10	0.0702	0.042	0.215	1.66	82	.101	.022
How often sees friends	6.22(b)	0.1258	0.105	0.110	1.20	82	.234	.011
Category	—	-0.0638	0.085	-0.097	-0.75	82	.454	.005

Regression constant = -1.846

Multiple correlation squared = 0.347 F = 8.73 with 5 and 82 DF (*P* under .001)
Multiple correlation = 0.589
Standard deviation of residuals = 0.654

Last step increased R^2 by less than 0.010
Partial correlations with dependent variable for variables not entered

Family status	1.5,1.6	0.020
Level of schooling	1.1	0.051
Where grew up: north/south	7.12	0.063
Father's occupation	7.13	-0.049

[a] Degrees of freedom.

Many of the parents of the technicians in our sample made the leap from a rural to an urban occupation, from peasant to worker, while others rose across the manual–nonmanual line. Yet some of the basic political attitudes of the respondents have presumably remained unchanged from the grandparents' generation.

The 88 technicians had a total of 176 grandfathers. Surprisingly, a few people do not know what one or the other or both of their grandparents did for a living. But we do have information on the occupations of 161 of the 176 grandfathers. Seventy-two of those mentioned (44.7%) were peasants. Yet only 9 of the fathers (10.3%) are peasants. In the fathers' generation there is also some mobility from the working class to the lower middle class, although the shift is less dramatic: Only 28.0 percent of the grandfathers mentioned were lower middle class, whereas 35.6 percent of the fathers are.

This mobility in the fathers' generation obscures a relationship presumably existing in the grandfathers' generation between attitudes broadly definable as political and class position. Not only is there less variance in class position in the fathers' generation than in the grandfathers', but, in addition, the infusion via mobile individuals of new values and political outlooks into previously more homogeneous subcultures reduces the effects of class on attitudes in the fathers' generation. Just as the change in the sons' circumstances has left their political attitudes basically similar to their fathers' political attitudes (a point documented in the following paragraphs), so the change in the fathers' generation must be assumed to have left *them* relatively unchanged relative to *their* parents. It is only when we go back two generations that we find correlations between class position, on the one hand, and strike participation and political position, on the other.

This explanation presupposes a time two and more generations ago, in the grandfathers' generation, when familial values coincided with class values and with a class situation. Whether these values developed over generations during a time of lower social mobility or whether they gelled during a period of "organic crisis," when values were in flux, we cannot say.[4] In any case, we can assume that these values were deeply felt and were transmitted to individuals finding themselves in quite different situations.

This finding is not particularly surprising. The transmission of political values from generation to generation is thoroughly documented by over 100 studies in several Western nations. Dawson and Prewitt, in their review of the literature on political socialization, report that, "Overwhelmingly, these investigations have shown that individuals tend to have political attitudes and values like those of their parents. . . . [O]n the whole, the associations are strong."[5] Less well documented are the processes of change, showing how groups make enduring shifts in their political allegiances.

Geographical mobility. Thirty-eight of the men in our sample grew up in Milan (43.7%). The others come from all over Italy. The immigrants are less likely to participate in strikes than those from the Milan area (r = .320). This variable adds 12.1 percent to the variance explained when it is added into the stepwise regression. The Milanese emerge as more class solidary in other respects as well. Although hardly more leftist than the rest of the sample, they tend to join unions more. And, interestingly, they are less likely to have changed their political sympathies from their fathers'. If they *have* changed, chances are better than even that they have moved to the left, whereas the mobile tend to have moved to the right (Table 6.2). The immigrants have become less class solidary in the course of their experience.[6]

Several plausible explanations for these differences were considered and rejected. The Milanese do not feel more secure in their jobs, nor are

Table 6.2. *Change in political position by where respondent grew up.*

Change in political party	Milan	Elsewhere	Total
Unchanged	81.1%[a]	71.4%	75.9%
	30	30	60
Left to center/right	8.1%	21.4%	15.2%
	3	9	12
Center/right to left	10.8%	7.1%	8.9%
	4	3	7
Total	46.8%	53.2%	100.0%
	37	42	79

[a]The upper entries are percent of column totals; the numbers below are units.

they more integrated into the social environment at work. They are as likely to feel that they have been upwardly mobile (as measured by responses to Cantril's ladder), although they have lower expectations for future mobility than do the immigrants. This may account in part for their greater strike participation.

Finally, the immigrants tend to be more educated, and the more educated strike less. However, it would seem that geographical mobility is a more important determinant of strike participation than is education, and that the correlation between education and strike participation is partially spurious and partially mediated through attitudinal variables entered in the second regression equation.

In fact, the zero-order correlation between mobility and strike participation is slightly higher than that between education and strike participation (the coefficients are .320 and .285, respectively). Furthermore, in the stepwise regression, the item on geographical mobility is entered before the item on level of education. Once geographical mobility is partialled out, the correlation between education and strike participation drops, and it drops still further when pay and contractual category are entered into the regression equation.

Looking ahead to the following regressions (see Tables 6.3 and 6.4), we may note that geographical mobility remains a significant predictor. By contrast, level of education would not be entered into the second equation, even were we to remove the item on geographical mobility. The partial correlation between it and strike participation goes down to .137 after the second and third variables, both attitudinal items, are entered. The partial correlation with geographical mobility remains high ($r = .296$).

These results indicate that geographical mobility is an important determinant of strike participation independent of its correlation with level of education.

We can only conclude by reaffirming the fact that immigrants strike less than do Milanese. We cannot give a satisfactory explanation of this difference from the data at hand.

Pay. The variable amount of pay adds 9 percent to the variance explained when it is entered into the regression equation. Although the beta weight attached to this variable is not statistically significant, pay merits discussion as a determinant of strike participation because of its prima facie importance and because of its high zero-order correlation with strike participation ($r = .306$). As we will see shortly, those who perceive their pay to be unfairly low *are* significantly more likely to strike. But those who say their pay is unfair are not concentrated among those who earn less.

In reality, amount of pay seems to be a cover variable for level in the company hierarchy. Pay is a finer measure of level in the hierarchy than is contractual category. The two variables are very highly intercorrelated ($r = .700$). The zero-order correlations between pay and strike participation and between category and strike participation are virtually the same ($r = .306$ and $r = .307$, respectively). The lower categories are more solidaristic in their orientations. A glance through the correlation matrix in Appendix B will show that category and pay are strongly related to those attitudinal items measuring solidarity with peers and ambitions to advance. In turn, these items are strong predictors of strike participation, causing pay to drop out of the equation when they are introduced. The lower categories include the fourteen blue collar workers in the sample, while many of the higher category and higher paying jobs are those of group leaders or technicians aspiring to promotion.

Other structural variables. What about the other "objective" variables in the regression? All except father's occupation are also correlated with strike participation, although they do not add much if anything to the variance explained by the equation. Family status (single/married/married with children) emerges as a significant predictor in the following equations and is discussed below under *Attitudes toward pay.*

One variable that does add a little bit to the variance explained (1.3%; the coefficient is not significant) is how often the interviewee sees friends. Those who see friends more often tend to strike more ($r = .237$). This supports the contention that those who are more integrated into their social environments strike more. Needless to say, the environment into which they are integrated is not irrelevant, but the evidence suggests that most of the technicians' environments, particularly in the lower job categories, are likely to be supportive of strike participation.

We have already discussed the negative correlation between level of education and strike participation. To the extent that education is important as a determinant of striking, it is because of its association with some of the attitudinal variables introduced in the next equation. The very narrow range of educational attainments in our sample is no doubt one reason for the unusually slight impact of this variable.

Attitudinal variables

The introduction of attitudinal variables into the regression equation almost doubles the amount of variance explained. The "objective" variables accounted for 34.7 percent of the variance. By adding the attitudinal items, 70 percent of the variance is explained. The first three items entered into the stepwise regression are all attitudinal ones. They alone explain 52.6 percent of the variance. The final step in this regression is reproduced in Table 6.3. We discuss below each of the newly introduced items.

Political position. By far the most important variable in accounting for strike participation is the political position of the interviewee. It alone explains 29.2 percent of the variance in the strike participation scale. The zero-order correlation between political position and strike participation is also high ($r = .541$).

The sample as a whole is surprisingly leftist considering that it is 84 percent white collar. The political inclinations of the technicians were compared with the results of the parliamentary elections of May, 1972, for the province of Milan. The item on party preference was dichotomized for the purposes of our data analysis, grouping together as left the Italian Socialist Party (PSI) and the political organizations to the left of it, and grouping together as center/right the others, including those who said they felt close to no party. For the sake of ease of expression and because the right is so small, this group will also be referred to simply as center. This division conveniently splits the sample approximately in half: 49 percent center/rightists and 51 percent leftists. More importantly, it expresses the fundamental cleavage between the Marxist and the non-Marxist parties.

The left is much more strongly represented in the sample than in the population of the province (60.6% vs. 41.5%). Within the left, the extremist groups and the moderate left are greatly overrepresented, whereas the Communist Party is underrepresented. This pattern is not surprising among a group of white collar technicians jealous of their autonomy. The image of the Communist Party is still that of a monolithic organization, and its strength is greatest in the traditionally proletarian sectors.[7]

The center is slightly underrepresented in the sample (35.6% vs. 43.6). The ranks of the rightists dwindle into insignificance (three people, or 3.9% of those in the sample who express a preference, vs. 13.2% of the votes cast in the province).

Table 6.3. *Regression of strike participation scale on background, structural, and attitudinal variables.*

Variable description	Item no.	Coefficient	Standard error of coefficient	Standardized coefficient	t test	DF[a]	Significance	Unique variance
Political position	6.13	-0.5402	0.112	-0.345	-4.82	77	under .001	.091
Would like become boss	3.1	-0.2154	0.116	-0.138	-1.86	77	.068	.013
More collaboration useful	1.16	-0.3096	0.105	-0.197	-2.94	77	.005	.034
Where grew up: Milan/elsewhere	1.5,1.6	0.3919	0.102	0.249	3.86	77	under .001	.058
Favors merit raises	2.11	-0.2191	0.120	-0.137	-1.83	77	.071	.013
Sum of grandfathers' occupations	7.14	0.0630	0.032	0.135	1.99	77	.050	.016
Important to improve position	3.2	-0.1669	0.058	-0.194	-2.87	77	.006	.032
Pay important and unfair	1.9,4.10,4.12	0.1468	0.052	0.198	2.82	77	.007	.031
Family status	1.5,1.6	0.1164	0.061	0.139	1.92	77	.059	.014
Category	—	-0.0693	0.045	-0.105	-1.54	77	.129	.009

Regression constant = 0.877

Multiple correlation squared = 0.700 F = 17.96 with 10 and 77 DF (P under .001)
Multiple correlation = 0.837
Standard deviation of residuals = 0.458

Last step increased R^2 by less than 0.010
Partial correlations with dependent variable for variables not entered

Level of schooling	1.1	0.019
Pay now	4.10	-0.038
How often sees friends	6.22(b)	0.042
Father's occupation	7.14	0.033
How to get ahead	4.13	-0.026

[a] Degrees of freedom.

Eleven people in the sample say they do not feel close to any party or refuse to answer the question on party preference. They are excluded from the percentage calculations because they are the equivalent of nonvoters.

To gain a clearer understanding of how strike participation is related to political position, we cross-tabulated the political position item by the strike participation scale divided into quartiles. Nearly all (95.7%) of those who strike most often (i.e., who scored in the highest quartile on the strike participation scale) are leftists. Given the questions in the scale about participation in political strikes and in strikes for the reforms, this result was to be expected. However, many leftists do not usually strike, and some centrists strike often.[8]

Because political position is such an important determinant of strike participation, its relation to background variables is of some interest. We remarked earlier that political position is related to grandfathers' class positions but not to father's class position. There is, however, a strong relationship between the respondents' political positions and their fathers' political positions. Dichotomizing the fathers' positions in the same manner as the respondents', we find them to be highly correlated ($r = .497$). Of those for whom we have data, only 24 percent switched their allegiance from one side to the other of the political spectrum (see Table 6.2). This relative stability is in spite of a considerable amount of upward mobility from the fathers' generation. Fifty-eight percent of the fathers were blue collar workers or peasants, whereas only 16 percent of our sample are blue collar workers. This observation lends weight to our argument that values are transmitted across generations, despite the different class situations in which people find themselves.

Of those who switched their political allegiance, nearly twice as many moved from left to right as from right to left. Considering that so many are upwardly mobile, this is hardly surprising. On the contrary, it is noteworthy that one-half of the sample is still leftist.

As mentioned earlier, there is some difference on this point between the Milanese and the immigrants. The former are slightly more likely to have changed from right to left, whereas the latter are more likely to have changed from left to right. However, the numbers are too small to draw any certain conclusions from this finding.

The discussions of the effects of grandfathers' class positions and of the respondents' own political positions indicate that a good part of the technicians' willingness to strike may be attributed to the fact that so many of them have leftist working class or peasant roots and grew up in working class milieux.

Mobility orientation and solidarity with peers. Any social system can hold out to a few individuals the possibility of rewards far exceeding those it can offer to collectivities. It can also withhold the possibility of rewards from those who do not conform. Chances for upward mobility may be few. But to many it must certainly seem irrational to sacrifice even the unlikely possibility of a big win for participation in a collective effort, in which any one person's contribution seems dispensable and whose benefits are relatively slight in the short run.

The more people join together to improve their situation, the more difficult it becomes for management to discriminate against those who participate in the collective struggle. Nonetheless, the data suggest that such discrimination is still effective. In the minds of the technicians, they face a choice between an individual strategy and a collective strategy. Several items concerning attitudes toward mobility are highly correlated with strike participation. These items are also correlated with one another and with the item on solidarity with peers.[9]

Two of the items on mobility aspirations are in the regression equation: "Would you like to become a boss?" and "Is it important to you to improve your position in the company?" The first adds 17.3 percent to the total variance explained when it is entered into the equation; the second adds 1.9 percent.[10] These items are negatively correlated with strike participation ($r = -.488$ and $r = -.292$, respectively). Those people to whom upward mobility is important and those people who believe in the openness of the company are less likely to strike than those to whom mobility is less important and those who do not believe in the openness of the system.

Solidarity with peers is not related in any necessary way to mobility orientation. Empirically, however, the two are related. Those who trust their co-workers to decide their merit raises and those who favor the abolition of merit raises tend not to be interested in individual mobility within the company. The item on solidarity with peers adds 4.1 percent to the variance explained.

Mobility orientation and solidarity with peers are important enough to warrant a closer look at the individual level. For some employees, advancement in the company hierarchy provides the self-esteem that cannot be obtained from the job itself or from association with colleagues. This status striving has entered the folklore of our times as one of the more repugnant aspects of white collar alienation. An example is provided by one of the testers, who sees this situation as entirely natural.[11]

The person who at a certain point gets ahead in the company, who improves constantly, he's satisfied with himself. . . . Take the case of someone who never gets ahead, who always stays in the same spot, who never got promoted, such a person denigrates himself. On the other hand, the person who sees his position in the company improving, who gets ahead, he feels himself to be an important person, so he is stimulated to produce better, to work harder, to lead a more organizational [sic] life, a more working life. (Brunelli)

Others stress the importance of the higher pay they would get were they to be promoted. Those technicians who have children at a young age, when their salaries are still quite low, find this argument quite compelling.

See, career is very much tied to pay. I'm working incredibly hard now in hopes of getting promoted to the second category and getting a raise. . . . I assure you, it's tough supporting a family, wife and two kids, it's very tough. I promise you, I'd love to come home, having finished everything, to play with my kids, to go out in the middle of a field with my kids. I like work, but I'm not a fanatic, and still I come home at midnight, one o'clock, I work Sundays. . . not out of egoism, not so I can have a bank account, because I swear to you that I don't save a cent, but to support my family. (Berardelli)

This attitude puts them in conflict with the leftists who are not only ideologically opposed to careerism, but who also champion the abolition of overtime as a means of encouraging the shift of jobs to Southern Italy.

We have noted that those who attribute a great deal of importance to mobility tend to be less solidaristic in their orientations toward their co-workers. Their unwillingness to be judged by their peers sometimes reflects a somewhat cynical attitude toward human nature. "People are selfish, so it's better to have someone who is above it all to decide on these things [merit raises] ." (Berardelli)

Then there are some people who see mobility as important but are unwilling to behave in the ways that they think they would have to behave in order to advance up the company hierarchy (see, for example, the quotation from Iuteri, under *Attitudes toward individual mobility,* in Chapter 4). School provides an alternative avenue of mobility for these technicians. Although few actually will finish a degree in night school, many work toward the light at the end of the tunnel. Asked whether it was important to him to improve his position within the firm, one man replied,

To improve, of course, it's pretty important. You can't do a job starting out with the idea of not improving, it's natural in man to want to improve. . . . Everyone would like to improve, but let me be clear, I don't want to become a boss in order to dominate. . . I'd rather be a bum than dominate others. (Terri)

This same man was quoted previously (Chapter 5, *Patterns of life outside the workplace*), saying that he is going to school, not because he is careerist, but because he is interested in learning more. His need to justify himself reflects the negative valuation placed by many of his colleagues on the careerist attitude. But going to school is not only a way he can deepen his knowledge and improve his position in society without compromising his principles. He realizes that he would not go far without a university degree even if he were willing to compromise himself by resorting to careerism.

These same considerations are voiced by those who disclaim all interest in mobility within the firm: They do not want to do what they would have to do to get ahead; they do not like the idea of dominating others; and no real career is possible anyway for people without university degrees. There are two aspects to the first points. First, some people see themselves as temperamentally unsuited to be in positions of authority. This may simply be an observation of a state of fact, or it may be phrased as the lack of some desirable quality. For Mongillo becoming a boss is undesirable, while for Cassella it is desirable but unattainable:

I don't think it's pleasant [to be a boss], because there's the pressure of work, work becomes an obsession, you think about it even when you're in bed, you think of it when you go to the beach. I just want to live in peace. (Mongillo)

I admit that I would be incapable of coordinating the work of others. I wouldn't know how to make myself obeyed, I wouldn't have the courage, the brazenness. . . (Cassella)

The feeling that the job of a boss is an undesirable one shades over into a second reason for not wanting to become a boss – principled opposition to careerism. "I don't know why, but 'the possibility of getting ahead'. . . it suggests. . . I think of those people who, in order to get ahead, grab onto everyone, or climb over things, pushing others down. . . I don't know, in practice I guess that's how it is" (Serano). In the Special Systems Laboratory, wanting to get ahead is so looked down upon that few people will admit to it: "If you ask anybody in here, 'Are you interested in getting ahead?' he'll say, 'No, I couldn't care less,' whereas in reality if someone isn't interested in getting ahead, he's certainly interested in money, at least so far as I have seen" (Massa). Yet, this same technician admits that, even though getting ahead in the Lab is as much a struggle as it is elsewhere, in the Lab it is carried on more honestly.

The last and most important reason for the disinterest in getting ahead is that there is a ceiling above which a technician cannot rise. This is true even in the Special Systems Laboratory.

In Italy to get ahead, both in economic terms and otherwise, the famous sheepskin is still necessary. . . . For me it's pretty annoying from a psychological point of view to know, as is recognized by everyone, that I do the job of a university graduate, but am given the economic treatment and prospects of a technician. . . . In general, in the company, there is a ceiling, especially in the first years. After that it remains to be seen, but it certainly is true that for the technician, even if he's the most brilliant person in this world, the difficulties are much greater than for any engineer. . . . This is true at the macrolevel of Siemens as a whole, but it is not insignificant even in the Lab. No one can come and tell me that if someone is good in here, it doesn't make any difference if he's an engineer or a technician. It just isn't true. (Massa)

One of the technicians from GT&E sees the situation in even bleaker terms: "In practice I do the work of an engineer. This stuff isn't called Systems Engineering for nothing. So actually I'm exploited. . . . I think I'll die without making it to 'director' [a high managerial category]. This is because the degree one has is considered all-important" (Alicea).

If these views represent reality, there is little to be lost by participating in strikes. But the very fact that desires for mobility within the company weigh on some people as an incentive not to strike implies that there are *some* opportunities for mobility. The technicians were asked how high in the company they thought they could get with their educational backgrounds. Twenty-six percent said nowhere, 12 percent said that they had already risen as far as they could, and a further 27 percent thought that it might be possible to rise somewhat higher than their present position, but not much. Eighteen percent thought that there was no absolute ceiling, but emphasized the unlikelihood of mobility for a technician. Only 15 percent visualized an open path for those with ability.

These answers present a mixed picture. They range from those who see no limits to their aspirations to those who see no possibilities for mobility at all. However, it is clear that a majority of those interviewed do not think that they can get very far without further education.

Much has been written in Italy about the proletarianization of technicians. One cause of proletarianization is the bureaucratization and rationalization of the workplace, itself a consequence of the increasing scale of investments in technology. Careers come to be restricted by rules. Experience no longer suffices to propel one across critical boundaries; instead, the academic degree becomes the ticket to the next level. We have no way of estimating how much the career opportunities of technicians have changed over the years. It is a safe guess, however, that these opportunities are fewer now than in the years when technicians were scarce, engineers above them were scarcer, and products were less sophisticated. This change provides one very plausible explanation for the increase in strike participation in recent years.

In Chapter 4 we discussed the relationships between attitudes toward mobility and toward peers and the job a man does. We found that the employees of the GT&E commercial offices were the most individualistic in their orientations and that the technicians at GT&E were generally more individualistic than their counterparts at Siemens. We noted too that the employees of the GT&E commercial offices were one of the groups lowest in discontent with the organization and strike participation. But the technicians working in the very solidaristic environment of the development labs at Siemens also scored low on these scales. Although an individualistic orientation may inhibit participation in strikes, a solidaristic one does not necessarily result in strike participation. Such participation will be contingent upon the mobilization of this solidarity through discontent with the organization or other impelling forces.

Objective variables other than the job someone does or the norms of his work environment also affect mobility aspirations and solidarity with peers. The technicians who receive the lowest pay are more junior and are lower in the company hierarchy, tend to express less desire to become bosses, and tend to be more solidaristic in their answers to the question on merit raises.[12] The effects of the objective variables of pay and contractual category on strike participation appear to be mediated almost entirely through these attitudinal variables. The partial correlations between pay and strike participation and between category and strike participation drop very substantially when the variables on mobility orientation and solidarity with peers are introduced in the step-wise regression. Only category is entered into the equation but the coefficient is not significant.

Again it is easy to come up with an ex post facto explanation (or even several) for why this should be. It may be that those in the higher pay brackets and the higher contractual categories got there because of their strong aspirations for mobility within the firm and their individu-alistic attitudes. Or it may be that, as time brings the technician closer to promotions or substantial merit raises, he abandons his earlier col-lectivist attitude for a more individualistic one. The proper testing of such hypotheses requires a research design rarely carried out: the panel study over time. Given the data at hand, this author favors the first hy-pothesis, according to which mobility orientation is seen as the chicken in what is admittedly a chicken-and-egg kind of circular interaction. At GT&E in particular, many interviewees emphasize the clientelistic character of the organization. Merit raises and promotions are seen as dependent on having the proper attitude toward one's boss and a cor-respondingly proper, that is, individualistic and competitive, attitude toward peers. These attitudes lead to isolation from one's peers and ac-ceptance by one's boss, in turn reinforcing the attitudes.

The need for more collaboration on the job. The question, "Do you think it would be useful to do more work in groups?" is the third item to be entered in this stepwise regression. The people who feel the need to work in groups are more likely to strike than are those who already work in groups or those who do not feel the need to do so. The item adds 6.1 percent to the variance explained, and the zero-order correla-tion between it and strike participation is .403.

The reader may remember that this question is included in the scale measuring discontent with the organization. It is the only item in the interview guide that is strongly related both to the job someone does and to whether he strikes or not. For this reason it has received our spe-cial attention. A detailed analysis indicates that it measures primarily a need to work in groups arising from the kind of work the person does. The two job groups in incongruent situations, those doing technical jobs in GT&E and those doing routine jobs in Siemens, express the greatest need to work more in groups. Those in the sales offices in GT&E do not feel a need to do more group work, whereas those who work in the development sections in the Special Systems Laboratory say they already work in groups. The correlation between the group-work item and the ORGDISC scale without this item is .280. Responses to this question are less a measure of a generalized solidaristic attitude than they are a measure of a felt need determined by the nature of the work task.[13]

The low but significant individual-level correlation between ORGDISC and the strike participation scale (r = .231) may be traced largely to the effect of the groupwork item. What remains to be explained is why negative attitudes toward the organization are not more consistently translated into strike participation. This issue is addressed at the end of the chapter.

Attitudes toward pay. We have seen that absolute level of pay is an indicator of level in the company hierarchy and that its effects on strike participation are mediated almost entirely through variables measuring career aspirations and solidarity with peers.

But attitudes toward pay do have a direct, even though slight, effect on strike participation. The technicians were asked what they thought would be a fair pay for their job. The percent difference between actual pay and what would be considered fair pay was computed for each person. A second measure of attitudes toward pay, described in the analysis of prior orientations to work (see Chapter 4), combines perceived unfairness with a measure of the importance of pay to the person in order to obtain a new variable. Thus, those who are highly dissatisfied with their pay and consider pay to be important are coded 1, those who are highly dissatisfied but do not consider pay to be important are coded 2, and so on, up to those, coded 5, who consider pay to be important and are completely satisfied.

Both these measures emerge with significant coefficients when one or the other is included in otherwise identical regression equations. Those who feel that their pay is unfairly low tend to strike more. The second variable adds 2 percent to the explained variance when entered into the stepwise regression, whereas the first adds only 1.5 percent. The standardized coefficient for the second variable is also slightly larger. A small addition in predictive power can be obtained by taking into account whether or not pay is important to the person. The zero-order correlations between these two variables and strike participation are .238 and .292, respectively. The two measures obviously overlap a great deal, and so only the second was included in the final regressions.

The more children a technician has the more dissatisfied he will be with his pay. Those who consider pay to be important in choosing a job also tend to be more dissatisfied, and the importance attributed to pay is itself dependent on marital status and number of children. There are conflicting pressures at work among the married and those with children. On the one hand, they feel more injustice regarding their pay, but, on the other hand, the wages lost through strike participation are more important to them. They are more likely to have experienced mobility at work and to be optimistic about the possibilities of getting ahead. Because of these conflicting tendencies, family status (single, married, or married with children) did not emerge as a significant variable in the first equation, and only enters the equation after attitudes toward pay are controlled for. Controlling for attitudes toward pay, those who are married and have children are less likely to strike than the single men. Family status adds 2.2 percent to the variance explained.

Dissatisfaction about pay explains a surprisingly small amount of variance after other attitudinal items have been entered into the equation. Were it not for the fact that organizational variables are not much more useful than pay in explaining strike participation, the relative unimportance of feelings about pay might be taken as support for the contention of the new working class theorists that pay is not a central issue for this type of worker.

Union membership

In the final regression equation, the variable of union membership was added. This last regression equation explains 72.1 percent of the variance in strike participation, a modest improvement over the 70.0 percent of the previous equation. However, the item on union membership is the third variable to be entered, and adds 7.8 percent to the variance explained by the first two (see Table 6.4).

Union membership is neither an attitudinal variable nor an objective aspect of the person's situation acting upon him. Rather, it is the result of a conscious decision, itself determined by the person's background, his current situation, and his attitudes. Once someone has joined a union, he feels obligated to strike as nonmembers do not.

The objection might be raised that union membership may play a greater role as a determinant of attitudes rather than vice versa. This does not seem plausible for two reasons, both alluded to briefly in

Table 6.4. *Regression of strike participation scale on background, structural, and attitudinal variables plus union membership.*

Variable description	Item no.	Coefficient	Standard error of coefficient	Standardized coefficient	t test	DF[a]	Significance	Unique variance
Political position	6.13	-0.4408	0.116	-0.282	-3.79	76	under .001	.053
Would like become boss	3.1	-0.2412	0.113	-0.154	-2.13	76	.037	.017
Union member	6.8	0.1722	0.072	0.189	2.40	76	.020	.021
Favors merit raises	2.11	-0.2764	0.118	-0.173	-2.33	76	.023	.020
Where grew up: Milan/elsewhere	7.12	0.3235	0.103	0.205	3.15	76	.003	.036
Family status	1.5,1.6	0.1303	0.059	0.155	2.21	76	.031	.018
Pay important and unfair	1.9,4.10,4.12	0.1391	0.051	0.187	2.75	76	.008	.028
Important to improve position	3.2	-0.1439	0.057	-0.167	-2.51	76	.015	.023
Sum of grandfathers' occupations	7.14	0.0571	0.031	0.122	1.86	76	.068	.013
More collaboration useful	1.16	-0.2021	0.112	-0.128	-1.81	76	.075	.012
Category	—	-0.0492	0.045	-0.075	-1.10	76	.274	.004

Regression constant = 0.364

Multiple correlation squared = 0.721   *F* = 17.86 with 11 and 76 DF (*P* under .001)
Multiple correlation = 0.849
Standard deviation of residuals = 0.444

Last step increased R^2 by less than 0.010
Partial correlations with dependent variable for variables not entered

Level of schooling	1.1	-0.011						
Pay now	4.10	-0.034						
How often sees friends	6.22(b)	0.082						
Father's occupation	7.14	0.038						
How to get ahead	4.13	-0.071						

[a] Degrees of freedom.

Chapter 5. First, the decision to join the union is entirely voluntary, and, second, union membership only exceptionally implies an active commitment. More usually it is a gesture of solidarity. The union member allows a small sum to be deducted from his paycheck as dues, but other than that his commitment is only symbolic. These circumstances indicate that union membership is a dependent variable in relation to the other variables discussed above.

With the introduction of union membership into the regression, the partial correlation between the groupwork item and strike participation goes down from .338 to .222. The groupwork item is highly correlated with union membership ($r = .411$) as well as with strike participation ($r = .403$). However, union membership is not correlated with the item on solidarity with peers, reinforcing our conclusion that the groupwork item is measuring a need determined by the nature of the work task.

Much of the effect of the groupwork item on strike participation is mediated through union membership, that is, those who most feel the need to work in groups tend to join unions and, therefore, to strike. In the final equation, the coefficient of the groupwork item is significant only at the .075 level.

Other variables in the equation. Four objective variables are entered into the equation, two with coefficients significant below the .05 level. One of these two, family status, did not explain enough variance to be entered in the first regression. Geographical mobility remains a significant predictor, and the variable of grandfathers' class positions is just above the .05 level of significance.

All of the attitudinal variables entered in the previous equations are retained with some minor changes of sequence. Only the groupwork item is clearly demoted by the introduction of union membership.

Discussion of the regression results

Four different types of variables are important contributors to the total variance in strike participation explained by the final regression equation.

The first type consists of those items concerning the interviewee's political position, his father's political position, and his grandfathers' class positions. The striking technician tends to be a leftist whose grandparents were workers or peasants. Chances are that his father was also a leftist (but knowledge of this fact will not increase the accuracy of our prediction of strike participation once we already know the interviewee's own political position).

A second type of variable concerns mobility aspirations and solidarity with peers. The striking technician tends to be relatively unconcerned about, if not actively rejecting of, upward mobility within the company. His alliances are with his peers rather than with the hierarchy. If he is interested in mobility, it is through night school, rather than by direct competition for advancement within the company.

The third type of variable is related to the job itself. The striking technician is likely to feel a need for more collaboration in order to do his job. He is also more likely to be a union member.

Fourth, the man who is dissatisfied with his pay is more likely to strike, particularly if pay is important to him.

If we are to explain the increase in the militancy of technicians over the past few years, we must relate it to changes that have occurred in recent years. The most important explanatory variables according to the preceding analysis are those related to political attitudes. These attitudes are largely formed by the time the person begins his working career. Of course, they may be changed by adult experience. Immigration to Milan, for example, seems to have some effect, but this effect is such as to make the immigrant less rather than more militant. There is no evidence that political position is affected by the work situation.

The relationships found here among political attitudes, work, and strike participation go counter to the Marxist assumption that the work situation has a strong effect on political views. Cotgrove and Vamplew report similar results from their study of process workers in five British plants. "[A]ttendance at union meetings, a dichotomous view of industrial relations, solidaristic reasons for joining a union, and support for collective action – all appear to be as much reflections of political socialization as they are of the objective conditions in the work situation."[14] Only in the case of one plant, where a recent strike had led to strained relations between workers and management, did they find effects in the other direction as well.

The political and social backgrounds of the technicians have contributed to their new militancy. With the rapid increase in the absolute number of technicians and white collar workers, more and more of them are recruited from blue collar and peasant families. The political traditions they bring with them predispose them favorably toward collective action.

Mobility aspirations and attitudes toward peers may also be assumed to have changed over the years. Possibilities for upward mobility "through the ranks" have become fewer with the bureaucratization of the technician's work environment and the increasing number of trained people graduating from schools. The value of the technician's degree has been diminished by its commonness. Under these circumstances, it is less of a sacrifice to opt for a collective strategy than it once was.

In making this point we assume that mobility aspirations diminish as opportunities for mobility become fewer. Our data support this assumption, at least so far as the relationship between aspirations and *perceived* opportunities is concerned. Those who perceive fewer opportunities for mobility also express less interest in the prospect.[15] But, it may be objected that perceptions of mobility opportunities, and mobility aspirations as well, are affected by reference groups, group norms, and many other factors besides real opportunities for mobility. We presented data earlier (see Chapter 4, *Attitudes toward individual mobility*) showing that mobility aspirations are related to organizational climate, although perceptions of mobility opportunities are not. We have no objective data on mobility in the organizations from which we drew the samples. It is reasonable to assume, however, that despite the effects of reference groups and subgroup norms, gross changes in opportunities for mobility are reflected in changes in the perceptions of these opportunities and in levels of aspiration.

Pay differences between blue collar and white collar workers were declining in the years preceding the research, in part as a result of union action specifically directed toward pay equalization and in part as a result of market forces. Some commentators have suggested that white collar strike actions came in an effort to maintain traditional differentials. Our findings do not support this view. Asked to comment on the decreasing differential, only two people in the sample can bring themselves to say that it is unfair, and only seven qualify their endorsement. Ninety-five percent of the sample say that blue collar and white collar workers share the same interests, and only 20 percent will qualify this statement. Technicians whose leftist political views and solidaristic attitudes incline them toward participation in strikes are also those least likely to feel that the gains of blue collar workers are unjustified. By contrast, those who view pay as important are often interested in getting ahead and tend to have a generally individualistic approach to work. This is why feelings about pay explain so little of the variance in strike participation. Nevertheless, some strikers are primarily interested in monetary gain, but these are likely to be among the followers, not the leaders.

Although pay is of modest importance as a determinant of strike participation, it deserves more attention than it has received in most writings on the new working class. Concerns about pay are among the issues underlying the ambivalence we have described in some white collar strikes (see Chapter 3, Recent conflicts at SIT Siemens). Bearing this in mind, the solidaristic responses of the men in our sample provide a remarkable illustration of the impact of a hegemonic working class organization such as the metalworkers' union in Italy.

What about the changes in technology and in the nature of jobs mentioned by so many of the authors discussed in Chapter 1? Only one of the many items pertaining to the job itself and to attitudes toward the organization is an important predictor of strike participation: the need for more collaboration on the job. The fact that this item expresses a grievance regarding the constraints of organizational structure supports the claims of the new working class theorists, who emphasize the high aspirations of technicians and the contradiction between involving jobs and confining organizational structure, as opposed to those who would emphasize worsening conditions and the increasingly routine nature of technical work. It is, nonetheless, surprising that most of the items on attitudes toward the job and the organization are not correlated with strike participation.

The weakness of links between attitudes about work, organization, and pay, on the one hand, and strike participation, on the other, implies that militancy, as defined at the beginning of this chapter ("the willingness to take action in the furtherance of one's interests"), is not very important in explaining individual participation in strikes. In fact, all but two of the variables in the regression equations tell more about why people refrain from participating in strikes than about why they participate. The items on working in groups and on fairness of pay are the only ones among the significant predictors of strike participation that provide a clue as to the underlying reasons motivating a technician to strike. The other items – political position, mobility aspirations, and solidarity with peers – are potential barriers to participation, whose presence or absence may discourage or permit participation, but they do not provide us with clues as to what it is that the technician is striking for. People do not initiate a strike because they are of working class origins, or because they have leftist political sympathies, or because they feel solidaristic with their colleagues. These preconditions might make a person unwilling to break through a picket line, but they do not explain the occurrence of militant strikes such as those at GT&E in the period preceding our study.

If the regression results suggest that it is primarily those who have a particular reason not to strike who do not do so, this is confirmed by the frequency distributions of responses to the interview items as well as by the data on actual strike participation at GT&E. Only 21 percent of the sample reject the strike on principle. Eighty-seven percent say that they participated in at least some strikes, and 66 percent say that they participated in *all* the strikes for the last contract. Turning back to the data on actual strike participation presented in Chapter 3, the level of participation in the 1970 strikes at GT&E averaged 76 percent among white collar workers as a whole, and was probably higher among white collar technicians.

In short, the great majority of technicians participate in contract strikes. The variance in the strike participation scale seems to distinguish among those who, either for fear of damaging their chances of promotion or on principle, do not strike, those who participate in all or almost all contract strikes, and those who participate in political strikes and strikes for reforms as well as contract strikes. The questions do not clearly separate those who participate because they are discontent with various aspects of their work situation and strongly support the demands from those who merely go along with the strike because they are sympathetic and feel that they have little to lose.

Our failure to discover more about the immediate causes of strikes, as opposed to the preconditions preventing or encouraging participation, may be explained by the character of the strikes that occurred in GT&E and SIT Siemens just prior to and during the period of the research. At GT&E, despite the rapid increase in the rate of strike participation among technicians, nuclei of union activists maintained control over the strikes, formulating the demands and the tactics for each struggle. Although the strikes elicited an unprecedented amount of support, they did not break out suddenly and spontaneously, nor were they provoked by pressing organizational problems, takeover threats, or mismanagement as were many of the more publicized cases of new working class unrest. Because the strikes were not the immediate expression of demands particular to GT&E, individual participation was less strongly linked to immediate issues in the plant.

In the Special Systems Laboratory of SIT Siemens, the situation was

different, although the consequences were similar. The issues under negotiation between unions and management at SIT Siemens often seemed
irrelevant and distant to the technicians of the Special Systems Laboratory. Because of the isolation and exceptional nature of the Lab, the
immediate grievances of its workers were not expressed in the issues of
collective bargaining in the plant as a whole. Here, even more than at
GT&E, there was a gap between immediate issues such as those expressed
in the interviews and the possible gains through strike participation.

In both cases, the technicians perceived the setting of strike objectives
and the control of strike actions to be in the hands of the unions and a
small number of active rank-and-file members. The strike demands addressed marginally, if at all, the organizational issues raised by the technicians quoted in Chapter 4. Most of these issues are squarely in the area
of "managerial prerogative." Although the unions have begun to nibble
at the edge of this area, they still cannot realistically hope to bargain on
many matters. It is hardly surprising, then, to find that political attitudes are more closely linked to strike participation than is discontent
over organizational issues.

Although the data do not suggest that organizational factors are irrelevant as causes of strikes, they do lead to the conclusion that such
factors are less important in explaining the new militancy of technicians
than the new working class theorists would have us believe. By contrast,
these theorists do not give sufficient importance to changes in patterns
of recruitment to technical occupations and declining opportunities for
mobility within increasingly large and bureaucratic organizations. The
significance of these changes is attested to by the regression weights of
social origins, political attitudes, and perceptions of opportunities for
internal mobility.

The contradiction between an involving job and an organizational
structure placing narrow limits on this involvement is stressed by the
new working class theorists and by the technicians themselves. This and
other work-related discontents may be among the precipitating factors
leading to strikes and, where union organization is weak, to greater
union penetration. They may affect the quality of strike participation
more than the extent of participation. Yet they are not key factors in
most people's decisions about whether or not to strike. Without the
changes in recruitment patterns and in opportunities for mobility, strike
participation would be much lower than it is.

We have pointed to the significance of preconditions facilitating individual participation in strikes. However, it is obvious that strikes such as those described in Chapters 2 and 3, with their innovative emphasis on participation, cannot be explained solely by reference to the preconditions necessary for strikes in general. The goals of the strikers, the immediate causes of the strike, must be part of any explanation. A precise assessment of the relative importance of preconditions and causes would require a sample of plants in addition to a sample of individuals. However, the literature on industrial relations provides abundant evidence for the importance of both. An example of the importance of preconditions is the finding that work groups in critical points of the production process are often strike-prone simply because they are in a position to gain their objectives more easily. An example of the importance of immediate causes is the observation that British mining strikes declined precipitously after the abolition of piecework.[16]

The new working class theorists focused on the plant and the strike as units of analysis. They paid special attention to the most spectacular new working class strikes. These usually broke out spontaneously, with no prior organizing activity, in firms low in union membership. The firms were often highly bureaucratized, and employed large numbers of technicians and white collar workers. The immediate causes of the strikes were far more visible in these cases, evident from the situation that had provoked the strike and reflected in the demands of the most articulate activists. These causes were discontents often similar to those expressed by the technicians in our sample quoted in Chapter 4.

Taking the individual as our unit, and considering plants in which the strike is more institutionalized, our analysis of individual strike participation reveals the importance of preconditions favorable to massive participation in strikes. These preconditions originate outside the plant (social background, political views) as well as inside (opportunities for internal mobility). The findings obtained by the two methods are complementary rather than contradictory.

Summary

Individual decisions to strike or not to strike are conditioned by five factors.

The first factor is related to the person's social background: Strikers are leftists, they tend to come from leftist families, and their working class or peasant roots often go back at least two generations.

A second factor is the choice of a collective or an individual strategy within the organization: Strikers feel solidaristic with their peers and are not striving for upward mobility within the company hierarchy.

The third factor, much less consistently important than the others, is the job itself: The striker is likely to feel that there is not enough collaboration in getting the job done.

Fourth, and also clearly of lesser importance, the striker is apt to be dissatisfied with his pay.

Finally, not surprisingly, union members are more likely to strike than nonmembers.

Preconditions encouraging strike participation emerge clearly from these results. These preconditions are the increased recruitment of technicians from the working class, many of them with leftist family traditions; and the increasing bureaucratization of firms with the consequent decline in possibilities of mobility within the hierarchy for technicians.

We have learned less about the immediate causes of strikes and the goals of strikers. The changing preconditions that make strike action seem possible and reasonable are at least as important in explaining the new militancy of technicians as the contradictions in the job situation emphasized by the new working class theorists. Preconditions are especially important in workplaces where a union already exists and where union activists play a dominant role in the key decisions regarding strike action. However, it must also be noted that in focusing on the individual's decision to participate or not to participate in an on-going strike, our methodology has inevitably underestimated the importance of militancy on workplace issues. Comparative case studies using the factory as the sampling unit are needed to complement studies of individuals such as this.

Turning from the strike as a collective phenomenon back to the individual, we note that the impact of the work situation on political attitudes is hard to discern, but the impact of politics on industrial behavior is very strong. Similar findings are cited from the United Kingdom, but this pattern is probably even more marked in Italy, where industrial relations are highly politicized.

Marx saw economic interests as shaping the consciousness of individuals. But our evidence shows that ideology can define people's perceptions of their economic interests. Attention is thus directed toward how consciousness changes – a process still little understood despite the attention political scientists and psychologists have given to it. In the concluding chapter, we offer some speculations as to the probability that the new working class will become class conscious.

7. The new working class: a revolutionary vanguard?

In the late sixties and early seventies there was a notable increase in strike participation among technicians and white collar workers. Strikes were often characterized by new kinds of demands and new forms of struggle. The new working class thesis tried to explain these happenings by reference to changes in the labor force and in the structure of industry, placing them in the context of the historical development of capitalism. In this view, the rapid postwar growth of technologically advanced industries employing large numbers of technicians and professionals, and the still more rapid increase in the numbers of technicians and professionals graduating from schools and universities, set the stage for the outbreak of militant collective action. Mallet and others described the swelling group of technicians as the vanguard of a reborn revolutionary movement.

The new working class theorists accepted much of the analysis of changes in advanced capitalism presented by proponents of the embourgeoisement thesis. But the conclusions they drew were different. A more highly educated labor force, more involving jobs, advanced technologies employing work teams, the greater integration of the worker into the firm, all were seen by the new working class theorists as leading to militancy and the demand for participation rather than to acceptance of the organizational hierarchy.

In two ways, the new working class thesis differed from previous positions in the debate on the role of the working class as a force for change. First, it saw positive involvement in work as a possible source of militancy. Second, it bridged the gap between the heretofore separate debates on blue collar and white collar workers simply by declaring it irrelevant in the advanced sectors. In these two respects, the new working class thesis not only reflected the mood of the supposed "affluent societies" of the sixties, but also made a lasting contribution to the debate.

The more specific propositions of the thesis must be examined in the light of empirical data and historical events. This we have sought to do

207

here, prying, within the limits of decency and of our resources, into every relevant aspect of the lives of the technicians in the sample in order to understand the causes and possible consequences of the changes in their behavior. This concluding chapter reviews some of our major findings, relates them to the results of recent French research, and suggests their implications for the organization of work and for the interpretation of the political and trade-union situation of the new working class.

We begin with the results on strike participation, discontent with the organization, and organizational structure, and what these findings indicate as to the future of conflict between technicians and management within organizations. We then take up the question of whether conflict within the firm is likely to spread beyond the boundaries of the firm itself to encompass larger political issues in Italian society. After reviewing our own findings and those of French studies on this point, we criticize some of the theoretical arguments that see the politicization of the conflict as inevitable. Finally, having rejected these deterministic notions, we discuss the possibility of such politicization.

Strike participation and organizational discontent

Strikes: causes and preconditions

The analysis of strike participation presented in Chapter 6 shows the necessity of distinguishing the immediate causes of a strike from the preconditions that make workers open to the idea of participating in a strike. The novel and daring qualities of many of the white collar strikes of this period stood out in the eyes of observers. Yet the data on individual participation in the strikes studied here suggests that the high level of participation is due to the existence of preconditions similar to those in large blue collar workplaces. These preconditions have so eroded the white collar worker's traditional unwillingness to strike that the strike has become generally accepted, and those who do not strike have particular reasons for not doing so.

Two preconditions are especially important. The first of these is the prevailing social milieu. As the number of technicians and white collar workers grows, they are perforce increasingly recruited from blue collar or peasant backgrounds. About 60 percent of the technicians in the sample are of working class or peasant origins. Half are leftists. Although immigration from the South, the Center, and the rural areas of the North to the northern cities may have a slightly conservatizing effect on political beliefs, the most notable tendency is one of continuity across generations, both in explicitly political beliefs and in general attitudes relevant to politics. The new working class's willingness to turn to collective action in their struggle against management is partly explained by the technicians' political and social roots.

The second precondition is the bureaucratization of the places where technicians work, and the accompanying reduction in opportunities for upward mobility within the company. Those who are solidaristic in their attitudes toward their peers and who are uninterested in being promoted (although they may be trying to rise by going to night school) are more likely to participate in strikes.

It is very difficult to organize a group for collective action if the same problems can be resolved by individual action. The fact that technicians have organized and acted collectively in itself constitutes evidence of low opportunities for mobility within the firm. This is confirmed by the perceptions of the men in the sample.

To some extent, the basic ambivalence of the traditional white collar worker remains. Some technicians have opted for the path of upward mobility within the firm. These men tend not to strike. It is probable, however, that the need to choose between an individual and a collective strategy is becoming a dilemma of the past. Strike participation among technicians is rapidly becoming "normal." Only a few years ago management kept lists of white collar strikers. Now, if they keep records on such matters at all, it is to record the names of the nonstrikers. Strikers no longer lose their chances for promotion as they once did. And, in any case, technicians' chances for upward mobility within the firm are decreasing as firms grow larger and more bureaucratized.

In the firms studied here, discontent over immediate organizational issues was not strongly related to strike participation. In both plants, the setting of strike objectives and the control of strike actions were in the hands of the unions and their activists within the plant. This situation tends to minimize the relevance of immediate issues while maximizing that of the preconditions just noted.

In contrast, those firms in which new working class militancy was most dramatic were unionized only weakly if at all. Many were threatened by foreign takeover or by layoffs due to mismanagement, or confronted by otherwise unusual situations. The immediate organizational issues, which under normal circumstances would never be subject to collective bargaining, now became subject to bargaining. In some cases, it was clear to all employees that their jobs were at stake, and middle management participated along with technicians, engineers, and blue collar workers. The new militancy of technicians on issues of control was evident in these cases. Our decision not to study the sites of the most publicized new working class strikes has thus affected our findings in this area.

In the more common, but less dramatic, cases of new working class militancy, the role of the unions in organizing and expressing demands is much greater. The white collar strike becomes institutionalized. The spontaneity of the early strikes is reduced by the diffusion of demands and tactics from other plants and by the strength of the existing union organization. The importance of political attitudes, closely related to attitudes toward the unions, and of other preconditions for a collective strategy is accordingly greater, and the importance of immediate causes is reduced.

Studies of new working class militancy taking the plant as their unit of analysis and focusing primarily on the more spectacular strikes have emphasized organizational issues. In our study, taking the individual as our unit and focusing on less dramatic cases, the preconditions favoring individual participation stand out as more important. Unfortunately, there are no studies on the plant level convincing enough in their methodology to enable us to say anything precise about the importance of organizational issues. Although some of the French studies that we describe below provide interesting information tending to confirm the significance of organizational variables, they do not provide any data specifically on strike participation.

The new working class theory has clearly underestimated the significance of the preconditions encouraging strike participation while overestimating the significance of immediate causes such as the tension between an involving job and a hierarchical organizational structure. Nevertheless, it must be pointed out that the new aspects of the new working class strikes, namely, the emphasis on participation as a means of governing the strike and as a strike objective, cannot be explained by reference to the preconditions that have always been necessary for any kind of strike. To explain these new aspects, we must turn to the concerns that set technicians apart from other workers, the immediate issues underlying strikes. These may be important only to a minority of strikers. They may not have a strong effect on the overall level of strike participation, particularly in unionized firms where the white collar strike is already commonplace. But the level of discontent over organizational issues provides an indication of the reservoir of feeling that can be tapped in moments of collective action.

Organizational discontent and organizational structure

The attitude of discontent with the organization is an active, demanding, even militant stance, often accompanied by a good deal of anger. In addition to the effects it may have on strike activity, it has obvious consequences for the way in which the work is carried out, especially if the job requires a commitment of the worker, as do many technicians' jobs in the electronics industry.

In Chapter 4 we illustrated the hypothesis that discontent with the organization is a function of the interaction of two factors: the job itself and the organizational structure within which the job is nested. Strike participation shows a similar, though weaker, relationship to these two factors.

Groups in *congruent* situations, that is, situations in which the job is involving and the organization is participatory or situations in which the job is uninvolving and the organization is hierarchical, tend to voice little discontent with the organization. If they are in the first type of congruent situation, they will be committed and satisfied; if they are in the second, they will be dissatisfied, withdrawn, and apathetic.

Groups in *incongruent* situations tend to be more demanding. If the job is involving and requires a commitment from the employee, he will come into conflict with a rigid organization in the course of trying to do his job well. This type of incongruence gives rise to positive, constructive demands of the kind described by Gorz and Mallet as typical of the new working class. In our sample, it is exemplified by the testers and lab technicians at GT&E.

Another type of incongruence, exemplified by the draftsmen at Siemens, exists between an uninvolving, closely controlled job and a participatory organization. The militant attitude in this situation is a reaction to the negative aspects of the control system and a striving toward the freer situation enjoyed by other workers in the same organization. It does not arise from a desire to do one's job better. It is, accordingly, less creative than the attitude arising from the first type of incongruence.

The schema developed in Chapter 4 made reference to three variables (see Table 4.6): the amount of commitment or involvement demanded by the job, the extent to which the organization is participatory or hierarchical, and the closeness of control over a particular job. To draw out the broader implications of the findings summarized in the preceding paragraphs, it is necessary to introduce one further distinction. Tasks vary in the extent to which what is demanded of the worker is structured, in other words, defined, predictable, and routine. A task may be judged to be structured or unstructured by considering it in the abstract, quite apart from how it is designed in a particular case or the character of the particular organization within which it is inserted. The distinction is a normative one in that it indicates to the designer of an organization how he should build both the jobs and the organization to do a given task. The term *task* suggests the abstract concept of work to be done as well as the concrete activity of a worker in an organization denoted by the term job. Because "task" carries the abstract connotation, we prefer to speak of structured and unstructured tasks rather than structured and unstructured jobs.

Research on small-group problem solving as well as research on organizational structure at the macrolevel indicates that hierarchical, centralized structures are more efficient in handling structured tasks, which are well-defined, routine, and predictable. More open, participatory organizations are more efficient in dealing with unstructured tasks requiring creativity and involvement.[1]

In many situations, the distinction between a structured and an unstructured task coincides with the distinction between an uninvolving and an involving task. In other words, most structured tasks are uninvolving, and most unstructured tasks are involving. However, there are exceptions to this rule, and the exceptions grow more numerous in advanced technology industries employing a highly educated labor force. We can diagram the relationships between these variables, placing the various groups in our sample in the appropriate cells (see Table 7.1).

In designing an organization, management is guided by two rules, which may on occasion lead to conflicting prescriptions. Taking into consideration the distinction between structured and unstructured tasks, the logical course for management is to allow greater control over the work situation to those workers doing unstructured tasks, while main-

Table 7.1. *Job groups and characteristics of the task.*

	Unstructured	Structured
Involving	Lab technicians	Testers
Not involving		Draftsmen, commercial office employees

taining more hierarchical structures for those workers engaged in more structured tasks. Following this rule, management will attempt to rationalize the structured tasks as much as possible. However, the distinction between involving and uninvolving tasks suggests a more pragmatic rule. As was shown in Chapter 4, workers who are more involved in their jobs will be more actively discontent if they are constrained by the organization than workers who are similarly constrained but uninvolved. Taking this into account, management will allow greater control over the work situation to those doing involving tasks whether they are structured or not, while reserving the hierarchical structures for those workers whose tasks are not only structured, but also uninvolving.

A glance at Table 7.1 shows that the conflict between the two rules concerns only the testers. Both rules prescribe a participatory organization for the upper left cell and a hierarchical one for the lower right cell. Both rules would suggest that a hypothetical job belonging in the lower left cell, now empty, might best be inserted in a participatory organization (because the rule on involving versus uninvolving jobs prescribes that involving jobs be done in participatory organizations, but it does not prescribe that uninvolving jobs necessarily be done in hierarchical organizations). But the testers would be placed in a hierarchical organization if the structure of the task were the only consideration, and in a participatory organization if their potential for militancy were given greater weight.

In Chapter 1 we noted the contrasting tendencies, on the one hand, toward increasing rationalization of jobs, hence proletarianization, and, on the other hand, toward more involving jobs, hence incongruence between job and organization if the organization is rigid. These two tendencies are reflected in the duality of the science of administration. The industrial engineers, operations researchers, and efficiency experts represent one of its poles; the practitioners of group dynamics and human relations represent the other. Although they often see themselves as opposed to one another and, in certain situations, may indeed be opposed, these approaches complement one another. The efficiency experts break down the structured organizational task, removing all discretion and, therefore, also all responsibility from the worker. In so doing, they render the outcome controllable and predictable. But even the simplest task requires a minimum of commitment from the worker – a commitment no longer obtainable solely by the threat of negative sanctions. So enter the experts on organizational behavior to recompose the task, to give back to the worker a measure of autonomy and responsibility, so that he will once again display that minimal commitment which is essential.

Also in Chapter 1 we discussed two different versions of the new working class thesis, roughly paralleling these contrasting tendencies in the design of jobs. Gorz and Mallet stress the conflict between involving work and rigid organizations. They see work becoming involving for more and more people. Other writers stress proletarianization and rationalization. They note the increasing division of labor, and ever closer controls over white collar work. It was pointed out that both theories might be right – they may simply describe different situations, or different aspects of the same situations.

Turning back to Table 7.1, we can see that it is the structured tasks that are most subject to proletarianization. In these cases there is a definite conflict between management's interest in productivity and the worker's interest in doing a job that is satisfying and will allow him to develop professionally. Any improvement in the situation of the worker is made at the expense of efficiency and managerial control. This is not to say that such improvements may not be initiated by management. However, management is only interested in improvements to the extent that they decrease militancy, absenteeism, turnover, and so forth.

The theory of conflict between an involving job and a rigid organization applies to a different, partially overlapping, set of situations, that is, the involving jobs, whether or not the tasks are structured. If the task is unstructured, there is no necessary conflict between worker and boss so far as the organization of work is concerned. The professional development of the worker constitutes an investment for the company, and his involvement in the job contributes to the quality of the product. An improvement in his situation results directly in a more productive organization. Under these circumstances the concept of alienation becomes rather abstract. But if the task is structured, then the job is in theory "rationalizable," and there is a conflict between workers and management. This is the case, for example, with the job of the tester.

Testers are likely to be particularly militant in their attitudes because of two elements in their situations: their jobs are involving and they tend to be closely controlled. Their militant stance includes the positive component derived from involvement in work and the negative component derived from close control. They exemplify a dilemma for management. They are more interested in learning on the job than in testing as many transmitters as possible. Because their goals do not coincide with those of management, giving them autonomy will not harness their creative energies in the service of higher productivity. Yet not giving them autonomy is damaging because of their active discontent.

Of course, the tendency toward increased rationalization meets with resistance from all categories of workers, although groups such as the testers may express their discontent more forcefully. In the case of less involved workers, resistance takes the form of high rates of absenteeism and turnover.

In the two right-hand cells of Table 7.1, there exists a conflict of interest between management and workers concerning the organization of work. The issue in both these cases is well described by those writers who see a process of proletarianization. In the upper right cell, the conflict is exacerbated by the involving character of the work.

Conflict is inherent in the situations of those performing structured jobs, be they testers, draftsmen, commercial office employees, or other low-level technicians. One-sided attempts at resolution are bound to be manipulative, papering over the potential conflict.

In the cases of those performing unstructured jobs, such as the lab technicians, the conflict is at least in principle resolvable to the advantage of both parties. Yet even when there is in principle no conflict of interest and where a more participatory organization is theoretically appropriate for the achievement of objectives, management may find it difficult to change existing structures in this direction. Fear of setting in motion a process that may accelerate beyond their control leads management to resist demands for greater participation. Their initial resistance brings about a situation in which their fear of loss of control becomes a self-fulfilling prophecy. This is particularly likely in Italy, where the tyranny and class stratification of bureaucratic hierarchies have their counterparts in the utopian aspirations of subordinates.

One solution to the problem of organizing these different tasks would be to split the productive unit in two. In drawing the dividing line, consideration might be given not only to the difference between structured and unstructured tasks, but also to the difference between workers who feel strongly the need for control over their work and those who do not. This would mean following the second of the two rules enunciated above. All those doing involving work would be in participatory units, whereas those doing uninvolving, structured jobs would be in hierarchical units. In our sample, lab technicians and testers would be the fortunate ones, whereas draftsmen and administrative workers would be less fortunate.

A serious problem with this solution from management's standpoint is the loss of efficiency in the work of those technicians, such as the testers, whose jobs fit into the upper right-hand cell of Table 7.1. Yet the solution is not so far-fetched as it might at first seem. Companies such as IBM pursue expensive personnel policies within their own plants while contracting out routine work where possible. Only the most critical parts and those requiring highly skilled labor or advanced technology are produced by IBM itself.[2]

This practice contributes to the balkanization of labor markets, the segregation of undesirable jobs in the secondary labor market, and the consequent unemployment, discussed in Chapter 2. The growth of dual labor markets is self-reinforcing. Workers in the secondary labor market lose all commitment to their work. A vicious cycle sets in: Rationalization leads to withdrawal on the part of the worker, leading to further rationalization, and so on. Finally, organizations adapt so as to deal with two different kinds of workers. One kind is treated with the care and respect of human capital in which an investment has been made; the other is primarily the object of discipline because his tenure in the organization is expected to be short and his job is designed to minimize the costs of rapid turnover.[3]

In some cases, physical separation is not possible. It is then difficult to prevent the freer organization from raising the aspirations of workers in other parts of the factory. Inspired by fear that this might happen, the Siemens management keeps the Special Systems Laboratory as segregated as possible. But such segregation makes the application of research findings to production problematic.

There are costs to management in all these solutions. Even expensively paternalistic personnel policies will not guarantee labor quiescence, particularly as such policies become commonplace. Conflict is latent in all those situations where jobs are structured. The probability that it will become manifest increases substantially where large numbers of people are grouped together with few channels for upward mobility within the organization. Even in the cases of those jobs where there is, in principle, no conflict of interest, conflict is likely if the organization has a history of rigidity and authoritarianism.

In short, the new working class will be involved in conflicts with management. The character of those conflicts will vary. They will be positive and creative to the extent that the participants are involved in their work; they will be negative (in the sense of being directed *against* some feature of the environment judged to be oppressive) to the extent that the participants are closely controlled. The most militant workers will be those whose involvement in their jobs is combined with resentment against close control.

A comment on the convergence of blue collar and white collar jobs

Our analysis of the relationships between the nature of the task and the design of the job casts some light on the debate between those authors, such as Crozier, who see the jobs of blue collar workers becoming increasingly similar to those of white collar workers, and those authors, such as Goldthorpe, Lockwood, et al., who on the contrary see the jobs of white collar workers becoming more similar to those traditionally associated with blue collar work. The variables determining the design of a job are ones regarding the nature of the task: whether it is structured or unstructured, involving or uninvolving. These distinctions increasingly crosscut the manual–nonmanual line. Accordingly, some white collar workers, particularly low-level office workers, find their jobs becoming proletarianized, while, at the same time, the number of unstructured technical and management jobs also grows. In the case of blue collar workers, the progress of automation seems to point less equivocally in the direction of more autonomous and enlarged jobs with greater responsibility. Perhaps, instead of speaking of convergence, we should emphasize the blurring of the manual–nonmanual line as it ceases to coincide with the separation between autonomous and interesting jobs, on the one hand, and narrow, repetitive jobs, on the other hand. There are still good jobs and bad jobs, but the manual–nonmanual distinction, so important for centuries, is losing all meaning in our technological age.

Recent research on the new
working class in France

A number of empirical studies of the new working class began to appear in France in the late sixties and early seventies. The findings are in striking agreement with our own on many points. In this section we deal only with the conclusions on involvement in work and on militancy. They tend to confirm the importance of involvement in work as a determinant of other attitudes. They suggest that technicians are on the whole highly involved in work, and that this involvement often leads to "conflictual participation" (i.e., a committed but demanding and critical attitude toward work and toward the organization) and to militancy.

The most thorough and interesting research for our purposes is Claude and Michelle Durand's survey of 1,300 employees in five factories.[4] Numerous open-ended interviews added to the depth of their knowledge of individual situations. Interviews were conducted at all levels of the hierarchy from unskilled workers to *cadres.* (For a definition of the French term *cadres,* see Chapter 1, p. 21.) Four of the five plants were in advanced sectors. The sample included 263 technicians and 210 *cadres.*

The study has a number of weaknesses: the perhaps inevitable avoidance of any explicitly political questions; the occasionally confusing and unsatisfactory analysis of the data; and the failure to draw upon any of the open-ended material to illustrate the array of tables that sometimes appears to befuddle the authors as much as they do the reader. Despite these weaknesses, it contains much interesting observation and analysis grounded on a more satisfactory foundation of data than any of the other studies reviewed.

One of the scales developed by the Durands measures involvement in work.[5] The technicians are more similar to the *cadres* (a group including numerous engineers in this case) than to the blue collar workers in their high involvement in work. The white collar workers resemble the semi-skilled in their low involvement. Considering a wide range of attitudes related to success, promotion, the importance of work in general, and evaluation of and involvement in one's own work, the Durands conclude that technicians and *cadres* share a professional as opposed to an economic conception of work.[6]

By contrast, in many attitudes toward life outside work and in their views on class conflict, inequality, and mobility, the technicians are closer to the blue collar workers than to the engineers and other *cadres,* whereas the clerical workers are closer to the *cadres* than to the semiskilled. In these more general questions, then, class origin reemerges as the most important determinant of attitudes.

The Durands show how the technician's involvement in work together with his working class outlook lead to a militant attitude. They also note, as we have, that organizational structure and personnel policy constitute intervening variables.

On the first point, the Durands find that technicians and *cadres* tend to participate actively (as measured by willingness to suggest changes in their company's training and promotion policies), whereas the semiskilled and the clerical workers tend to be retreatist. In all five firms, technicians are the most demanding group. Furthermore, among technicians even more than among *cadres,* participation is linked to involvement in work and is independent of attachment to the firm. In contrast, among semiskilled and clerical workers, participation is linked to the striving for upward mobility.[7]

In areas more directly related to militancy, the Durands find that those employees who have a professional rather than an economic view of promotion tend to be more pro-union. Technicians are the group most distrustful of management's motives in sponsoring training programs and tend to agree with blue collar workers that promotion policies should seek to develop the possibilities of all rather than to recompense the best. Like blue collar workers, technicians favor consultation with the unions on promotions and tend to describe the role of top management (*le patron*) in negative and exploitative terms.[8]

In the Durand study, personnel policy, organizational structure, and technology emerge as intervening variables. The Durands describe four different situations. In one of the most technologically advanced plants, with a combative union and a moderately bureaucratized organization, demands regarding training and promotion policies center around matters of power and control. In a second advanced technology firm, the union is weak, personnel policy is paternalistic, and the employees tend to be conformist. Here dissatisfaction centers on individual injustices resulting from the workings of the promotion system. The third plant uses a more traditional mass production technology and employs a high proportion of semiskilled workers. Demands are couched in terms of pay. Finally, in the two more democratically organized firms, whose technology is also advanced, one of which has a very strong union organization, the other a slightly weaker one, the level of dissatisfaction is low. Those individuals who are unhappy with their lot complain, but, unlike in the second plant, their discontent is not ideologically grounded.[9] These situations parallel our categories of active discontent, retreatism, and satisfaction.

In an article on professionalism based on the same data, Michelle Durand states more explicitly the possibility of conflict between work and organization. Durand finds that the data on professional involvement and organizational involvement (cosmopolitan and local orientations) cannot be adequately interpreted using the concepts of socialization and role conflict. The nature of work itself is important. As Durand puts it, "the history of professionalization is like a struggle between work and the collective organization of work. . . . Professionalization develops only when the job is to some extent autonomous."[10] Thus, clerical workers do not become professionalized because their work situation lacks autonomy. Durand sees autonomy of work as a principle of opposition to the organization. For example, cosmopolitans are more aware than locals of an exploitative relationship at the workplace. This does not, however, affect their allegiance to the enterprise, which takes the form of "conflictual participation."

Although we agree with Michelle Durand that autonomy of work may sometimes constitute an oppositional principle, as we have already indicated, this is by no means always the case.

In sum, there are a number of points on which the Durands' research supports the conclusions of the previous section. Comparing different categories of employees, they find involvement in work to be an important determinant of participation and militancy and of retreatism and withdrawal. Organizational structure is a significant intervening variable. The concordance of the Durands' results and those of this research are noteworthy, the more so as the present author did not come across the Durands' book until after having written the first version of this manuscript.

Another organizational study was conducted by Renaud Sainsaulieu.[11] The monograph is based on about 1,800 questionnaires and numerous open-ended interviews. The subjects are technicians, blue collar workers, and *cadres* in several departments of a large manufacturer of electrical and electronic equipment. Unlike the *cadres* in the Durand study, these *cadres* are all line managers. Few engineers in this sample are involved in research.

The study is concerned primarily with personal relations among the employees and with styles of interaction within the work group. The technicians represent the highest level of nonmanagerial employee in the sample. Insofar as the findings are comparable, they partially contradict ours and those of the Durand study.

Sainsaulieu distinguishes between highly skilled blue collar electronics workers (blue collar technicians), similar to the testers in our sample, and technicians proper (white collar technicians), including draftsmen, lab technicians, and others. The work situation among the first group is very similar to that of the testers in our sample. At least one of the research labs of the second group sounds much like the research lab at GT&E. The draftsmen's offices are also similar to those at GT&E and SIT Siemens. The descriptions of interpersonal relations and attitudes toward work of all these groups are often like those given in Chapter 4.

Sainsaulieu emphasizes the lack of solidarity among the new working class categories. Although small friendship groups exist, based on shared professional interests, there is little broader solidarity. Interestingly, the technicians in this sample show strong desires for more collegial cooperation much as do the militant technicians in our sample. The blue collar technicians are the most discontent group of all on a number of work-related dimensions. The white collar technicians are less dissatisfied. However, unionization is weak in both groups. Among the blue collar technicians there are quite a few union activists, but the percentage of union members is lower than in most other groups. Among the white collar technicians, unionization is lower still, although again the number of activists is comparatively high.

Sainsaulieu attributes the weakness of the unions among the new working class to their high mobility aspirations, their competitive attitudes toward one another, and their patterns of relationship based more on shared interests than on some more general affective solidarity. Yet he sees their attitudes toward unionism as "difficult to interpret," and asks whether changes may not be in the making. In this connection, he notes the freer atmosphere among the technicians since May 1968.

Sainsaulieu's technicians differ from those in our sample in their uniformly low solidarity. Yet their discontents are remarkably similar to those voiced by our sample. Maybe the difference can be explained by the fact that the technicians in the firm he studied had not had experiences of collective action to increase their solidarity. Had we interviewed the technicians in our sample a few years earlier, they might have sounded much like Sainsaulieu's. This possibility is in fact suggested by the author himself.

One earlier study is that by Marc Maurice. Because its focus is on mobility orientations, it will be discussed in the following section.

Finally, there are a number of analyses of the Events of May 1968. These suffer from all of the problems of retrospective research, but they have the corresponding advantage of being studies of behavior as much as of attitudes – a not inconsiderable advantage when militancy is one of the major variables of interest. Given the general consensus among these analyses, we will discuss only two of them here. Again, one of the most thorough studies is that by Claude Durand.[12] This is a study of eight large plants, four with traditional mass-production technologies and four in the advanced sectors. All eight experienced great worker militancy in May 1968. Thirty open-ended interviews were conducted with activists who had played important parts in the Events in their workplaces. Pamphlets and other documents were also collected.

This study tends to confirm the new working class thesis, although generalization of the struggle beyond the firm appears problematic. The innovative aspects of the May Events are described as originating in, and usually limited to, the advanced sectors, where technicians played key roles. These innovations included the development of participatory processes in conducting the struggle (the use of assemblies as decision-making bodies and the wide-ranging theoretical and intellectual activities of various study groups meeting during the strike) and the raising of demands challenging management's rights to make certain decisions unilaterally and asking for more control by the employees.

The form and rhetoric of the May strikes was more revolutionary than the demands made. With a few exceptions in the advanced sectors, the innovative demands challenging managerial prerogative were not acceded to. Although there was a highly politicized minority in the advanced sectors, political goals were rejected by the union leadership as well as by the base in both sectors. The general strike had an implicit political meaning recognized by all the activists, but any attempt to give the strike political goals outside the workplace failed. Nonetheless, almost all the activists felt that the May Events had led to a politicization of the base.

The same volume contains another study, by Renaud Dulong, on the actions of the *cadres* in May 1968.[13] The so-called malaise of the *cadres* has been the subject of much discussion in France since the mid-sixties. The increasing participation of this group in union activities is noteworthy in light of their previous complete identification with management. The development of large research and development laboratories and the expansion of company bureaucracies have led to the creation of *cadre* jobs that are not part of the line hierarchy. Young engineers are prominent among the militant *cadres*. A small number of activists are ideologically sophisticated and are trying to develop an alliance with the working class. All the studies on this subject seem to agree, however, that the participation of *cadres* in collective actions does not signify an unambiguous alliance of this type. The complaints of *cadres* are often identical to those of the technicians in our sample. But their actions are rather attempts to define their own position within the enterprise, both in relation to the technicians, clerical workers, and blue collar workers below them and in relation to top management above them.[14]

It is significant that there now exists a minority of militant young engineers allied with the labor movement. This personal ideological stand does not presage the conversion of all the *cadres* to the same position. But, as Dulong points out, it has on occasion led the engineers of research labs to follow the more militant actions of the technicians.

The French research confirms the view of technicians as a militant group, their militancy related to their involvement in work. Technicians emerge as exceptionally concerned about participation and about issues related to the organization of work, although less radical than blue collar workers in their political views and images of society.

The literature underscores the importance of the job and the organizational environment as determinants of attitudes and behavior independent of social origins and the individual meanings attached to work. This point is made explicitly by Sainsaulieu and is implicit in all the studies showing consistent variations in attitudes and behaviors between job groups in different plants throughout France.[15] The Durands, for example, consistently find greater differences between professional categories than between plants.

Two variables not related to the job or the organizational structure, which are given great importance by all who discuss the situation of technicians, are social background and upward mobility aspirations. We too have found these to be very important. Their importance is also discussed below.

The generalization of conflict
from the firm to society

A summary of the findings of this study

Given that conflict within the firm is likely, what are the prospects for the development of true class conscious action among the new working class? We begin to answer this question by reviewing our findings on the origins and traditions the technicians bring with them, their perceptions as to the possibilities for upward mobility, and their life style and images of the class structure.[16] We then return to the French studies cited in the previous section, to see what they have to say about the effects of upward mobility and high levels of aspiration on class consciousness. A full answer, however, must draw upon a view of long-term social and economic trends in the society as a whole, and even in the world. Here the objective weighing of the evidence bearing on a particular hypothesis must give way to an informed judgment guided by political values. The reader will make this judgment in accordance with his own views, and our final interpretation is not the only possible one. We will, nonetheless, present one interpretation, and criticize others.

In the discussion of strike participation, we noted that a majority of technicians are of working class or peasant origins and that about half of them support the Socialist or Communist parties. These facts suggest an openness to leftist political action going beyond the workplace.

We noted also the declining opportunities for a technician to work his way up in the organizational hierarchy. By contrast, opportunities for mobility via education are greater now than in the past. In fact, the technicians in the sample are slightly more optimistic about their possibilities for mobility in the society than they are about their chances for progress within the firm.

The strongest evidence for the technicians' belief in the openness of the society comes from the figure on night-school attendance. Twenty-nine percent of the sample go to night school. Night school is seen as a way to get ahead without compromising oneself as one would have to in order to advance in a bureaucratic setting. Night-school attendance is not associated with conservative political views, money models of the class structure, or nonparticipation in strikes. In contrast, aspirations for mobility within the firm *are* associated with money models and nonparticipation in strikes. They are also negatively associated with dichotomous class images.

Attendance at night school is consistent with the technicians' images of the class structure. A predominant feature of these class images is a large central class within which there is a range of inequality, but with no sharp boundaries. Mobility is possible within the large central class. It is important less for the higher status it brings than because it leads to a higher-paying and more satisfying job. Status considerations would not appear to be very important determinants of school attendance.

The apex of the stratification hierarchy tends to be seen as a power elite sharply disjunct from the other classes. Mobility is possible up to, but not into, this class.

Such a view of the class structure is compatible with collective action against the power elite as well as with projects of individual mobility within the large central class. Along with their considerable interest in mobility outside the firm, the technicians manifest a great deal of solidarity with the working class. Forty-nine percent of the sample identify as working class rather than middle class, even though only 16 percent of them are actually blue collar workers. The majority do not see another class below the one in which they place themselves. When told that the salary gap between blue collar and white collar workers has been narrowing in recent years and then asked whether they think this is fair, only two people can bring themselves to say that it is not, and only seven people add a qualification to their endorsement. Only 5 percent of the sample say that blue collar and white collar workers do not have the same interests, and only 20 percent will even qualify the statement that they do. Not all of the technicians interviewed seem wholly committed to reducing the gap between blue collar and white collar workers. But those whose support of this goal is less than wholehearted are reluctant to admit as much. Ideology and common struggle create and sustain these solidaristic norms.

As to the technicians' patterns of life outside of work, they neither exclude nor imply the inevitability of the development of class consciousness. The single men participate in a very loose form of occupational community. The lives of the married men tend to be privatized. But, as we stressed earlier, the privatized life style was not chosen by these men – it simply happened to them. Certainly, the technicians' lives outside of work are very different from the life of the traditional working class community with its ritualized interaction patterns and cohesive groups. There is little here to foster this kind of solidary collectivism. Yet we must not be too quick to see in this situation the inevitable end of solidarity and ideology. Privatized lives generate new social needs. How these are formulated and articulated will be critical for the nascence of a renewed socialist movement.

The findings of recent French research

We return now to the French studies cited earlier. Organizational in their focus, these studies have little to say about life outside the workplace. They do, however, pay a good deal of attention to two important variables: social origins and mobility aspirations.

The findings show that technicians are often upwardly mobile in relation to their origins and that they have high aspirations for mobility in the future. Forty-six percent of the technicians in the Durand study are of working class origins. Maurice, who sampled 416 technicians in the Chemical Industries Union of the CFDT, found over 60 percent to be upward mobile. Sainsaulieu finds a smaller percentage to be of working class origins (somewhere around 35%, so far as one can tell) although 70 percent had worked in the shop before moving up to the labs. Barrier, with 154 questionnaires from traditional skilled workers and new working class employed by the Electricité de France, also finds less upward mobility. Although she does not give any figure, she does say that most of the new working class subjects in her sample were of lower middle class origins.[17] These figures may be compared with the 49 percent of our sample who are of working class origins, plus 9 percent of rural origins, adding up to nearly 60 percent who are intergenerationally mobile.

There is less variation in the findings of high aspirations for the future. Thirty-six percent of the technicians in the Durands' sample are taking courses, as are 22 percent of those in Sainsaulieu's sample.[18] It will be remembered that the comparable figure for our sample is 29 percent. The other two studies do not provide figures, but both stress the high level of aspirations of the technicians, as do Durand and Sainsaulieu.

What are the effects of this high level of upward mobility and of the perhaps even higher level of aspirations? On the one hand, the orientation toward upward mobility does not seem to make the technicians less militant. On the other hand, to the extent that they believe such mobility to be possible, the radicalism of their perspectives on society appears to be tempered. It remains to be seen whether these aspirations can be met given the rapid increase in the number of technicians.

The major dependent variables in the Durand study are attitudes and behaviors related to continuing education and to promotion. Once again, their study is the most thorough, but once again the wealth of data they present is marred by unexplained contradictions. For example, the technicians are described as being optimistic about possibilities for promotion within the firm, yet pessimistic about possibilities for mobility in the society at large. Such seemingly contradictory findings, unreconciled in the text, make interpretation difficult.

The Durands' own view is that the technicians have a particular kind of class consciousness resulting from a strong interest in mobility together with a heightened awareness of the difficulties of such mobility. In their sample, the intergenerationally upwardly mobile technicians are more class conscious than the stable. Among the mobile, identification with a social group above their own (i.e., engineers or *cadres*) does not diminish their class consciousness (as measured by coding their descriptions of *patron* and worker), and among the stable such identification actually increases class consciousness.[19] In other words, high aspirations lead to heightened awareness of the barriers to mobility.

The Durands' data on the characteristics of those taking courses add to this picture. They find that the type of person who takes courses varies according to the personnel policies of the firm. In those firms with paternalistic personnel policies, taking courses and showing interest in promotion are negatively correlated with class consciousness. Support for the firm's training and promotion policies is linked to ideology in all firms except those with democratic personnel policies.[20] These results parallel our own findings regarding the negative effect on strike participation of aspirations toward mobility within the firm (as opposed to mobility through education).

The type of person who takes courses also varies by professional category. Among technicians, those taking courses tend to be critical of the company and aware of the difficulties of social mobility. They tend to describe the engineers and *cadres* in favorable terms and to identify with groups above themselves.[21] The characterization is not dissimilar from that of the technicians as a group: the perceptions of a conflict with the company and of the difficulties of mobility are associated with an identification with the categories above their own.

Sainsaulieu describes both the blue collar and the white collar technicians as having high aspirations to move up in the company – aspirations that may conflict with the adoption of a collective strategy. He finds considerably more discontent among the blue collar technicians who often work closely with the white collar technicians and find themselves correcting the mistakes of the latter, but have relatively limited opportunities for mobility. Within the category of the white collar technicians, there is some form of hierarchy they may ascend, and their discontent is accordingly lower.[22] Unfortunately, Sainsaulieu did not collect any data on political attitudes or views of society outside the workplace.

The study by Marc Maurice indicates that intergenerational upward mobility does not reduce militancy among technicians. Maurice argues that politicization among technicians is associated with high levels of aspiration and participation rather than with the traditional class consciousness of the blue collar worker. These suggestions support the Durands' findings. However, the attempt to read meaning into an assortment of tables with no other data available beyond the forced-choice responses to a questionnaire is a hazardous project.[23]

*Mobility aspirations, labor market
situation, and class consciousness*

The French studies just reviewed depict the technicians as militant because of, rather than in spite of, their mobility aspirations, However, both the French research and our own suggest that mobility aspirations can also reduce militancy under certain circumstances: when promotion policies discriminate against those who are militant and when mobility is seen in terms of advancement within the firm.

The technicians in these samples do not tend to share the simple dichotomous oppositional view of society of the blue collar worker. They see the social structure as more open, while remaining very much aware of the difficulties of mobility. A militant attitude at the workplace is linked to a more moderate view of the society at large. These findings are very similar to our own.[24]

The high aspirations of technicians are related to the involving character of their work and to their constant contacts with engineers as much as to their educational levels. But what are their real chances for mobility, and how can the technicians be expected to respond as their situation on the labor market worsens?

The men in our sample are relatively optimistic in their perceptions of the labor market despite the gloomy figures on the objective situation presented in Chapter 2. Forty-six percent think it would be easy to find another job as good as their present one, 14 percent think they would find one, although not with ease, and 35 percent think it would be difficult. This optimism may reflect the special labor market situation of young technicians who have had some on-the-job training and experience in advanced firms in the electronics industry.

As was pointed out in Chapter 2, the worsening labor market situation may not lead to a decline in militancy. The investment in training each of these workers is considerable. Union strength and legal protection add to their job security. Furthermore, technicians are likely to move into jobs at lower levels rather than remain unemployed. This too will reduce the effect of oversupply on bargaining power. And at these lower levels, the conflicts between aspirations and jobs will be still greater.

The Durands have described the type of class consciousness corresponding to this situation. It is close to what Germani and others have described as the result of partially blocked mobility. "The rising expectations of newly educated groups remain unsatisfied because other groups . . . virtually monopolize the higher positions available in the society, or because the new supply of educated persons exceeds the demand. . . ."[25] This process may lead to the radicalization of educated groups. Although the new working class is not a distinct group outside the workplace, and cannot be expected to organize as such, it would be fallacious to argue that mobility or the aspiration to mobility will automatically lead to the dissipation of class consciousness.[26]

The theories of Gorz and Mallet

The weakest point in the new working class theorists' arguments is their conceptualization of the relationship between the work situation and the political situation. For them, the sources of militancy are exclusively internal to organizations. Gorz and Mallet use somewhat different reasonings, but both see the generalization from trade-unionistic goals to revolutionary goals as inevitable. Their arguments are curiously devoid of any references to the individual or collective histories of workers, their social backgrounds, their political attitudes, and their prior orientations to work. The causal links between life at work and life outside of work are all in one direction: from work to other realms. Our findings show, however, strong causal relationships only in the opposite direction: from attitudes acquired outside the work situation to militancy in the work situation.

The deductive leap from the work situation to the political situation is questionable on logical as well as empirical grounds. Mallet's argument starts with the observation that the firm is no longer simply an economic unit subject to the vicissitudes of the market; it is a political unit as well. The development of planning at the firm level and the dependence of working conditions on the plan force the union to take an interest in all areas of management policy making. In a parallel way, the development of planning at the national level and the relatedness of the economic choices of the large firms to the national plan must necessarily lead the trade-union movement to take an interest in national economic issues that are really political issues.

So far, Mallet's argument is supported by data. The trade-union movement is taking a growing interest in working conditions at the plant level. And it is true that the new working class has on a number of occasions taken an interest in management policy in the broadest sense. But in these cases, which were among the most clamorous cases of new working class unrest, the companies were floundering under bad management or threats of dismemberment. The demand for workers' control was invariably present. The lines of conflict were drawn so as to include among the "workers" everyone from just below top management on downward. Mallet's argument applies very well here. We do, however, question the conclusion that the demand for control is an *inevitable* result of the extension of technocratic planning within the firm.

Mallet correctly points out the increased mutual interdependence of the state and the labor unions. This tendency began with the development of industrial unionism and economic planning based on a Keynesian model. It has been documented for the United States as well as for many Western European countries.[27]

The final step in Mallet's argument is the most problematic one. After admitting that the demands of the new working class have not thus far been revolutionary, he falls back upon a modified version of deterministic Marxism. Even while recognizing the narrow self-interested character of some of the new working class struggles, he states that this character

. . . cannot resist in the deepening crisis of neo-capitalism. The modern working class has an immediate interest in uninterrupted technological development and in its benefits: a substantial reduction in working hours, professional advancement, possibilities for change within the productive sphere. Capitalism, on the contrary, tends to retard the development of the forces of production insofar as their development leads to declining rates of profit and the use of socialistic measures whose effects may be uncontrollable.[28]

In trying to prove that the new working class is perforce "revolutionary," Mallet reverts to the dubious argument of the breakdown of the capitalist system. There is one new element however: the idea of the contradiction between a rational technological development championed by the new working class and the irrationality of a system based on profit maximization.

This idea is central to André Gorz's early reasoning on this subject. For Gorz, it is precisely its technical training that gives the new working class a privileged role in his strategy.

The fundamental contradiction is that between the

requirements and criteria or profitability set by monopoly capital and the big banks on the one hand, and on the other the inherent requirements of an autonomous, creative activity which is an end in itself: an activity which measures the scientific and technical potential of an enterprise in scientific and technical terms and which sees . . . the possibility of conquering new domains of knowledge . . . destroyed by the barbaric commands of financial profit. . . . To men who give all of their creative capacities to a task . . . capital suddenly says: "Stop; what you are doing is worthless. . . . From now on you will mass produce components designed in Minnesota."[29]

This quotation echoes the words of many of the technicians in our sample. Here too, however, we must take issue with the notion of the *inevitability* of this contradiction. To see this situation as the evidence of a universal contradiction pitting bourgeois rationality, the rationality of profit maximization, against the higher rationality of a presumably socialist science and technology is an error. There may be such contradictions, particularly in the cases of floundering companies such as mentioned above. In such cases, technicians will be moved to defend their jobs. Their defense may be in the name of science as Gorz argues; or it may be in the name of planning and national priorities as Mallet argues. But these cases do not provide evidence for concluding that capitalism is less able to further the development of science and technology than is socialism. The directions of scientific development may differ. If, under capitalism, these directions are dictated by considerations of profit, under socialism, they may be dictated by social needs. In neither case, however, does science develop autonomously, guided by dictates internal to itself.

The equation of science with social rationality and rationality with socialism is one pole of the error that Angelo Dina has called "the illusion of the objective rationality of technology."[30] The other pole of this same error is Marcuse's and Habermas's equation of science with technocracy and of technocracy with capitalism.

The technical training that gives the new working class a privileged position in Gorz's analysis leads Habermas to disqualify the technician from a vanguard role. For Habermas, science and technology constitute the basis of legitimation of the capitalist system:

Relative growth of the productive forces no longer represents "eo ipso" a potential that points beyond the existing framework with emancipatory consequences, in view of which legitimations of an existing power structure become enfeebled. For the leading productive force – controlled scientific-technical progress itself – has now become the basis of legitimation.[31]

Habermas describes "technocratic consciousness" as a seemingly non-ideological ideology, veiling political choices with claims of scientifically determined inevitability. A true rationalization at the level of the "institutional framework," the level at which political choices are made, cannot occur without a demystification of this ideology. The only groups able to see through the veil are the students in the social sciences and humanities.

For the moment we can put aside the position taken by Habermas and, even more extremely, by Marcuse. (Habermas does not go as far as Marcuse, who argues that science and technology are bound up with capitalism in a *necessary* way.) If anything, the evidence presented up to now has shown that at least some technicians are class conscious: Consciousness is not the privilege of marginal groups. This is not to say that there is no substance to Habermas's thesis. Indeed, it does afford a partial explanation as to why students in the social sciences and humanities were the leaders in protests and why the scientific faculties were generally the refuge of the most inactive students. However, a useful approach must also explain why within the factory the technicians and engineers have been more militant than the administrative employees.

Such an approach must consider the belief systems of various groups in relation to their immediate situations and their prospects for the future.

Gorz and Mallet's analyses on this point must be taken more seriously, especially because they are shared by many groups on the left in Italy. At the risk of being repetitive, we can do no better than to quote Angelo Dina's rejection of their position:

We are convinced that the myth of objective rationality will not be overcome by focusing on the internal contradictions that place the technician in opposition to the capitalists, that is, the contradictions between greater or lesser efficiency, between short term or long term profits, between temporary imbalances and structural imbalances, no matter how sharp these contradictions may be. . . . This is not to say that there are no contradictions through which the technician can play a revolutionary role. . . . But these contradictions are not those between technically correct choices and profit-maximizing choices. . . . For such contradictions a solution is always at least conceivable within the system. . . . The fundamental contradiction for the technician is that between the decision-making power given to him and the ends of these decisions.[32]

Dina correctly rejects the deterministic view of an inevitable conflict. He wrongly concludes that the technician will become militant only by a voluntaristic decision. The basis for the collective action of the new working class, as of any other group, lies in their immediate situation. Ideology and organization are crucial if this action is to generalize beyond narrow self-interested demands. One function of such an ideology would be to make the technician aware of the ends of his work in terms of the social system. But such awareness will not come spontaneously or inevitably. This is why the hegemonic role of a working class party is so rightly stressed by Perry Anderson.[33]

In fact, Gorz appears to have changed his position considerably since the publication in 1964 of the work we have cited. In a 1971 article on technicians, he no longer sees the conflict between the ends of technical work and those of the capitalist enterprise as an important source of radicalization.[34] Quite to the contrary, he accepts Habermas's view that technology plays an ideological role in legitimating the division between mental and manual labor, thanks to which control and hierarchy are maintained at the workplace. It is the function of at least some technicians to organize this division of labor, and the radicalization of these can only occur, says Gorz, if they themselves can challenge their roles in the division of labor. Furthermore, insofar as all technicians perform mental work, it can be argued that they and all white collar workers have a stake in the existing division of labor.

This view is very similar to that of Dina and the Olivetti Manifesto group.[35] It suggests that the political behavior of technicians will be ambiguous, a hypothesis discussed in the following section.

The political role of the new working class

It is time to return to the question posed by Mallet in his introduction to the second edition of *The New Working Class:* Is the new working class revolutionary?

The question is deceptively simple. In its turn it raises another question: What is meant by "revolutionary"? Faced with a gradually metamorphosing capitalist society already described by various authors as "postcapitalist" or "postindustrial," some theorists of the new left have sought to move away from the concept of revolution as cataclysm, based on the examples of the French and Russian revolutions. Essential to this new position, advocated by Gorz and Mallet among others, is the idea that the transition from capitalism to socialism will be a gradual one. Socialism is to grow within the slowly dissolving capsule of capitalist society. Bourgeois democracy is accepted as a starting point from which to move toward a more fundamental democratization.

André Gorz has stated the strategy accompanying this analysis:

Is it possible *from within* – that is to say, without having previously destroyed capitalism – to impose anti-capitalist solutions which will not be immediately incorporated into and subordinated to the system? This is the old question of "reform or revolution." This was (or is) a paramount question when the movement had (or has) the choice between a struggle for reforms and armed insurrection. Such is no longer the case in Western Europe. . . . The question here revolves around the possibility of "revolutionary reforms," that is to say, of reforms which advance toward a radical transformation of society. . . .

[A revolutionary reform] is one which is conceived not in terms of what is possible within the framework of a given system and administration, but in view of what should be made possible in terms of human needs and demands. . . . It bases the possibility of attaining its objective on the implementation of fundamental political and economic changes.[36]

The revolutionary reform must be implemented or controlled by those who demand it. It leads to the restriction of the power of the state or of capital and the extension of popular power.

The new working class demand for more control at the workplace is revolutionary in this sense. The ultimate end of this movement is complete workers' control. The issue is whether it will attain this ultimate end or whether it will expend itself short of these goals.

The same question might have been asked by a hypothetical sociologist analyzing the role of craftsmen in the labor movement of a century ago. Mallet explicitly recognizes the parallels between craft unionism and the new working class unionism. Their common characteristics are

a high level of participation in union activities, debureaucratization through a renewal of the union at the shop level, and an orientation toward control [over the job situation]. There is also another common characteristic: the mistrust of traditional politics, and the trust in union action instead. People have spoken about the rebirth of a modern anarchosyndicalism. . . .[37]

Having drawn this parallel, Mallet proceeds to explain why the unionism of the new working class, unlike craft unionism, must inevitably become political. The parallel to craft unionism is apt, but the sleight of hand at the end is unworthy of the argument as a whole.

Rejection of this deterministic view does not imply acceptance of the extreme empiricist criticism of the new working class thesis summarized by Reynaud (see Chapter 1, *The new working class thesis*).[38] Reynaud argues that the variations between new working class groups in different jobs and in firms with different personnel policies are more pronounced than their commonality. In answer, we note, first, that Reynaud's definition of the new working class is much broader than that of Mallet, including engineers and *cadres* as well as all kinds of technicians; and, second, that studies of different groups of skilled, semiskilled, or any other kind of worker inevitably find a considerable range of variation. In fact, the agreement among the various studies of the new working class, extending even across national boundaries, is striking to this author, and provides strong evidence for the importance of the job as a determinant of attitudes and behaviors. There is no reason to assume, as Reynaud does, that an interpretation in terms of the strategies of particular groups within organizations is incompatible with an interpretation in terms of class struggle. Nor need we assume, as Reynaud does, that upward mobility aspirations are incompatible with class consciousness.

What about the argument of Gorz and others that the technicians' position in the division of labor makes them unreceptive to a truly class conscious appeal? Gorz's own article is highly contradictory in its statements about the political role of technicians. Although he begins by arguing that their behavior is ambiguous at best, by the end he concludes that as a result of the rapidly proceeding automation of production they are fast becoming a part, although not the vanguard, of the revolutionary proletariat.

Some technicians do play a role in the division of labor that limits their solidarity with the working class. Those whose jobs consist of removing the intellectual component from a task (for example, the technicians who design an assembly-line process) fall into this category. But those who fill the subordinate jobs in plants employing primarily very highly trained workers do not benefit in any obvious way from the division of labor. Not only are their jobs without authority over others, but they often contain a manual component such as assembling and/or testing a piece of equipment. The analogy with craft work seems apt here. And, indeed, our data show that the technicians seek if anything to deny the importance of the manual–nonmanual division.

Pursuing the parallel between craft unionism and new working class unionism further, we can begin to look at how the role of the new working class on the political stage will vary from country to country according to its own social origins, its goals, and the setting in which it finds itself. In some countries, technicians may join together with young semiskilled workers, students, and other marginal groups in a mass-based socialist party to demand structural reforms that will fundamentally alter the nature of capitalism. Italy and France present the most immediate possibilities for such an alliance. In other countries, such as the United States, the legacy of past history makes the task of welding together a "historical bloc" of this kind more difficult.

In an interesting article, Perry Anderson has applied a set of concepts developed by Gramsci to the analysis of how such a historical bloc might be built in England. He correctly lays great stress, as did Gramsci and as does Gorz, on values and ideology:

In Western Europe today, any true socialist party must present itself unambiguously as a hegemonic force. That is to say, it must propose a coherent, global alternative to the existing order, and represent a permanent drive towards it. . . . The battle for the working class can, as we have seen, only be won on the plane of ideology.[39]

The historical bloc led by the party of the working class is not a coalition in the usual sense of the term. Its program is not based on the lowest common denominator uniting the various groups, but rather on an alternative vision of society. This vision is superordinate to the specific interests of particular groups within the bloc.[40]

Some of the latent interests of the new working class may be narrowly self-interested. The role of a socialist party would be to nurture and express those demands that are in accordance with the aims of the bloc as a universal force in society.

It is possible to recognize that there is much that is new and even revolutionary in the technicians' struggles without claiming that the new working class is in some sense privileged as the vanguard of a revolutionary socialist movement. Craftsmen contributed cadres, organization, and ideology to the labor movement. Yet in many ways they were in effect a moderating influence on the more radical and more politicized unskilled and semiskilled laborers.[41] Similarly, the new working class may contribute cadres, objectives, and ideology to a socialist movement. The ambivalence inherent in their intermediate position may be submerged by the hegemony of a class conscious organization. Their expressions of solidarity with the blue collar working class cited a few pages earlier illustrate this point. Their ambivalence nonetheless remains a factor to be reckoned with.

In short, groups in society play different roles in the movement for the transformation of that society. Workers who are worse off are likely to be more violent in their opposition to the status quo, but they lack the organizational resources and the ideological creativity of the slightly more privileged groups.

Under ordinary circumstances, these counterbalancing characteristics prevent the broad development of revolutionary class consciousness.[42] This contradiction is implicit in Marx's idea of alienation. Those workers who have the strongest interest in revolution are the most alienated and the least able to act. Those who are more autonomous in their work are less alienated and more capable of action, but they have interest only in fairly limited changes.

The innovative militancy of the Italian labor movement since 1968 may be explained partly by the conjunction of a number of changes in the society in the previous years: the rapid growth of manufacturing in the North and the concomitant immigration from rural areas of the South to the industrial cities of the North; and the increase in the student population and in the number of technicians in the advanced sectors of industry. The spread of values particular to the postindustrial society thus coincided with the large influx of young immigrants into semiskilled jobs. In Britain or the United States, these changes were separated by at least a generation. Their overlap proved to be an explosive situation.

It remains to be seen whether the unions and parties of the Italian left will be able to fuse these disparate groups together into a historical bloc. Because structural change in Italian society would of necessity be a gradual and democratic process, the unity of the bloc would have to be strong enough to withstand the setbacks and the turmoil accompanying such change. The example of Chile can hardly make one optimistic. Ironically, Gramsci, a Marxist, may have overestimated the power of ideas and underestimated that of narrow economic self-interest. However, the fragility and interdependence of the world economy is today so apparent that it would be foolhardy to predict the continuing stability of the status quo.

Alain Touraine has gone beyond the stress on ideology and organization as the binding cement holding together the diverse sources of protest in postindustrial societies to point out the emergence of new, structurally determined, lines of cleavage. The fundamental conflict in postindustrial society, he says, is not that between labor and capital, but rather that between the technocratic centers of economic and political power, interested in economic growth above all else, and those who are manipulated into a "dependent participation," a pseudoparticipation, in the system:

The principal opposition between the two great classes or groups of classes does not result from the fact that one possesses wealth or property and the other does not. It comes about because the dominant classes dispose of knowledge and control information. . . . The one who controls exerts influence on the systems of social relations in the name of their needs; the one who is controlled constantly affirms his existence. . . as an autonomous unit whose personality does not coincide with any of his roles. This is the reason – in our eyes justified – why the idea of *alienation* is so widespread. . . . What dominates our type of society is not the internal contradictions of the various social systems but the contradictions between the needs of these social systems and the needs of individuals. . . .

In modern societies, a class movement manifests itself by direct political struggle and by the rejection of alienation: by revolt against a system of integration and manipulation. What is essential is the greater emphasis on political and cultural, rather than economic, action. This is the great difference from the labor movement, formed in opposition to liberal capitalism. Such movements are scarcely beginning, but they always talk about power rather than about salaries, employment, or property. . . . The principal objective of modern social movements is more the control of change than the struggle against profit.[43]

In his rejection of the classical Marxist contention that the labor movement is still the primary driving force toward the basic transformation of society, Touraine shares common ground with pluralist authors such as Dahrendorf. His position is different in that he continues to see an objective unifying element in the protests of the postindustrial society. He has merely substituted "relationship to the means of decision and control" for "relationship to the means of production."

Although Touraine sees the labor movement losing its primary role in the struggle as decision centers move out of the firm to the level of the state, the role of the new working class is pivotal in his theory. It is among this group, at the heart of the organizations of production and economic decision making, that the contradiction between organizational interests and personal autonomy is most directly manifested.[44] Touraine, like Mallet, draws on the analogy between skilled workers and the new working class. Both groups, "in their opposition to those who hold power, use the instruments of production which their opponents claim to control."[45]

Touraine also stresses, as we have, the need for the creation of a historical bloc that will overcome the narrowly self-interested tendencies of the various groups, joining them together in the drive toward a more participatory society:

In the nineteenth century, massive movements dedicated to social change were formed by the combination of the craftsmen's resistance with the realization of exploitation on the part of certain categories of unskilled workers. Likewise, one can predict that, today and tomorrow, these opposition elites [technicians and students] must form the avant-garde of new movements for social change by mobilizing those communities which are in a state of decline: older workers who are victims of change and the "users" of hospitals, housing projects, and mass transportation.[46]

We have quoted Touraine at such length because his analysis is supported at many points by our own findings. Old distinctions such as that between manual and nonmanual work are breaking down, and new distinctions based on power differences are becoming more salient. The emergent importance of power differences is apparent among the technicians interviewed here, both from the prominence of class imagery including a power elite and from the importance of problems of power and control at the level of the job.

There is a tendency in postindustrial societies toward the raising of the lower levels of income and education. This tendency increases the capacity and desire of people at these levels to participate, and makes extreme differences in power, even if presumably meritocratically determined, more and more difficult to legitimate.

An open question is whether it will be possible to unify the conflicts of the postindustrial society so that the gains of privileged groups such as the new working class are shared by the marginal groups.[47] Ideology, organization, and leadership will be important in determining the outcome. Finally, this question will be answered by the socialist movement.

Appendix A: The attitude scales

Attitudes toward task and organization

Two scales were constructed to measure attitudes toward the task and the organization (see Chapter 4). They are based on the factor analysis mentioned on page 74. It includes all items on attitudes toward the task and the organization. Table A.1 gives the principal components factor loadings and the rotated factor loadings (Varimax rotation). The two factors account for 39.5 percent of the variance of the rotated factors. They were used to create the scales on attitudes toward the task (work discontent or WKDISC) and attitudes toward the organization (discontent with the organization or ORGDISC), respectively.

The items for the scales were chosen by considering their loadings on the factors, the item-to-item correlations, and the content of the items. The scales were constructed by standardizing each item, weighting it by its rotated factor loading, and taking the mean of all the items in the scale. (The weighted items do not give very different results from the unweighted items. However, given the availability of the weights, it was decided to use these for the slight addition in precision.)

Table A.2 shows the item-to-item and item-to-scale correlations for the WKDISC scale. The average item-to-item correlation is .41.

Table A.3 shows the same information for the ORGDISC scale. The average item-to-item correlation is .28. This is not as high as might be desired, as it lowers the correlations between the scale and other variables. However, in the absence of any good reason for excluding one or the other items, it was decided to include all of them in the scale.

Strike participation

The factor analysis presented in Table A.4 was used to construct the strike participation scale discussed on page 179. The first factor explains 36.2 percent of the variance. The next factor is not interpretable. Loadings on the first factor were one of the criteria used in choosing

Table A.1. *Factor analysis of items concerning attitudes toward the task and the organization.*

Variable description	Item no.	Principal components factor loadings					Communality
		1	2	3	4	5	
Is work interesting	1.11	-0.754	0.203	-0.051	0.056	0.058	0.619
Possibility for learning on job	1.12	-0.665	0.329	-0.225	-0.171	0.150	0.653
Increase in knowledge required	1.20	-0.549	0.280	-0.334	0.331	-0.147	0.622
Is your knowledge utilized	1.21	0.526	-0.473	-0.168	0.011	-0.056	0.532
Orders changed without explanation	2.3(a)	0.419	0.490	-0.286	-0.111	0.286	0.592
Do things without knowing why	2.3(b)	0.586	0.156	-0.307	0.000	0.282	0.541
Is work repetitive	2.6	0.702	-0.329	0.034	0.018	-0.214	0.648
More collaboration useful	1.16	0.345	0.391	0.220	0.595	-0.239	0.732
Reaction to organizational problems	2.1	-0.113	-0.430	0.086	0.457	0.681	0.877
No contacts is problem	2.4	0.456	0.306	-0.352	0.505	0.084	0.687
Work group does good job	2.5	-0.471	-0.504	0.292	0.310	0.077	0.663
Should employees have more say	2.12	0.074	0.481	0.688	0.202	-0.039	0.753
Your advice unsought	2.13	0.335	0.333	0.518	-0.343	0.351	0.732
Latent roots		3.279	1.854	1.376	1.227	0.916	8.651
% of variance explained		25.2	14.3	10.6	9.4	7.0	66.5

Variable description	Item no.	Rotated factor loadings (varimax)		
		1	2	Communality
Is work interesting	1.11	−0.748	−0.223	0.610
Possibility for learning on job	1.12	−0.739	−0.069	0.550
Increase in knowledge required	1.20	−0.614	−0.050	0.380
Is your knowledge utilized	1.21	0.696	−0.126	0.501
Orders changed without explanation	2.3(a)	0.099	0.638	0.416
Do things without knowing why	2.3(b)	0.416	0.441	0.367
Is work repetitive	2.6	0.770	0.089	0.601
More collaboration useful	1.16	0.088	0.514	0.272
Reaction to organizational problems	2.1	0.130	−0.425	0.197
No contacts is problem	2.4	0.227	0.500	0.302
Work group does good job	2.5	−0.136	−0.677	0.476
Should employees have more say	2.12	−0.190	0.448	0.237
Your advice unsought	2.13	0.110	0.459	0.223
Sum of squares		2.886	2.247	5.133
% of variance explained		22.2	17.3	39.5

Table A.2. *Item-to-item and item-to-scale correlations for work discontent (WKDISC) scale.*

Variable description	Item no.	Correlation coefficients					
		1.11	1.12	1.20	1.21	2.6	WKDISC scale
Is work interesting	1.11	1.000	0.506***	0.358***	0.295**	0.610***	0.772***
Possibility for learning on job	1.12	0.506***	1.000	0.397***	0.358***	0.500***	0.763***
Increase in knowledge required	1.20	0.358***	0.397***	1.000	0.326**	0.323***	0.633***
Is knowledge utilized	1.21	0.295**	0.358***	0.326**	1.000	0.465***	0.666***
Is work repetitive	2.6	0.610***	0.500***	0.323***	0.465***	1.000	0.813***
WKDISC scale	—	0.772***	0.763***	0.633***	0.666***	0.813***	1.000

Variable description	Item no.	No. of units					
		1.11	1.12	1.20	1.21	2.6	WKDISC scale
Is work interesting	1.11	88	87	88	87	86	88
Possibility for learning on job	1.12	87	87	87	86	86	87
Increase in knowledge required	1.20	88	87	88	87	86	88
Is knowledge utilized	1.21	87	86	87	87	85	87
Is work repetitive	2.6	86	86	86	85	86	86
WKDISC scale	—	88	87	88	87	86	88

** Significant at the .01 level.
*** Significant at the .001 level.

Table A.3. Item-to-item and item-to-scale correlations for scale on discontent with the organization (ORGDISC).

Correlation coefficients

Variable description	Item no.	2.3(a)	1.16	2.4	2.5	2.3(b)	ORGDISC scale
Orders changed without explanation	2.3(a)	1.000	0.185	0.279*	0.418***	0.279**	0.715***
More collaboration useful	1.16	0.185	1.000	0.344**	0.123	0.181	0.534***
No contacts is problem	2.4	0.279*	0.344**	1.000	0.294*	0.369**	0.658***
Work group does a good job	2.5	0.418***	0.123	0.294*	1.000	0.358***	0.725***
Do things without knowing why	2.3(b)	0.279**	0.181	0.369**	0.358***	1.000	0.624***
ORGDISC scale	—	0.715***	0.534***	0.658***	0.725***	0.624***	1.000

No. of units

Variable description	Item no.	2.3(a)	1.16	2.4	2.5	2.3(b)	ORGDISC scale
Orders changed without explanation	2.3(a)	88	82	74	84	88	88
More collaboration useful	1.16	82	82	70	78	82	82
No contacts is problem	2.4	74	70	74	70	74	74
Work group does a good job	2.5	84	78	70	84	84	84
Do things without knowing why	2.3(b)	88	82	74	84	88	88
ORGDISC scale	—	88	82	74	84	88	88

*Significant at the .05 level.
**Significant at the .01 level.
***Significant at the .001 level.

Table A.4. *Factor analysis of items regarding political position and participation in various kinds of strikes.*

Variable description	Item no.	Principal components factor loadings					Communality
		1	2	3	4	5	
Opposing interests	4.1	0.272	0.531	0.348	-0.391	-0.203	0.672
Follows Works Council activities	5.7	0.492	-0.327	0.274	-0.104	0.391	0.588
Favors abolition of lowest grades	5.9	0.620	-0.181	-0.232	0.194	-0.136	0.527
Favors abolition of overtime	5.10	0.349	0.202	-0.007	0.284	-0.746	0.800
Struck in last struggle	6.1	0.690	0.171	-0.281	0.274	0.134	0.678
Struck for housing	6.4(a)	0.745	0.229	-0.101	-0.030	0.075	0.624
Favors union political ties	6.7	0.606	-0.088	0.314	-0.475	-0.220	0.747
Interested in politics	6.9	0.587	-0.221	0.502	0.404	-0.076	0.814
Talks about politics	6.11	0.544	0.078	0.532	0.310	0.155	0.706
Thinks strike is useful	5.5	0.793	0.101	-0.103	-0.045	0.035	0.653
Remembers demands	5.8	0.385	0.664	0.094	0.057	0.271	0.674
Do you strike?	5.11	0.756	0.135	-0.281	0.084	0.005	0.676
Strikes in political strikes	6.4(b)	0.740	-0.024	-0.092	-0.051	0.051	0.561
Favors union political action	6.5	0.577	-0.390	0.156	0.016	0.012	0.510
Favors unions' reform strikes	6.6	0.578	-0.147	-0.346	0.018	0.067	0.480
Union member	6.8	0.607	0.076	-0.158	-0.325	0.126	0.521
Political position	6.13	0.603	0.406	0.094	0.302	0.236	0.683
Latent roots		6.157	1.421	1.258	1.054	1.024	10.914
% of variance explained		36.2	8.4	7.4	6.2	6.0	64.2

Table A.5. *Item-to-item and item-to-scale correlations for strike participation scale (STRIKES).*

Correlation coefficients

Variable description	Item no.	6.1	5.5	5.11	5.9	6.4(a)	6.4(b)	STRIKES scale
Struck in last struggle	6.1	1.000	0.556***	0.567***	0.465***	0.532***	0.536***	0.775***
Thinks strike is useful	5.5	0.556***	1.000	0.641***	0.478***	0.611***	0.623***	0.827***
Do you strike?	5.11	0.567***	0.641***	1.000	0.442***	0.549***	0.765***	0.828***
Favors abolition of lowest grades	5.9	0.465***	0.478***	0.442***	1.000	0.423***	0.449***	0.699***
Struck for housing	6.4(a)	0.532***	0.611***	0.549***	0.423***	1.000	0.581***	0.780***
Strikes in political strikes	6.4(b)	0.536***	0.623***	0.765***	0.449***	0.581***	1.000	0.828***
Six-item strike scale	—	0.775***	0.827***	0.828***	0.699***	0.780***	0.828***	1.000

No. of units

Variable description	Item no.	6.1	5.5	5.11	5.9	6.4(a)	6.4(b)	STRIKES scale
Struck in last struggle	6.1	84	82	84	84	83	61	84
Thinks strike is useful	5.5	82	86	86	86	85	63	86
Do you strike?	5.11	84	86	88	88	87	64	88
Favors abolition of lowest grades	5.9	84	86	88	88	87	64	88
Struck for housing	6.4(a)	83	85	87	87	87	64	87
Strikes in political strikes	6.4(b)	61	63	64	64	64	64	64
Six-item strike scale	—	84	86	88	88	87	64	88

***Significant at the .001 level.

247

items for the scale. Again, item-to-item correlations and the meaning of the item were also taken into consideration.

Because the items used loaded fairly equally on the first factor, weights were not attached to the items in computing scale scores. Each item was standardized. The mean of the standardized items gives the individual's scale score.

Table A.5 shows the item-to-item and item-to-scale correlations for the strike participation scale. The average item-to-item correlation is .55.

Note that, because of the arbitrary coding of many items, the signs of the correlation coefficients are not meaningful.

Appendix B: Correlation matrix for strike participation regressions

The correlation matrix (Table B.1) on the following page includes all variables used in the regressions described in Chapter 6. Once again, we note that because of the arbitrary coding of many items, the signs of the coefficients are not meaningful.

Table B.1. *Correlation matrix for strike participation regressions.*

Variable description	Item no.	6.13	3.1	1.16	7.12	2.11	7.14	3.2	Category	1.5,1.6	1.1
Political position	6.13	1.000	0.141	0.126	-0.089	0.355	-0.276	0.079	0.147	0.056	-0.127
Would like become boss	3.1	0.141	1.000	0.249	-0.153	0.302	-0.201	0.259	0.298	-0.177	-0.248
More collaboration useful	1.16	0.126	0.249	1.000	-0.095	0.118	-0.142	0.037	0.034	-0.049	-0.185
Where grew up: Milan/elsewhere	7.12	-0.089	-0.153	-0.095	1.000	0.010	-0.076	-0.019	-0.097	-0.067	0.395
Favors merit raises	2.11	0.355	0.302	0.118	0.010	1.000	-0.161	0.216	0.211	-0.325	0.014
Sum of grandfathers' occupations	7.14	-0.276	-0.201	-0.142	-0.076	-0.161	1.000	-0.043	-0.022	0.111	0.084
Important to improve position	3.2	0.079	0.259	0.037	-0.019	0.216	-0.043	1.000	0.060	-0.117	-0.012
Category	—	0.147	0.298	0.034	-0.097	0.211	-0.022	0.060	1.000	-0.277	-0.400
Family status	1.5,1.6	0.056	-0.177	-0.049	-0.067	-0.325	0.111	-0.117	-0.277	1.000	-0.060
Level of schooling	1.1	-0.127	-0.248	-0.185	-0.095	0.014	0.084	-0.012	-0.400	-0.060	1.000
Pay now	4.10	-0.001	-0.355	-0.173	-0.087	-0.361	0.106	-0.124	-0.700	0.539	0.195
How often sees friends	6.22(b)	-0.071	-0.298	0.064	0.102	-0.211	0.115	-0.012	-0.175	0.400	0.045
Father's occupation	7.13	-0.085	-0.044	0.007	-0.072	-0.010	0.473	0.121	0.025	0.018	0.166
How to get ahead	4.13	0.319	0.258	0.103	-0.117	0.470	-0.285	0.080	0.251	-0.341	-0.011
Pay important and unfair	1.9,4.10,4.12	-0.102	-0.200	-0.264	0.042	-0.072	0.153	0.178	0.012	-0.181	0.090
Union member	6.8	-0.386	-0.121	-0.411	0.303	0.005	0.154	-0.115	-0.164	-0.122	0.332
Six-item strike scale	—	-0.541	-0.488	-0.403	0.320	-0.467	0.346	-0.292	-0.307	0.213	0.285

Variable description	Item no.	4.10	6.22(b)	7.13	4.13	1,9,4.10, 4.12	6.8	STRIKES scale
Political position	6.13	-0.001	-0.071	-0.085	0.319	-0.102	-0.386	-0.541
Would like become boss	3.1	-0.355	-0.298	-0.044	0.258	-0.200	-0.121	-0.488
More collaboration useful	1.16	-0.173	0.064	0.007	0.103	-0.264	-0.411	-0.403
Where grew up: Milan/elsewhere	7.12	-0.087	0.102	-0.072	-0.117	0.042	0.303	0.320
Favors merit raises	2.11	-0.361	-0.211	-0.010	0.470	-0.072	0.005	-0.467
Sum of grandfathers' occupations	7.14	0.106	0.115	0.473	-0.285	0.153	0.154	0.346
Important to improve position	3.2	-0.124	-0.012	0.121	0.080	0.178	-0.115	-0.292
Category	–	-0.700	-0.175	0.025	0.251	0.012	-0.164	-0.307
Family status	1.5,1.6	0.539	0.400	0.018	-0.341	-0.181	-0.122	0.213
Level of schooling	1.1	0.195	0.045	0.166	-0.011	0.090	0.332	0.285
Pay now	4.10	1.000	0.168	0.055	-0.206	0.100	0.030	0.306
How often sees friends	6.22(b)	0.168	1.000	0.105	-0.205	0.093	-0.124	0.237
Father's occupation	7.13	0.055	0.105	1.000	-0.133	0.233	0.015	0.119
How to get ahead	4.13	-0.206	-0.205	-0.133	1.000	-0.065	-0.008	-0.412
Pay important and unfair	1,9,4.10,4.12	0.100	0.093	0.233	-0.065	1.000	0.162	0.292
Union member	6.8	0.030	-0.124	0.015	-0.008	0.162	1.000	0.493
Six-item strike scale	–	0.306	0.237	0.119	-0.412	0.292	0.493	1.000

Appendix C: The interview guide*

1.1 Let's begin with some biographical data. Are you a *perito* now? What type of school did you attend?

1.2 Was it a day school or a night school?

1.3 On the whole, did you have good marks or not?

1.4 Before starting (professional school, technical institute), did you ever think of going into a different line of work?

1.4a Are you going to school now?

1.5 Are you married?

1.6 [*If yes*] Do you have children?

1.7 Do you have any brothers?

1.8 [*If yes*] What kind of work do they do?

1.9 If you had to say what the most important characteristics of a job are, which would you choose as the most important? And the second most important?
(a) Interest and variety
(b) Good pay
(c) Good workmates
(d) A strong union
(e) Possibility of advancement

1.10 So far as (the first/second characteristic chosen) goes, would you say that your job is good? so-so? not very good?

1.11 Would you say that your job is interesting?
(a) It is very interesting.
(b) It is quite interesting.
(c) It is not very interesting.
(d) It is not at all interesting.

1.12 In the course of your work, do you have the opportunity of improving your professional knowledge?

*Translated from Italian.

252

1.13   [*If no*] Why not?

1.14   Exactly what do you do in your work?

1.15   Is it a job that you do relatively independently or does it require your collaboration with others?

1.16   Would it be useful for you to collaborate (more) with others?

1.17   What did you do in your first job?

1.18   And when you were hired here, what was your job?

1.19   How many years ago was this?

1.20   Would you say that your present job requires more knowledge than the job you had when you were first hired here?

1.21   Do you think that your job could be done by someone with less technical education than you have?

2.1   It sometimes happens that the organization of work is not very rational. This can cause difficulties for the worker. Which of the following formulas corresponds best to your situation?
(a) I don't encounter any particular difficulties in doing my work well.
(b) I encounter some difficulties, but I don't get annoyed by this.
(c) I encounter some difficulties, and I get quite annoyed about this.

2.2   [*If (b) or (c)*] What type of difficulty do you encounter?

2.3   Does it ever happen that you
(a) have too much work at some times and not enough at others?
(b) have to do something without knowing exactly what it's for?

2.4   In the execution of a project, every worker deals with a certain phase of the job. In the course of your work, do you have contacts with those who execute the preceding and succeeding phases? [*If no*] Do you miss not having these contacts?

2.5   On the whole, would you say that your work group manages to do its job
(a) very well?   (b) quite well?   (c) with difficulty?

2.6   Would you say that your work is repetitive, that is, that you encounter the same problems over and over, or would you say that the problems you must deal with change?

2.7   How long does it take you to (complete one cycle of your job)?

2.8   In situations such as yours, what is the boss for?

(a) He is needed to put his knowledge and experience at the service of the group.

(b) He is needed to make sure that people do their work.

(c) He is needed to take care of the administrative aspects of the group.

(d) He isn't really necessary at all.

2.9   Do you think he performs this function well?

2.10a Do you think he should follow his employees more closely?

2.10b Do you think he should give them more autonomy?

2.11   Some people say that the merit of each worker should be judged by his colleagues and that raises should be given according to this judgment rather than according to the judgment of the boss. What do you think of this idea?

2.12   Do you think that the employees should have more say in the decisions that are made in the company?

2.13   [*If yes*] Can you give me an example of a decision concerning you that was taken without consulting you?

2.14   If you could have more say in the determination of the general objectives of the firm, to which of the following objectives would you give priority?

(a) Contribute to the economic development of the country.

(b) Give the highest possible wages to the workers.

(c) Provide a significant professional experience to the workers.

(d) Maximize profits.

3.1   Would you like to become a supervisor even if this meant leaving a technical job for an administrative job?

3.2   Is it very important for you to improve your position in the company?

(a) Yes, it is very important.

(b) Yes, it is quite important.

(c) No, it is not very important.

(d) No, it is not at all important.

3.3   [*If it is not important*] What is it that you wouldn't like about a higher position?

(a) I don't want to do what I would have to do to get there.

(b) I wouldn't like to have so much responsibility.

(c) It would be too much work.

(d) I wouldn't want to leave my workmates.

(e) I wouldn't like to leave the technical work for administrative work.

3.4 Do you expect to be promoted soon?

3.5 How high up in this company do you think someone with your background can get?

3.6 Do you think you could find another job as good as your present one easily?

3.7 Have you ever thought of leaving?

3.8 Which of the following characteristics helps most in getting ahead in this company?

(a) Being good at one's work

(b) Knowing the right people

(c) Working hard

(d) Being lucky

(e) Being an apple-polisher

3.9 Do you think that the salary range in the company is

(a) too wide?

(b) about right?

(c) not wide enough?

3.10 Do you think the salary differences correspond to differences in merit?

3.11 Do you sometimes compare yourself with others in terms of professional capacity?

3.12 Do you talk to your workmates much? once in a while? almost never?

3.13 Are you good friends with any of your workmates?

3.14 [*If yes*] How many of them do you see outside work?

3.15 How would you judge the climate in your section so far as relations between workmates is concerned?

(a) Very competitive

(b) Quite competitive

(c) Of reciprocal indifference

(d) Quite cooperative

(e) Very cooperative

3.16 Which of the following alternatives best expresses your thought?

(a) The company does all it can for its employees.

      (b) The company does a certain amount for its employees.

      (c) The company does as little as possible for its employees.

4.1   Do you think workers and management have opposing interests or not?

4.2   If you could go back in time and choose again, would you still choose this type of work?

4.3   Are you satisfied with your salary?

4.4   [*If not*] Is this because you think the work you do is worth more money, or because you need more money?

4.5   Do you sometimes compare your salary with that of other individuals or groups?

4.6   [*If yes*] With whom?

4.7   [*If R mentions only people within the company*] And outside the company, do you make any comparisons between your own standard of living and that of others?

4.8   Do you think that among the groups listed here there are any that earn more than it would be fair for them to earn? Or any that earn less than would be fair?

	Earn too much	Earn about right	Earn too little
(a) Free professionals	————	————	————
(b) Dependent technicians	————	————	————
(c) Administrative employees	————	————	————
(d) Skilled workers	————	————	————
(e) Semiskilled workers	————	————	————

4.9   Could you tell me how much you used to earn two years ago?

4.10   And now, how much do you earn?

4.11   How much do you expect to earn five years from now?

4.12   How much do you think you ought to earn, considering the job you do now?

4.13   Do you think that anyone in Italy who is intelligent and willing to work can get ahead on his own, or do you think that one can only get ahead through connections?

4.14   One hears a lot these days about social classes. Do you think there are social classes in Italy?

4.15 How many classes would you say there are?

4.16 What would you call them?

4.17 What is it that puts someone in one class or another?

4.18 Where would you put yourself?

4.19 If you had to say middle or working class, which would you say?

4.20a Which group in Italian society do you think leads the most enviable life?

4.20b Which group in Italian society do you think is most open to criticism?

5.1 Here is a drawing of a ladder with ten rungs. If the top rung represents the highest social position in Italian society and the bottom rung represents the lowest position, where would you put yourself
(a) now?
(b) five years ago?
(c) five years from now?

5.2 Could you tell me if you think technicians are at the same level, or above, or below each of the following groups [on a ladder going from +5 to −5]?
(a) Engineers
(b) Administrative employees
(c) "The political class"
(d) The managerial class
(e) The proletariat
(f) The middle class

5.3 Do you think that inequality is inevitable?

5.4 Here are some things which one often hears said. Tell me if you think they are true or false.
(a) The pay of blue collar workers has gone up in recent years compared to that of white collar workers.
[*If yes*] What do you think of this?
(b) Marx was right when he said that blue and white collar workers are both employees with similar interests.

5.5 I'd like to go back to the situation in your company a minute to ask you a few questions on the unions' demands. First of all, do you think that the strike is a valid means for you to obtain improvements in your situation?

5.6   Do you think that the technicians would be better off with a category union that would defend their interests independently of those of semiskilled workers and administrative employees as happens in other countries?

5.7   Do you follow what the Works Council is doing?

5.8   In the last contract struggle, was there any particular demand that interested you especially?

5.9   In the last struggles, the unions made demands for the elimination of the lowest categories and equal raises for all, demands that would decrease the pay differentials in the company. Do you think it is fair to try to decrease these differences or do you think that it is unfair toward those who contribute more?

5.10 One of the demands in the platform for the last contract was the demand for a regulation of overtime. As you may know, the main reason for this request is that by diminishing or even abolishing overtime, the company is forced to hire more people, thus decreasing unemployment. But there are situations in which people need the money they earn through overtime. Do you think everyone should be allowed to do as much overtime as he wants to or not?

5.11 Did you ever strike?

6.1   [*If yes*] Did you strike for the last company contract? and for the reforms?

6.2   [*If R struck*] Why did you strike?
      (a) Because there were pickets
      (b) Because I agreed with the demands
      (c) For solidarity

6.3   [*If R did not strike*] Why didn't you strike?

6.4   Did you strike for the housing bill on April 7th?

6.5   Do you think it is right that the unions support political measures favoring the workers?

6.6   Do you approve of the unions' fight for the reforms?

6.7   [*If yes on No. 6.6.*] Do you think that the unions should have ties with political parties or not?

6.8   Were you ever a union member?
      [*If yes*] Which union were you a member of? When?

[*If R is no longer a member*] Why aren't you enrolled anymore?

6.9 Would you say that you are interested in politics?

6.10 [*If yes*] Do you ever watch *tribuna politica* on TV?

6.11 Do you talk about politics with your friends?
(a) Often
(b) Once in a while
(c) Rarely

6.12 Do they have the same political ideas as you have?

6.13 Which party do you usually feel closest to?

6.14 Would you say that you feel very close, quite close, or not very close to this party?

6.15 Are you a member of this party?

6.16 [*If yes*] How many hours a week do you dedicate, on the average, to party activities?

6.17 Was your father interested in politics?

6.18 Which party did he sympathize with?

6.19 Now I'd like to ask you a few questions about how you use your free time. First of all, could you tell me who are the people who live in your household?

6.20 Apart from those who live with you, who are the two people you see most frequently?

6.21 [*If they are relatives*] Do you see friends sometimes?

6.22a Let's take the two friends you see most often. Could you tell me what kind of work they do?

6.22b About how often do you see each other?

7.1 Do you belong to any sports, recreational, cultural, or political associations?

7.2 What do you do in your free time after work? To take an example, what did you do last night? Was this pretty typical?

7.3 Does overtime take much of your free time?

7.4 Do you ever happen to read any science or electronics magazines? [*If yes*] Which ones? How often do you buy them?

7.5 Do you have friends with whom you talk about electronics, or aren't they interested in such things?

7.6 Do you have time to read books?

[*If yes*] What kind of books do you read? [Get examples.]

7.7   Do you buy a newspaper sometimes? Which one? About how often do you buy it?

7.8   Now I'd like to ask you a few questions about consumption. For each of the items listed here, could you tell me whether or not you have it; if you don't have it, could you tell me if you'd like it; and whether you think it is something most people can afford or whether it is something only a few can afford.

	Own	Would like to buy	Luxury?
(a) Dishwasher	____	_____	_____
(b) Fur coat for your wife	____	_____	_____
(c) Washing machine	____	_____	_____
(d) Vacation abroad	____	_____	_____
(e) Car	____	_____	_____

7.9   If you could buy a car without considering the expense, what kind of car would you buy?

7.10 In what year were you born?

7.11 Where?

7.12 Where did you grow up?

7.13 What did your father do?

7.14 Do you remember what your grandfathers did?

7.15a Are you religious?

7.15b Do you go to church regularly?

Notes

Chapter 1. The debate on the new working class and the
evolution of the class structure

1 V. I. Lenin, *Imperialism: The Highest State of Capitalism* (New York: International Publishers, 1939), p. 107.
2 Karl Marx, *Economic and Philosophical Manuscripts,* in T. B. Bottomore, ed., *Karl Marx: Early Writings* (New York: McGraw-Hill, 1964), p. 78.
3 See also Karl Marx, *Capital,* Vol. I (New York: International Publishers, 1967), pp. 677, 715-16.
4 Daniel Bell in turn cites Goetz A. Briefs as the source of this quotation. See Bell, *The End of Ideology* (New York: Free Press, 1962), p. 277.
5 For discussions of this literature, see Richard F. Hamilton, *Class and Politics in the United States* (New York: Wiley 1972), Chapter X; *Affluence and the French Worker in the Fourth Republic* (Princeton: Princeton University Press, 1967), Chapter VII; and James W. Rinehart, "Affluence and the Embourgeoisement of the Working Class: A Critical Look," *Social Problems,* 19 (1971), 149-62.
6 Daniel Bell, "The Post-Industrial Society: The Evolution of an Idea," *Survey* 79 (1971), 111. See Marx, *Capital,* Vol. III, p. 299.
7 Marx, *The Grundrisse,* translated and edited by David McLellan (New York: Harper & Row, 1971), p. 142.
8 Marx, *Capital,* Vol. III, p. 299.
9 See Michel Crozier, *The World of the Office Worker* (Chicago: University of Chicago Press, 1971), Chapter II, for a summary of Bernstein's position as well as some of the other positions discussed below.
10 Emil Lederer, "The Problem of the Modern Salaried Employee," mimeographed. (New York: Columbia University, Department of Social Science, 1937).
11 See particularly Emil Lederer and Jacob Marschak, "The Middle Class," mimeographed. (New York: Columbia University, Department of Social Science, 1937).
12 Gustav Schmoller, *Was verstehen wir unter dem Mittelstand* (Göttingen: Vanderhock and Ruprecht, 1897). For a summary see Roger Girod, *Etudes sociologiques sur les couches salariées* (Paris: Rivière, 1961).
13 Thorstein Veblen, *The Engineers and the Price System* (New York: Harcourt Brace Jovanovich, 1963).
14 Erich Fromm, Herbert Marcuse, and David Riesman are some of the more well-known authors who have written on this subject. Their works bridged the gap between the professional and lay audience.
15 Daniel Bell, "Labor in the Post-Industrial Society," *Dissent* (Winter, 1972), p. 171.
16 A. J. Jaffe and J. Froomkin, *Technology and Jobs* (New York: Praeger, 1968), p. 95.
17 G. B. Zorzoli, *La ricerca scientifica in Italia* (Milan: Franco Angeli, 1970), p. 25.
18 United States Department of Labor, Bureau of Labor Statistics, *Handbook of Labor Statistics, 1969* (Washington, D.C., 1970), Table 37, p. 80.

19 For 1951, see Istituto Centrale di Statistica, *Nono censimento generale della popolazione, Novembre, 1951* (Rome); for 1975, see Istituto Centrale di Statistica, *Annuario di statistiche del lavoro - 1976* (Rome), Table 6, p. 25.

20 See issues of Istituto Centrale di Statistica, *Annuario di statistiche del lavoro.* This is a percentage close to that of France or West Germany for the same measure. See ILO, *Yearbook of Labor Statistics, 1972* (Geneva, 1972). Table 2, pp. 150-277.

21 Marzio Barbagli, *Disoccupazione intellettuale e sistema scolastico in Italia* (Bologna: Il Mulino, 1974).

22 White collar and managerial personnel constituted 6.2% of the total employed in industry in 1951 and 11.2% in 1973. The comparable figures for "other activities" are 28.6% and 37.1%. Sources: for 1951, Istituto Centrale di Statistica, *Nono censimento generale della popolazione, Novembre, 1951* (Rome); for 1973, Istituto Centrale di Statistica, *Annuario di statistiche del lavoro - 1973* (Rome), p. 53.

23 The three industries with the highest percentages of white collar workers (chemicals, petroleum and coal derivatives, electrical and electronic machinery) are also the most advanced technologically. It is reasonable to conclude that a high percentage of white collar workers indicates a high percentage of technicians and other scientific workers.

24 Istituto Centrale di Statistica, *Quarto censimento generale dell'industria e del commercio, 16 Ottobre, 1961.*

25 These percentages are computed from data from Istituto Centrale di Statistica, *Quarto censimento generale dell'industria e del commercio, 16 Ottobre, 1961.*

26 Figures from issues of Istituto Centrale di Statistica, *Annuario di statistiche del lavoro* for the years 1959-73.

27 I do not propose to review the extensive literature on automation here. Two good annotated bibliographies are Philip Sadler, *Social Research on Automation* (London: Heinemann, 1968) and Irene Taviss and William Gerber, *Technology and Work* (Cambridge, Mass.: Harvard University, Program on Technology and Society, 1969).

28 Robert Blauner, *Alienation and Freedom* (Chicago: University of Chicago Press, 1964); Pierre Naville, "Divisione del lavoro e ripartizione dei compiti," in Georges Friedmann and Pierre Naville, *Trattato di sociologia del lavoro*, Vol. 1, (Milan: Edizioni di Comunità, 1963); Herbert A. Simon, *The Shape of Automation for Men and Management* (New York: Harper & Row, 1965); Alain Touraine, "L'organizzazione professionale dell'impresa," in Friedmann and Naville, *Trattato*, Vol. 1; James C. Taylor, *Technology and Planned Organizational Change* (Ann Arbor, University of Michigan, Institute for Social Research, 1971).

29 Ida Hoos, *Automation in the Office* (Washington, D.C.: Public Affairs Press, 1961); Friedrich Pollock, *Automation* (Frankfurt: Europäische Verlagsanstalt, 1964); Paul Blumberg, *Industrial Democracy* (London: Constable, 1968); James R. Bright, *Automation and Management* (Boston: Harvard Graduate School of Business Administration, 1958).

30 Thomas Whisler, *The Impact of Computers on Organizations* (New York: Praeger, 1970).

31 William A. Faunce, *The Problems of an Industrial Society* (New York: McGraw-Hill, 1968); Touraine, "L'organizzazione professionale dell'impresa"; Blauner, *Alienation and Freedom;* Hans Paul Bahrdt, *Industriebürokratie: Versuch einer Soziologie des industrialisierten Bürobetriebes und seiner Angestellten* (Stuttgart: Enke, 1958).

32 Bahrdt, *Industriebürokratie;* Faunce, *Problems of an Industrial Society.*

33 Ibid.

34 Touraine, "L'organizzazione professionale dell'impresa."

35 Warren G. Bennis, "Beyond Bureaucracy," in W. G. Bennis, ed., *American Bureaucracy* (Chicago: Aldine, 1970). See also G. Bennis and Philip E. Slater, *The Temporary Society* (New York: Harper and Row, 1968).

36 John H. Goldthorpe, David Lockwood, Frank Bechhofer, and Jennifer Platt, *The Affluent Worker in the Class Structure* (Cambridge: Cambridge University Press, 1969); FIM-FIOM, "Proposte di iniziative rivendicative per i tecnici e gli impiegati," Seminario Nazionale Unitario, 20-24 Aprile, 1970 (Ariccia).

37 Serge Mallet, *La nouvelle classe ouvrière* (Paris: Editions du Seuil, 1963); Blauner, *Alienation and Freedom*; John Kenneth Galbraith, *The New Industrial State* (Boston: Houghton Mifflin, 1967); Bell, "Labor in the Post-Industrial Society."

38 Goldthorpe, Lockwood, et al., *The Affluent Worker in the Class Structure.*

39 For the United States, see, for example, Kurt Mayer, "The Changing Shape of the American Class Structure," *Social Research*, 30 (1963), 458–68; for the United Kingdom, see David Lockwood, *The Blackcoated Worker* (London: Allen and Unwin, 1958); for a discussion of the French case, which is less clear, see Hamilton, *Affluence and the French Worker.*

40 Ente Nazionale Idrocarburi and Istituto per la Ricostruzione Industriale, "Risultati dell'indagine sulle retribuzioni di fatto: 1970," mimeographed, no date.

41 However, as a number of authors have pointed out, large differences in consumption persist and even outwardly similar patterns may be variously motivated [see Alessandro Pizzorno, "The Individualistic Mobilization of Europe," *Daedalus* 93 (1964), 199–224; Gerald Handel and Lee Rainwater, "Persistence and Change in Working Class Life Styles," in Arthur Shostak and William Gomberg, eds., *Blue Collar Worlds* (Englewood Cliffs, N.J.: Prentice-Hall, 1964); Goldthorpe, Lockwood, et al., *The Affluent Worker in the Class Structure*].

42 Figures on school enrollment have already been presented. As to urbanization, it will suffice to point out that between the 1951 census and the 1961 census the population of the city of Milan grew by 24.2% and the population of the city of Turin grew by 42.6%, while the population of the country as a whole grew by only 6.5%. Data from the present study also suggest that the blue collar–white collar status distinction is less important now than it once was.

43 A review of this literature may be found in Goldthorpe, Lockwood, et al., *The Affluent Worker in the Class Structure*, Chapter I; see also Hamilton, *Affluence and the French Worker.*

44 See Hamilton, *Affluence and the French Worker*; Bennett Berger, *Working Class Suburb* (Berkeley: University of California Press, 1960); Peter Willmott and Michael Young, *Family and Class in a London Suburb* (London: Routledge & Kegan Paul, 1960); Goldthorpe, Lockwood, et al., *The Affluent Worker in the Class Structure*; Handel and Rainwater, "Persistence and Change."

45 Goldthorpe, Lockwood, et al., *The Affluent Worker: Industrial Attitudes and Behavior* (Cambridge: Cambridge University Press, 1968a), *The Affluent Worker: Political Attitudes and Behavior* (Cambridge: Cambridge University Press, 1968b), *The Affluent Worker in the Class Structure.*

46 Lockwood, *The Blackcoated Worker,* and C. Wright Mills, *White Collar* (New York: Oxford University Press, 1951), describe a process of proletarianization, whereas Bahrdt, *Industriebürokratie,* and Crozier, *The World of the Office Worker,* are more optimistic.

47 Mallet, *La nouvelle classe ouvrière.*

48 Crozier, *The World of the Office Worker*; Nancy C. Morse, *Satisfactions in the White Collar Job* (Ann Arbor: University of Michigan, Institute for Social Research, 1953); Leonard Sayles, *The Behavior of Industrial Work Groups: Prediction and Control* (New York: Wiley, 1958).

49 Seymour Martin Lipset, *Union Democracy* (Glencoe, Ill.: The Free Press, 1956); Arnold Tannenbaum and Robert Kahn, *Participation in Union Locals* (Evanston, Ill.: Row, Peterson, 1958); Leonard Sayles and George Strauss, *The Local Union* (New York: Harper and Row, 1953); Lois R. Dean, "Social Integration Attitudes and Union Activity," *Industrial and Labor Relations Review*, 8 (1954), 48–58.

50 For a good summary of this literature, which does not, however, deal with political attitudes, see Victor H. Vroom, *Work and Motivation* (New York: Wiley, 1964).

51 Richard J. Hackman and Edward Lawler III, "Employee Reactions to Job Characteristics," *Journal of Applied Psychology*, Monograph 55 (1971), 259–86.

52 See Maurice Zeitlin, *Revolutionary Politics and the Cuban Working Class* (Princeton: Princeton University Press, 1967), Chapter IV, for a discussion of this problem.

53 Mallet, *La Nouvelle classe ouvrière;* André Gorz, *Strategy for Labor* (Boston: Beacon Press, 1967); S. Bologna and F. Ciafaloni, "I tecnici come produttori e come prodotto," *Quaderni piacentini* (March 1969), 52-72.

54 Serge Mallet, *La nuova classe operaia,* 2nd ed. (Turin: Einaudi, 1970), p. 23.

55 For a discussion of the views of Marcuse and Habermas, see Jürgen Habermas, "Technology and Science as 'Ideology,'" in Habermas, *Toward a Rational Society* (Boston: Beacon Press, 1970), pp. 81-122.

56 For a summary of some of these positions see Marcello Lelli, *Tecnici e lotta di classe* (Bari: De Donato, 1971), Chapter VIII.

57 However, Garaudy noted the rising skill levels of the working class as well as the proletarianization of white collar workers [see Roger Garaudy, *The Crisis in Communism: The Turning Point of Socialism* (New York: Grove Press, 1970)].

58 Mallet's vague and rather expansive usage of the term "new working class" has been followed by still vaguer and more expansive usage on the part of U.S. authors. As Aronowitz says, "When American writers deal with the new working class theory, they tend to equate the new working class with university-trained workers" [see Stanley Aronowitz, "Does the United States Have a New Working Class?" in G. Fischer, ed., *The Revival of Socialism in America* (New York: Oxford University Press, 1971), p. 197.] This is undoubtedly because technicians have not been as militant as other white collar workers in the United States.

59 André Gorz, "Techniques, techniciens, et lutte des classes," *Les temps modernes,* 301-2 (August-September 1971), 141-80. For similar positions, see Olivetti Workers, anonymous group, "La divisione del lavoro in fabbrica," *Il manifesto,* I (1969), pp. 28-37, and Angelo Dina, "Condizione del tecnico e condizione operaia in fabbrica: dall'oggettività alla scelta politica," *Classe,* 1 (1969), pp. 89-134.

60 Jean Daniel Reynaud, "Industrial Relations in France, 1960-1975: A Review," paper presented at the Harvard Conference on Industrial Relations, Cambridge, Mass., September 26-7, 1975, p. 6.

Chapter 2. The new working class in Italian society

1 For a summary of these two approaches, see Anthony Giddens, *The Class Structure of the Advanced Societies* (New York: Barnes and Noble, 1973).

2 Seymour Martin Lipset and Stein Rokkan, "Cleavage Structures, Party Systems, and Voter Alignments: An Introduction," in Lipset and Rokkan, eds., *Party Systems and Voter Alignments* (New York: Free Press, 1967), p. 38.

3 Ibid., p. 53.

4 I have relied primarily on the following sources concerning France in this discussion: Stephen S. Cohen, *Modern Capitalist Planning: The French Model* (Cambridge, Mass.: Harvard University Press, 1969); Mattei Dogan, "Political Cleavage and Social Stratification in France and Italy," in Lipset and Rokkan, eds., *Party Systems and Voter Alignments;* Reynaud, "Industrial Relations in France"; Philip M. Williams and Martin Harrison, *Politics and Society in De Gaulle's Republic* (London: Longman Group, 1971). See also Peter Gourevitch, "Reforming the Napoleonic State: The Creation of Regional Government in France and Italy," paper presented at the Ninth World Congress of the International Political Science Association, Montreal (August, 1973); Ezra N. Suleiman, *Politics, Power, and Bureaucracy in France* (Princeton: Princeton University Press, 1974); and current issues of *Sociologie du travail.* For an excellent summary of the differences between the Italian and French Communist Parties, see Sidney Tarrow, "Communism in Italy and France: Adaptation and Change," in

Donald L. M. Blackmer and Sidney Tarrow, eds., *Communism in Italy and France* (Princeton: Princeton University Press, 1975).

5 Another important reason for the choice of Italy was the author's attachment to a country where he had spent ten of his formative years.

6 Augusto Graziani, ed., *L'economia italiana: 1945-1970* (Bologna: Il Mulino, 1972), table 2, p. 370.

7 Mariano D'Antonio, *Sviluppo e crisi del capitalismo italiano, 1951-1972* (Bari: De Donato, 1973), table 2, p. 57.

8 Massimo Paci, *Mercato del lavoro e classi sociali* (Bologna: Il Mulino, 1973); David M. Gordon, *Theories of Poverty and Underemployment* (Lexington, Mass.: Heath, 1972).

9 Paci, *Mercato del lavoro e classi sociali*, p. 222.

10 Gordon, *Theories of Poverty;* Peter B. Doeringer and Michael J. Piore, *Internal Labor Markets and Manpower Analysis* (Lexington, Mass.: Heath, 1971).

11 This discussion follows Barbagli, *Disoccupazione intellettuale*, Chapter VIII.

12 For yearly figures on the numbers of graduates of various schools, see issues of Istituto Centrale di Statistica, *Annuario statistico dell'istruzione.*

13 Barbagli, *Disoccupazione intellettuale*, p. 354.

14 These points are supported by the very interesting research of Piergiorgio Corbetta, *Tecnici, disoccupazione e coscienza di classe* (Bologna: Il Mulino, 1975), which came to the author's attention as this manuscript was going to press (see Chapter 7, note 26, for a further exposition of his findings).

15 Barbagli, *Disoccupazione intellettuale*, pp. 342-51.

16 Peter R. Weitz, "Labor and Politics in a Divided Movement: The Italian Case," *Industrial and Labor Relations Review*, 28 (1975), 226-42.

17 Alessandro Pizzorno, "Resoconto sulla formazione delle ipotesi e sui primi risultati della ricerca," in Istituto per lo Studio della Società Contemporanea, *Rapporto sulla ricerca sull'evoluzione del potere sindacale*, mimeographed (1973).

18 D'Antonio, *Sviluppo e crisi.*

19 Our discussion relies primarily on D'Antonio, *Sviluppo e crisi.* See also Kevin Allen and Andrew Stevenson, *An Introduction to the Italian Economy* (New York: Harper and Row, 1975); Graziani, *L'economia italiana;* and Michele Salvati, *Il sistema economico italiano: analisi di una crisi* (Bologna: Il Mulino, 1975).

20 Graziani, *L'economia italiana*, table 9, p. 377.

21 For a summary, see ibid., part III.

22 Allen and Stevenson, *Italian Economy*, pp. 67-8; D'Antonio, *Sviluppo e crisi*, pp. 185-6.

23 Cited in D'Antonio, *Sviluppo e crisi*, pp. 172-4.

24 OECD, *Labour Force Statistics 1961-1972* (Paris: OECD, 1974).

25 See Giorgio Fuà. *Occupazione e capacità produttive: la realtà italiana* (Bologna: Il Mulino, 1976), and works cited therein.

26 Paolo Sylos-Labini, "Sviluppo economico e classi sociali in Italia," in Paolo Farneti, ed., *Il sistema politico italiano* (Bologna: Il Mulino, 1973); Saverio Caruso, *Burocrazia e capitale in Italia* (Verona: Bertani, 1974).

27 Suzanne Berger, "Uso politico e sopravvivenza dei ceti in declino," in Stephen R. Graubard and Fabio Luca Cavazza, eds., *Il caso italiano: Italia anni '70* (Milan: Garzanti, 1974).

28 Sylos-Labini, "Sviluppo economico e classi sociali in Italia"; Cohen, *Modern Capitalist Planning.*

29 Mallet, *La nouvelle classe ouvrière;* Claude Durand, "Ouvriers et techniciens en mai 1968," in Pierre Dubois et al., *Grèves revendicatives ou grèves politiques?* (Paris: Editions Anthropos, 1971); Renaud Dulong, "Les cadres et le mouvement ouvrier," in Dubois et al., *Grèves revendicatives ou grèves politiques?*

Chapter 3. Design, methods, and locales of the study

1 Pizzorno, "Resoconto sulla formazione delle ipotesi e sui primi risultati della ricerca"; Emilio Reyneri, "Caratteristiche e fattori dell'inizio del nuovo ciclo di conflittualità operaia," in Istituto per lo Studio della Società Contemporanea, Rapporto sulla ricerca sull'evoluzione del potere sindacale, mimeographed (1973).
2 For FIOM membership figures, see *Rassegna sindacale*, April 26, 1970.
3 The underestimation is by 11% for FIM and 19% for FIOM, accepting the union's figures as accurate.
4 For figures, see John Low-Beer, "The New Working Class in Italy," Ph.D. dissertation, Harvard University, Cambridge, Mass., 1974, p. 347.

Chapter 4. Life at work

1 This school, although similar to a three-year professional school, does not grant a publicly recognized degree.
2 Vroom, *Work and Motivation;* Edwin A. Locke, "The Nature and Consequences of Job Satisfaction," in Marvin D. Dunnette, ed., *Handbook of Industrial and Organizational Psychology* (Chicago: Rand McNally, 1973).
3 Crozier, *The World of the Office Worker*, table 1, p. 92.
4 The one exception is the only blue collar worker from this group in the sample.
5 Paul R. Lawrence and Jay W. Lorsch, *Organization and Environment* (Boston: Harvard University, Graduate School of Business Administration, 1967).
6 With modernization the externalization of control increasingly appears in other areas of society as well as in the factory. This is especially evident in the control of deviance.
7 Sayles, *Behavior of Industrial Work Groups.*
8 Given the differences in mobility aspirations among job groups, one would expect that there would also be differences among the groups in their perceptions of whether or not upward mobility is actually possible. However, the three items on this question do not show any such variation. If anything, the less career-oriented groups seem more optimistic about getting ahead, although the differences are slight. On the individual level, there are correlations between mobility aspirations and perceptions of career possibilities. Mobility aspirations are discussed further in Chapter 6 (see particularly pp. 189ff, 200, and note 15).
9 H. L. Wilensky, "Work, Careers, and Social Integration," *International Social Science Journal*, 12 (1960), 543-60.
10 Carole Pateman, *Participation and Democratic Theory* (Cambridge: Cambridge University Press, 1970).
11 Only 18% of the Siemens lab technicians felt that employees should have more say over decisions made in the company. No one in this group could cite an example of a decision on which he might have been consulted but had not been. The comparable percentages for the sample as a whole are 51% and 34%.
12 Fifty-eight percent of Special Systems Laboratory employees say that the company does as little as possible; the corresponding figure for GT&E is 60%.
13 The workers at GT&E (with the exception of those in the commercial offices) are much more likely to be union members than those in the Special Systems Laboratory. Forty-three percent of the GT&E sample is unionized. Taking into account that this is a largely white collar sample and that union membership is entirely voluntary, this percentage is quite high. In Siemens, only the draftsmen are slightly unionized. The differences between the two sites in union tradition and organization have been discussed in Chapter 3; some of the antecedents of union membership are discussed in Chapter 6. Here we would note that union

membership is significantly correlated with political beliefs and with place of origin. These factors, together with the level of discontent with the organization, explain the differences in unionization between the different jobs.

14 Fifty-two percent of the men in the Goldthorpe and Lockwood et al.'s manual sample do not belong to any formal associations; for nonmanual workers, the figure is 33%. See Goldthorpe, Lockwood, et al., *The Affluent Worker in the Class Structure*, p. 93.

15 Goldthorpe, Lockwood, et al., *The Affluent Worker: Industrial Attitudes;* Geoffrey K. Ingham, *Size of Industrial Organization and Worker Behavior* (Cambridge: Cambridge University Press, 1970); David Silverman, *The Theory of Organisations* (London: Heinemann, 1970).

16 Silverman, *Theory of Organisations*, pp. 208-10.

17 Ibid., p. 5.

18 For the cross-sectional study, see Melvin L. Kohn, *Class and Conformity* (Homewood, Ill.: Dorsey Press, 1969). Kohn reported on the findings of the longitudinal study at the 71st Annual Meeting of the American Sociological Association, New York, N.Y., September 2, 1976.

19 John H. Flavell, *The Developmental Psychology of Jean Piaget* (New York: Van Nostrand Reinhold, 1963), pp. 47-52.

Chapter 5. Life outside work and images of the class structure

1 From Charles Booth, *Life and Labour of the People of London*, cited in Lockwood, *The Blackcoated Worker*, p. 28.

2 Ralf Dahrendorf, *Class and Class Conflict in Industrial Society* (Stanford: Stanford University Press, 1959).

3 Among those who do not spend time with childhood friends, several have moved with their parents, whereas others never were part of this type of peer group.

4 It is true that only nine of the forty-three married couples never see relatives. Eight of these, we note, are not from the area. That leaves thirty-four couples who mention seeing relatives, but do not see relatives very frequently. Of the thirty-four, less than half (fifteen) make clear that they see relatives several times a week. Eleven see relatives no more than once a week and in some cases much less often. Eight respondents did not provide sufficient information to enable us to judge how often they see relatives.

5 Nine of the fifteen who rarely see friends also see relatives rarely or not at all. Among them there are, as noted earlier, five couples who see no one at all. Three of the fifteen see relatives, but how often they see them is unclear. Only three of the fifteen couples who rarely see friends mention that they see relatives a lot. Looking at these figures another way, nearly half (9/19) of those married men who do not see relatives or do not often see them also see friends rarely, whereas only one-fifth (3/15) of those who see relatives very frequently do not also see friends frequently.

6 Goldthorpe, Lockwood, et al., *The Affluent Worker in the Class Structure*, p. 93.

7 Looking at membership in specific kinds of organizations, some of the variables do seem to have an effect, but the number is too small to draw conclusions. Only for the case of union membership, the discussion of which we postpone to Chapter 6, can more be said.

8 Fifty-one percent of the sample have completed secondary school. Although 68% of this group mention seeing family and friends as their major leisure time activity, only 49% of the less educated mention this. Regarding electronics, however, there is evidence that the less educated are less interested: They read technical magazines less and talk less about electronics with their friends.

9 Robert Blauner, "Work Satisfaction and Industrial Trends in Modern Society," in S. M. Lipset and R. Bendix, eds., *Class, Status, and Power* (New York: Free Press, 1966), pp. 483-4.

10 David Lockwood, "Sources of Variation in Working Class Images of Society," in Joseph A. Kahl, ed., *Comparative Perspectives on Stratification* (Boston: Little Brown, 1968).
11 Ibid., p. 101.
12 Ibid., p. 104.
13 Ibid., p. 105.
14 Ibid., p. 107.
15 Ibid., p. 108.
16 Ibid., p. 114n.
17 Goldthorpe, Lockwood, et al., *The Affluent Worker in the Class Structure*, p. 181.
18 There seems to be a change in emphasis between Lockwood's earlier paper, first published in 1966, and Goldthorpe, Lockwood, et al.'s *The Affluent Worker in the Class Structure* (1969). Whereas Lockwood gives almost equal weight to the work situation and the community situation, the later book downplays the effect of the work situation while emphasizing more the community situation and the orientation the worker brings to this situation. The change in emphasis is related to what this author sees as the critical weakness in their research design. In choosing workers on the basis of their incomes rather than, say, on the basis of the kind of work they do, Goldthorpe, Lockwood, et al. obtained a sample that was attracted to those jobs because they paid well. These workers' orientations to their jobs are unusual in that not only are they earning relatively high wages, but they are particularly interested in wages per se.
19 Martin Bulmer, ed., *Working Class Images of Society* (London: Routledge & Kegan Paul, 1975).
20 Jim Cousins and Richard Brown, "Patterns of Paradox: Shipbuilding Workers' Images of Society," in Martin Bulmer, ed., *Working Class Images of Society*, pp. 79–80.
21 Goldthorpe, Lockwood, et al., *The Affluent Worker in the Class Structure*, p. 107.
22 Ibid.
23 These are, of course, the three dimensions of stratification first specified by Max Weber.
24 John H. Goldthorpe, "Images of Class Among Affluent Manual Workers," mimeographed (Cambridge: University of Cambridge, 1970), p. 12.
25 Goldthorpe, Lockwood, et al., *The Affluent Worker in the Class Structure*, Appendix C. One of Goldthorpe, Lockwood, et al.'s points was omitted. We did not ask respondents about the nature of ongoing changes in the class structure, primarily because of lack of time.
26 See Goldthorpe, Lockwood, et al., *The Affluent Worker in the Class Structure*, Chapter V, and Dahrendorf, *Class and Class Conflict*, Chapter VIII. One recent study of a "proletarian traditional" group seems to cast doubt upon the notion that the manual–nonmanual line is always of great importance to such workers. Cousins and Brown, "Patterns of Paradox," find that 8% of Tyneside shipbuilding workers *explicitly* include white collar employees in their large central class, and a further 12% *implicitly* include them. But the great majority of their sample simply do not mention the existence of a white collar middle class, seeing no major group between the "working class" and the elite. Whether or not their working class includes white collar employees cannot be ascertained from the data presented. It might be guessed that these workers, living in an environment with few white collar employees, omit them from their schemas or assimilate them to the elite. This is not equivalent to the explicit denial of the importance of the manual–nonmanual line found in our sample.
27 Goldthorpe, "Images of Class," 14n.
28 Seventy-one percent of type VI and type II respondents identify as working class, whereas only 31% of types I, IV, and V identify as working class.
29 Richard Centers, *The Psychology of Social Classes* (Princeton: Princeton University Press, 1949), table 20, p. 86.

30 Joseph Lopreato and Lawrence E. Hazelrigg, *Class, Conflict and, Mobility* (San Francisco: Chandler, 1972).

31 Ibid., Table VIII:9, pp. 202, 222.

32 This definition is a very narrow one: "two major classes, differentiated in terms of possession or non-possession of power and authority." Goldthorpe, "Images of Class," table 5.

33 It is not possible to derive a precisely comparable figure from the data presented.

34 Alfred Willener, *Images de la société et classes sociales* (Lausanne: Université de Lausanne, 1957); Goldthorpe, "Images of Class"; John L. Haer, "An Empirical Study of Social Class Awareness," *Social Forces*, 36 (1957), 117–21; Cousins and Brown, "Patterns of Paradox"; Peter Hiller, "Continuities and Variations in Everyday Conceptual Components of Class," *Sociology*, 9 (1975), 255–87.

35 These figures are adapted from Lopreato and Hazelrigg, *Class, Conflict, and Mobility*, Table VII:3, p. 167.

36 Ibid., Table VII:4, p. 355.

37 Willener's sample from French Switzerland is an exception in that the subjects seem to perceive a power elite about as frequently as the subjects in the Italian samples (see Willener, *Images*).

38 See, for example, Willener, *Images*, pp. 205–9; O. A. Oeser and S. B. Hammond, *Social Structure and Personality in a City* (New York: Macmillan, 1954), table 101, p. 273; Peter Hiller, "The Nature and Location of Everyday Conceptions of Class," *Sociology*, 9 (1975), table 4, p. 17.

39 Lopreato and Hazelrigg, *Class, Conflict, and Mobility*, Part II.

40 Goldthorpe, "Images of Class," Appendix, p. 2.

41 Lawrence Kohlberg, "Stage and Sequence: The Cognitive Developmental Approach to Socialization," in David A. Goslin, ed., *The Handbook of Socialization Theory and Research* (Chicago: Rand McNally, 1969).

42 Fifty-seven percent of those without class image and 50% of those with money models come from center/rightist families, as compared with 33% from such backgrounds in the sample as a whole. Only 17% of those with dichotomous images come from such families.

Chapter 6. Militancy, class consciousness, and the determinants of strike participation

1 Lopreato and Hazelrigg, *Class, Conflict, and Mobility*, p. 116.

2 For example, see John C. Leggett, *Class, Race, and Labor* (London: Oxford University Press, 1968). The distinction between class consciousness and class solidarity is also made by Lopreato and Hazelrigg, *Class, Conflict, and Mobility*.

3 Karl Marx, *Die Heilige Familie*, excerpts in T. B. Bottomore and Maximilien Rubel, eds., *Karl Marx: Selected Writings in Sociology and Social Philosophy* (New York: McGraw-Hill, 1964), p. 233.

4 The concept of "organic crisis" was developed by Antonio Gramsci. See Gramsci, *Selections from the Prison Notebooks*, edited and translated by Quentin Hoare and Geoffrey Nowell Smith (New York: International Publishers, 1971).

5 Richard Dawson and Kenneth Prewitt, *Political Socialization* (Boston: Little Brown, 1969), p. 111. It is true that research by Jennings and Niemi leads to some qualification of the statement about the strength of the associations. "The results of a whole set of analyses indicate that for high-school students at any rate, the student-'perceived parent' correlation is likely to overestimate the true student–parent correlation by about .1." See Richard G. Niemi, "Political Socialization," in Jeanne Knutson, ed., *Handbook of Political Psychology*

(San Francisco: Jossey-Bass, 1973), p. 127. However, the true correlation is still very high, $r = .47$, in the Jennings and Niemi study.

6 An alternative hypothesis is that the Milanese are, for historical reasons, more militant and more class conscious than the average for the country as a whole. Two points counsel rejection of this hypothesis. First of all, the fathers of the Milanese are slightly more likely to be centrist rather than leftist in their political orientations as compared to the fathers of those who grew up elsewhere: in other parts of the North, in the Center, or in the South (see *Political position*, this chapter, for definitions of left and center).

  Second, even in our sample the Milanese are not much more leftist than the sample mean. The Milanese differ from the rest of the sample only with respect to two characteristics: They are more likely to act on their convictions, both by joining a union and by striking, and they are more likely to have moved leftward relative to their fathers, or at least not to have moved rightward.

7 However, some of those who say they feel closest to the extraparliamentary groups probably vote for the PCI.

8 In fact, 28% of the leftists score in the lower half of the scale, and 11% score in the lowest quartile. Twenty-nine percent of the centrists score in the upper half of the scale, but all but one of them fall into the second quartile rather than the highest quartile.

9 The mean correlation among the three items on mobility (3.1, 3.2, and 1.9) is .260. The mean correlation between these three items and the item on solidarity with peers (2.11) is .261, and between these four and the strike participation scale is .441.

10 Because of the substantial overlap between these two items, the coefficient of the first one is not significant in this equation, although both coefficients are significant in the final equation.

11 For another example, see the quotation from the interview with Alicea in Chapter 4.

12 The correlations between pay, union category, and age, on the one hand, and desire to become a boss and desire not to have merit raises decided by peers, on the other hand, are .355, .298, .152 and −.361, −.211, −.275.

13 The question, "Do you think it would be useful to do more work in groups?" received three answers: "I already work in a group," "Yes, it would be useful," or, "No, I don't think it would be useful." There are three ways in which these categories might be grouped, linked with two different interpretations of the meaning of the question. One hypothesis is that the question is measuring solidaristic versus individualistic attitudes toward work. According to this interpretation, one would contrast those who say that it would be useful to work more in groups with those who say that it would not, putting those who say that they already do so in the middle or grouping them with those who say that they would like to do so. The other hypothesis is that the question is measuring a need to work in groups based on the kind of work the person does. The appropriate grouping would then be to contrast those who feel this need with those who do not, either because they already work in groups or because their work does not require a team effort. Grouping according to the second hypothesis yields higher correlations with almost all variables except those relating to solidarity with peers and aspirations for individual mobility. As these last correlations are very low anyhow, we are led to accept the second interpretation of the meaning of this item.

  There is also other evidence in support of the second hypothesis. Those who say that they already work in groups evince the least discontent with the organization, followed by those who say that it would not be helpful to do more groupwork. The most discontent are those who say more groupwork would be useful. The correlation between the groupwork item and the other items in the ORGDISC scale is .280. As remarked in Chapter 4, the pattern of variation of this item by job is similar to that of other items in the ORGDISC scale: The Siemens lab technicians and the employees of the GT&E sales offices feel the need for more groupwork least.

14 Stephen Cotgrove and Clive Vamplew, "Technology, Class, and Politics: The Case of the Process Workers," *Sociology*, 6 (1972), p. 179.

15 The matrix shown in the table to this note presents the correlations between the four items on opportunities for mobility and the three items on mobility aspirations:

	Mobility aspirations		
Mobility opportunities	3.1 Would you like to become a boss?	3.2 Is it important to you to improve your position in the plant?	1.9 What are the most important characteristics in a job? (mentions "the possibility getting ahead")
3.4 Do you expect to advance soon?	.064	.206	.299
3.5 How high can someone with an education like yours get around here?	.030	.278	–.001
3.8 Which of the following characteristics are most important for getting ahead around here?	.089	.119	.019
4.13 Do you think anyone with intelligence who is willing to work can get ahead in Italy, or do you think one needs connections?	.253	.078	.046

16 For an example of the first type, see Sayles, *Behavior of Industrial Work Groups;* for the second type, see Richard Hyman, *Strikes* (London: Collins, 1972), p. 29.

Chapter 7. The new working class: a revolutionary vanguard?

1 For the small-group level, see Victor H. Vroom, "Industrial Social Psychology," in Gardner Lindzey and E. Aronson, eds. *Handbook of Social Psychology*, Vol. 5 (Reading, Mass.: Addison-Wesley, 1970); for the level of organizational structure, see Tom Burns and G. M.

Stalker, *The Management of Innovation* (London: Tavistock Publications, 1961) and Lawrence and Lorsch, *Organization and Environment*.

2 IBM Workers and Emilio Reyneri, "IBM, stabilimento di Vimercate," pamphlet (Milan: Centro di Ricerche sui Modi di Produzione, 1971).

3 See Gordon, *Theories of Poverty*, for a summary of the literature on this subject.

4 Claude Durand and Michelle Durand, *De l'o.s. à l'ingénieur* (Paris: Les Editions Ouvrières, 1971).

5 Ibid., p. 94.

6 Ibid., pp. 106–7.

7 Ibid., pp. 119, 114, 121–2, 126, 121.

8 Ibid., pp. 90, 152, 161–2, 168, 178.

9 Ibid., p. 156.

10 Michelle Durand, "Professionalisation et allégeance chez les cadres et les techniciens," *Sociologie du travail*, 14 (1972), 211.

11 Renaud Sainsaulieu, *Les relations de travail à l'usine* (Paris: Les Editions D'Organisation, 1972).

12 Durand, "Ouvriers et techniciens en mai 1968."

13 Dulong, "Les cadres et le mouvement ouvrier."

14 On the "malaise of the *cadres*," see Jean E. Humblet, *Les cadres d'entreprises* (Paris: Editions Universitaires, 1966); Alfred Willener et al., *Les cadres en mouvement* (Paris: Editions de l'Epi, 1969); and the special issue, *Les cadres dans le mouvement syndical*, of *Sociologie du travail*, 10 (1968). On these last points, see particularly Dulong, "Les cadres et le mouvement ouvrier," pp. 167–81; Alfred Willener and Catherine Gajdos, "Les cadres en mouvement," in Willener et al., *Les cadres en mouvement*, p. 80ff.

15 Sainsaulieu, *Les relations de travail à l'usine*, p. 258.

16 On the origins and traditions of the men in the sample, see Chapter 5 (pp. 123–132, 136–7, 169–70) and Chapter 6 (pp. 180–4, 188–9, 198–9); on aspirations and perceptions of mobility, see Chapter 4 (pp. 105–7) and Chapter 5 (pp. 127–8, 170–1, 189–95, 199–204); on life style and images of the class structure see Chapter 5.

17 Durand and Durand, *De l'o.s. à l'ingénieur*, p. 198; Marc Maurice, "Determinants du militantisme et projet syndical des ouvriers et des techniciens," *Sociologie du travail*, 7 (1965), 256; Sainsaulieu, *Les relations de travail à l'usine*, pp. 178–9; Christiane Barrier, "Techniciens et grèves à l'Electricité de France," *Sociologie du travail*, 1 (1968), 63.

18 Durand and Durand, *De l'o.s. à l'ingénieur*, p. 45; Sainsaulieu, *Les relations de travail à l'usine*, p. 176.

19 Durand and Durand, *De l'o.s. à l'ingénieur*, pp. 211–12.

20 Ibid., pp. 146–82.

21 Ibid., pp. 271–4.

22 Sainsaulieu, *Les relations de travail à l'usine*, pp. 265–6.

23 This problem is even more apparent in the research of Christiane Barrier. See Barrier, "Techniciens et grèves à l'Electricité de France." We cite it only because we do not wish to appear to disregard data relevant to the new working class thesis. The article attempts to refute some of the hypotheses of Gorz and Mallet. Admittedly exploratory, it has a number of methodological weaknesses that make the conclusions questionable. Barrier argues that the new working class technicians show no sign of interest in control over the organization of work or in any of the other subjects discussed by Gorz and Mallet. They do show some interest in traditional trade unionism and a great interest in personal advancement.

The weaknesses of the study may be summarized briefly. Given that the sample is divided into three equal strata of traditional skilled workers, technicians, and engineers, it is too small (154 questionnaires). Many of the tables have numerous cells with less than five cases each. There is no in-depth material upon which to draw when contradictions and complexities appear in the tables. The way in which the single relevant question was posed made it extremely unlikely that the new working class thesis would be supported. Apparently, workers were simply asked, "What objectives would you be willing to strike for?" Of course, almost all replied, "Money." However, no exact data are given as to what the responses were. One can only hope that Barrier's recent book on this subject (unavailable to the author as of this writing) does not suffer from all these defects, although reviews suggest that it does.

24 There is no space here to relate these findings to the literature on social mobility and political attitudes. However, it might be pointed out that the findings are consistent with those of other European research according to which the upwardly mobile are intermediate in their attitudes between their class of origin and their class of arrival. See Durand and Durand, *De l'o.s. à l'ingénieur,* Chapter VIII, for further discussion.

25 Gino Germani, "Social and Political Consequences of Mobility" in Neil J. Smelser and Seymour Martin Lipset, eds., *Social Structure and Mobility in Economic Development* (Chicago: Aldine, 1966), p. 372.

26 Research by Piergiorgio Corbetta, which only came to the author's attention as this book was going to press, emphasizes the effects of partially blocked mobility. Corbetta's book, *Tecnici, disoccupazione e coscienza di classe,* is the only empirical study of Italian technicians the author knows of. Despite its unsophisticated methodology, which at times makes its assertions appear unconvincing, it is a most valuable contribution to the debate. Considering a sample of 945 graduates of technical high schools in various parts of Northern Italy, 245 from the classes of 1958 and 1959 and 700 from the classes of 1968 and 1969, Corbetta finds that those who were not able to get jobs "appropriate" to their degrees are more leftist in their political attitudes. This finding holds up even controlling for social class of origin. Looking at the 193 technicians from the classes of 1968 and 1969 who were still university students at the time of the survey, Corbetta shows that those who enrolled because of a lack of other options are more leftist than those who enrolled by choice. The unemployed technicians, surprisingly, are no more leftist than those employed in appropriate jobs. Corbetta argues that this last group is on the whole socially integrated, not radicalized. However, his ability to look at different job situations within this group is greatly hampered by the lack of detailed data about jobs as well as by the weakness of his methods.

27 See Alessandro Pizzorno, "Sull'azione politica dei sindacati," *Problemi del socialismo,* 12 (1970), for a general discussion. For the U.S. case see J. David Greenstone, *Labor in American Politics* (New York: Knopf, 1969).

28 Mallet, *La nuova classe operaia,* pp. 44-5.

29 Gorz, *Strategy for Labor,* pp. 103-4.

30 Dina, "Condizione del tecnico e condizione operaia nella fabbrica."

31 Habermas, "Technology and Science as 'Ideology,'" p. 111.

32 Dina, "I Tecnici nella società contemporanea," *Problemi del socialismo,* 9 (1967), 1415.

33 Perry Anderson, "Problems of Socialist Strategy," in Perry Anderson and Robin Blackburn, eds., *Towards Socialism* (London: Fontana Library, 1965).

34 Gorz, "Techniques, techniciens et lutte des classes."

35 Dina, "Condizione del tecnico e condizione operaia nella fabbrica"; Olivetti Workers, "La divisione del lavoro in fabbrica."

36 Gorz, *Strategy for Labor,* pp. 6-8.

37 Mallet, *La nuova classe operaia,* p. 91.

38 Reynaud, "Industrial Relations in France."

39 Anderson, "Problems of a Socialist Strategy," pp. 240, 265.

40 Garaudy has used Gramsci's concept of a "historical bloc" to refer to the strategic alliance

of white collar and blue collar workers, assigning an important linking role to technicians. See Garaudy, *The Crisis in Communism*, Chapter V. The interpretation of a historical bloc as coalition is, however, controversial.

41 Zygmunt Bauman, *Between Class and Elite* (Manchester: Manchester University Press, 1972); E. P. Thompson, *The Making of the English Working Class* (London: Gollancz, 1963).

42 Michael Mann makes the same point [see Mann, *Consciousness and Action in the Western Working Class* (London: Macmillan, 1973), p. 70.]

43 Touraine, *The Post Industrial Society* (New York: Random House, 1971), pp. 61, 73–4.

44 Ibid., p. 66.

45 Ibid., p. 64.

46 Ibid., p. 67.

47 In his more recent work, Touraine, expressing the mood of the mid-seventies, is more pessimistic about this possibility [see Touraine, "Les nouveaux conflits sociaux," *Sociologie du travail*, 17(1975), 1–17]. Here he expresses the view that the opposition groups share no common interests beyond their opposition. The concerns and power of the state now extend into all areas of life, and conflict, accordingly, tends to generalize. Although in *The Post Industrial Society* Touraine still saw the state as expressing the drive toward growth and economic development, in the more recent article he no longer seems to see the state as expressing the economic logic of advanced capitalism. This is why he no longer sees a common interest uniting the opposition groups, and denies the possibility of an alternative model of society. We cannot follow him to this conclusion.

References

Allen, Kevin, and Andrew Stevenson. 1975. *An Introduction to the Italian Economy*. New York: Harper and Row.

Anderson, Perry. 1965. "Problems of Socialist Strategy," in Perry Anderson and Robin Blackburn, eds., *Towards Socialism*. London: Fontana Library.

Aronowitz, Stanley. 1971. "Does the United States Have a New Working Class?" in George Fischer, ed., *The Revival of Socialism in America*. New York: Oxford University Press.

Bahrdt, Hans Paul. 1958. *Industriebürokratie: Versuch einer Soziologie des industrialisierten Bürobetriebes und seiner Angestellten*. Stuttgart: Enke.

Barbagli, Marzio. 1974. *Disoccupazione intellettuale e sistema scolastico in Italia*. Bologna: Il Mulino.

Barrier, Christiane. 1968. "Techniciens et grèves a l'Electricité de France," *Sociologie du travail*, 1 (January-March), 50–71.

Bauman, Zygmunt. 1960. *Between Class and Elite*. Translated by Sheila Patterson. Manchester: Manchester University Press, 1972.

Bell, Daniel. 1962. *The End of Ideology*. New York: Free Press.

——— 1971. "The Post-Industrial Society: The Evolution of an Idea," *Survey*, 79 (Spring), 102–68.

——— 1972. "Labor in the Post-Industrial Society," *Dissent* (Winter), 163–89.

Bennis, Warren G. 1970. "Beyond Bureaucracy," in W. G. Bennis, ed., *American Bureaucracy*. Chicago: Aldine.

——— and Philip E. Slater. 1968. *The Temporary Society*.

Berger, Bennett. 1960. *Working Class Suburb*. Berkeley: University of California Press.

Berger, Suzanne. 1974. "Uso politico e sopravivenza dei ceti in declino," in Stephen R. Graubard and Fabio Luca Cavazza, eds., *Il caso italiano: Italia anni '70*. Milan: Garzanti.

Blauner, Robert. 1964. *Alienation and Freedom*. Chicago: University of Chicago Press.

——— 1966. "Work Satisfaction and Industrial Trends in Modern Society," in S. M. Lipset and R. Bendix, eds., *Class, Status, and Power*, 2nd ed. New York: Free Press.

Blumberg, Paul. 1968. *Industrial Democracy*. London: Constable.

Bologna, S., and F. Ciafaloni. 1969. "I tecnici come produttori e come prodotto," *Quaderni piacentini* (March), 52–72.

Bright, James R. 1958. *Automation and Management*. Boston: Harvard Graduate School of Business Administration.

Bulmer, Martin, ed. 1975. *Working Class Images of Society*. London: Routledge & Kegan Paul.

Burns, Tom, and G. M. Stalker. 1961. *The Management of Innovation*. London: Tavistock Publications.

Caruso, Saverio. 1974. *Burocrazia e capitale in Italia*. Verona: Bertani.

Centers, Richard. 1949. *The Psychology of Social Classes*. Princeton: Princeton University Press.

Centro Karl Marx di Pisa. 1971. *Sviluppo capitalistico e forza-lavoro intellettuale*. Milan: Sapere.

Cohen, Stephen S. 1969. *Modern Capitalist Planning: The French Model*. Cambridge, Mass.: Harvard University Press.

Corbetta, Piergiorgio. 1975. *Tecnici, disoccupazione e coscienza di classe*. Bologna: Il Mulino.

Cotgrove, Stephen, and Clive Vamplew. 1972. "Technology, Class, and Politics: The Case of the Process Workers," *Sociology*, 6 (May), 169–85.

275

Cousins, Jim, and Richard Brown. 1975. "Patterns of Paradox: Shipbuilding Workers' Images of Society," in Martin Bulmer, ed., *Working Class Images of Society*, pp. 55-82. London: Routledge & Kegan Paul.

Crozier, Michel. 1965. *The World of the Office Worker*. Translated by D. Landau. Chicago: University of Chicago Press, 1971.

Dahrendorf, Ralf. 1959. *Class and Class Conflict in Industrial Society*. Stanford: Stanford University Press.

D'Antonio, Mariano. 1973. *Sviluppo e crisi del capitalismo italiano, 1951-1972*. Bari: De Donato.

Dawson, Richard E., and Kenneth Prewitt. 1969. *Political Socialization*. Boston: Little Brown.

Dean, Lois R. 1954. "Social Integration Attitudes and Union Acitivity," *Industrial and Labor Relations Review*, 8 (October), 48-58.

Dina, Angelo. 1967. "I tecnici nella società contemporanea," *Problemi del socialismo*, 9 (November-December), 1406-16.

   1969. "Condizione del tecnico e condizione operaia nella fabbrica: dall'oggettivita alla scelta politica," *Classe* (June). Milan: Dedalo Libri. pp. 89-134.

Doeringer, Peter B., and Michael J. Piore. 1971. *Internal Labor Markets and Manpower Analysis*. Lexington, Mass.: Heath.

Dogan, Mattei. 1967. "Political Cleavage and Social Stratification in France and Italy," in Seymour Martin Lipset and Stein Rokkan, eds., *Party Systems and Voter Alignments*. New York: Free Press.

Dulong, Renaud. 1971. "Les cadres et le mouvement ouvrier," in Pierre Dubois et al., *Grèves revendicatives ou grèves politiques?*, pp. 161-245. Paris: Editions Anthropos.

Durand, Claude. 1971. "Ouvriers et techniciens en mai 1968," in Pierre Dubois et al., *Grèves revendicatives ou grèves politiques?*, pp. 7-159. Paris: Editions Anthropos.

Durand, Michelle. 1972. "Professionalisation et allégéance chez les cadres et les techniciens," *Sociologie du travail*, 14 (April-June), 185-212.

Durand, Claude, and Michelle Durand. 1971. *De l'o.s. à l'ingénieur*. Paris: Les Editions Ouvrières.

Faunce, William A. 1968. *The Problems of an Industrial Society*. New York: McGraw-Hill.

Flavell, John H. 1963. *The Developmental Psychology of Jean Piaget*. New York: Van Nostrand Reinhold.

Fuà, Giorgio. 1976. *Occupazione e capacità produttive: la realtà italiana*. Bologna: Il Mulino.

Galbraith, John Kenneth. 1967. *The New Industrial State*. Boston: Houghton Mifflin.

Garaudy, Roger. 1969. *The Crisis in Communism: The Turning Point of Socialism*. Translated by Peter and Betty Ross. New York: Grove Press, 1970.

Germani, Gino. 1966. "Social and Political Consequences of Mobility" in Neil J. Smelser and Seymour Martin Lipset, eds., *Social Structure and Mobility in Economic Development*. Chicago: Aldine.

Giddens, Anthony. 1973. *The Class Structure of the Advanced Societies*. New York: Barnes and Noble.

Girod, Roger. 1961. *Etudes sociologiques sur les couches salariées*. Paris: Rivière.

Goldthorpe, John H. 1970. "Images of Class Among Affluent Manual Workers." Mimeographed. Cambridge: University of Cambridge, Department of Applied Economics.

Goldthorpe, John H., David Lockwood, Frank Bechhofer, and Jennifer Platt. 1968a. *The Affluent Worker: Industrial Attitudes and Behavior*. Cambridge: Cambridge University Press.

   1968b. *The Affluent Worker: Political Attitudes and Behavior*. Cambridge: Cambridge University Press.

   1969. *The Affluent Worker in the Class Structure*. Cambridge: Cambridge University Press.

Gordon, David M. 1972. *Theories of Poverty and Underemployment*. Lexington, Mass: Heath.

Gorz, André. 1964. *Strategy for Labor.* Translated by Martin Nicolaus and Victoria Ortiz. Boston: Beacon, 1967.

1971. "Techniques, techniciens et lutte des classes," *Les temps modernes,* 301–2 (August–September), 141–80.

Gourevitch, Peter. 1973. "Reforming the Napoleonic State: The Creation of Regional Government in France and Italy." Mimeographed. Paper presented at the IXth World Congress of the International Political Science Association, Sir George Williams University, Montreal, Canada, August 19–25.

Gramsci, Antonio, 1971. *Selections from the Prison Notebooks,* edited and translated by Quentin Hoare and Geoffrey Nowell Smith. New York: International Publishers.

Graziani, Augusto, ed. 1972. *L'economia italiana: 1945–1970.* Bologna: Il Mulino.

Greenstone, J. David. 1969. *Labor in American Politics.* New York: Knopf.

Habermas, Jürgen. 1968. "Technology and Science as 'Ideology'," in Jurgen Habermas, *Toward a Rational Society.* Translated by J. J. Shapiro. Boston: Beacon, 1970.

Hackman, Richard J., and Edward Lawler III. 1971. "Employee Reactions to Job Characteristics," *Journal of Applied Psychology,* Monograph 55 (June), 259–86.

Haer, John L. 1957. "An Empirical Study of Social Class Awareness," *Social Forces,* 36 (December), 117–21.

Hamilton, Richard F. 1967. *Affluence and the French Worker in the Fourth Republic.* Princeton: Princeton University Press.

1972. *Class and Politics in the United States.* New York: Wiley.

Handel, Gerald, and Lee Rainwater. 1964. "Persistence and Change in Working Class Life Styles," in Arthur Shostak and William Gomberg, eds., *Blue Collar Worlds.* Englewood Cliffs, N.J.: Prentice-Hall.

Hiller, Peter. 1975a. "The Nature and Location of Everyday Conceptions of Class," *Sociology,* 9 (January), 1–28.

1975b. "Continuities and Variations in Everyday Conceptual Components of Class," *Sociology,* 9 (May), 255–87.

Hoos, Ida. 1961. *Automation in the Office.* Washington, D.C.: Public Affairs Press.

Humblet, Jean E. 1966. *Les cadres d'entreprises.* Paris: Editions Universitaires.

Hyman, Richard. 1972. *Strikes.* London: Collins.

IBM workers and Emilio Reyneri. 1971. "IBM, stabilimento di Vimercate." Pamphlet. Milan: Centro di Richerche sui Modi di Produzione.

Ingham, Geoffrey K. 1970. *Size of Industrial Organization and Worker Behavior.* Cambridge: Cambridge University Press.

Jaffe, A. J., and J. Froomkin. 1968. *Technology and Jobs.* New York: Praeger.

Kahl, Joseph A., and James A. Davis. 1955. "A Comparison of Indexes of Socio-Economic Status," *American Sociological Review* 20 (June), 317–25.

Kohlberg, Lawrence. 1969. "Stage and Sequence: The Cognitive Developmental Approach to Socialization," in David A. Goslin, ed., *The Handbook of Socialization Theory and Research.* Chicago: Rand McNally.

Kohn, Melvin L. 1969. *Class and Conformity.* Homewood, Ill.: Dorsey Press.

Lawrence, Paul R., and Jay W. Lorsch. 1967. *Organization and Environment.* Boston: Harvard University, Division of Research, Graduate School of Business Administration.

Lederer, Emil. 1912. "The Problem of the Modern Salaried Employee." Mimeographed. Translated as part of W.P.A. Project No. 465–97–3–81. New York: Columbia University, Department of Social Science, 1937.

and Jacob Marschak. 1926. "The New Middle Class." Mimeographed. Translated as part of W.P.A. Project No. 465–97–3–81. New York: Columbia University, Department of Social Science, 1937.

Leggett, John C. 1968. *Class, Race, and Labor.* London: Oxford University Press.

Lelli, Marcello. 1971. *Tecnici e lotta di classe.* Bari: De Donato.

Lenin, V. I. 1939. *Imperialism: The Highest State of Capitalism.* New York: International Publishers.

Lipset, Seymour Martin. 1956. *Union Democracy.* Glencoe, Ill: The Free Press.

—— and Stein Rokkan. 1967. "Cleavage Structures, Party Systems, and Voter Alignments: An Introduction," in S. M. Lipset and S. Rokkan, eds., *Party Systems and Voter Alignments.* New York: Free Press.

Locke, Edwin A. 1973. "The Nature and Consequences of Job Satisfaction," in Marvin D. Dunnette, ed., *Handbook of Industrial and Organizational Psychology.* Chicago: Rand McNally.

Lockwood, David. 1958. *The Blackcoated Worker.* London: Allen and Unwin.

—— 1968. "Sources of Variation in Working-Class Images of Society," in Joseph A. Kahl, ed., *Comparative Perspectives on Stratification.* Boston: Little Brown. First published in *Sociological Review,* 14 (November 1966), 249–67.

Lopreato, Joseph, and Lawrence E. Hazelrigg. 1972. *Class, Conflict and Mobility.* San Francisco: Chandler.

Low-Beer, John. 1968. "Trends in Italian Trade Unionism." Unpublished paper. Harvard University, Cambridge, Mass.

—— 1974. "The New Working Class in Italy." Unpublished Ph.D. dissertation. Harvard University, Cambridge, Mass.

Lukács, Georg. 1923. *History and Class Consciousness.* Cambridge, Mass.: MIT Press, 1971.

Mallet, Serge. 1963. *La nouvelle classe ouvrière.* Paris: Editions du Seuil.

—— 1969. *La nuova classe operaia,* 2nd ed. Translated by G. Fofi. Turin: Einaudi, 1970.

Mann, Michael. 1973. *Consciousness and Action in the Western Working Class.* London: Macmillan.

Marx, Karl. 1844. *Economic and Philosophical Manuscripts,* in T. B. Bottomore, ed., *Karl Marx: Early Writings.* New York: McGraw-Hill, 1964.

—— 1845. *Die Heilige Familie,* excerpts in T. B. Bottomore and Maximilien Rubel, eds., *Karl Marx: Selected Writings in Sociology and Social Philosophy.* New York: McGraw-Hill, 1964.

—— 1867. *Capital.* New York: International Publishers, 3 vols., 1967.

—— 1971. *The Grundrisse.* Excerpts translated and edited by David McLellan. New York: Harper & Row.

Maurice, Marc. 1965. "Déterminants du militantisme et projet syndical des ouvriers et des techniciens," *Sociologie du travail,* 7 (July-September), 254–72.

Mayer, Kurt. 1963. "The Changing Shape of the American Class Structure," *Social Research,* 30 (Winter), 458–68.

Mills, C. Wright. 1951. *White Collar.* New York: Oxford University Press.

Morse, Nancy C. 1953. *Satisfactions in the White Collar Job.* Ann Arbor: University of Michigan, Institute for Social Research.

Naville, Pierre. 1961. "Divisione del lavoro e ripartizione dei compiti," in Georges Friedmann and Pierre Naville. *Trattato di sociologia del lavoro,* Vol. 1. Translated by M. Paci. Milan: Edizioni di Comunità, 1963.

Niemi, Richard G. 1973. "Political Socialization," in Jeanne Knutson, ed., *Handbook of Political Psychology.* San Francisco: Jossey-Bass.

Oeser, O. A., and S. B. Hammond. 1954. *Social Structure and Personality in a City.* New York: Macmillan.

Olivetti Workers, anonymous group. 1969. "La divisione del lavoro in fabbrica," *Il Manifesto,* Vol. 1, n. 5–6, pp. 28–37.

Paci, Massimo. 1973. *Mercato del lavoro e classi sociali.* Bologna: Il Mulino.

Pagani, Angelo. 1960. *Classi e dinamica sociale.* Pavia: Istituto di Statistica della Università di Pavia and Amministrazione Provinciale di Milano.

Pateman, Carole. 1970. *Participation and Democratic Theory.* Cambridge: Cambridge University Press.

Pizzorno, Alessandro. 1964. "The Individualistic Mobilization of Europe," *Daedalus,* 93 (Winter), 199-224.

1970. "Sull'azione politica dei sindacati," *Problemi del socialismo,* 12 (November-December).

1973. "Resoconto sulla formazione delle ipotesi e sui primi risultati della ricerca," in Istituto per lo Studio della Società Contemporanea, Rapporto sulla ricerca sull'evoluzione del potere sindacale. Mimeographed.

Pollock, Friedrich. 1964. *Automation.* Frankfurt: Europäische Verlagsanstalt.

Regini, Marino, and Emilio Reyneri. 1971. *Lotte operaie e organizzazione del lavoro.* Padua: Marsilio.

Reynaud, Jean Daniel. 1975. "Industrial Relations in France, 1960-1975: A Review," Mimeographed. Paper presented at the Harvard Conference on Industrial Relations. Cambridge, Mass., September 26-7.

Reyneri, Emilio. 1973. "Caratteristiche e fattori dell'inizio del nuovo ciclo di conflittualità operaia," in Istituto per lo Studio della Società Contemporanea, Rapporto sulla ricerca sull'evoluzione del potere sindacale. Mimeographed.

Rinehart, James W. 1971. "Affluence and the Embourgeoisement of the Working Class: A Critical Look," *Social Problems,* 19 (Fall), 149-62.

Sadler, Philip. 1968. *Social Research on Automation.* British Social Science Research Council. London: Heinemann.

Sainsaulieu, Renaud. 1972. *Les relations de travail à l'usine.* Paris: Les Editions d'Organisation.

Salvati, Michele. 1975. *Il sistema economico italiano: analisi di una crisi.* Bologna: Il Mulino.

Sayles, Leonard. 1958. *The Behavior of Industrial Work Groups: Prediction and Control.* New York: Wiley.

and George Strauss. 1953. *The Local Union.* New York: Harper and Row.

Schmoller, Gustav. 1897. *Was verstehen wir unter dem Mittelstand.* Göttingen: Vanderhock and Ruprecht.

Silverman, David. 1970. *The Theory of Organisations.* London: Heinemann.

Simon, Herbert A. 1965. *The Shape of Automation for Men and Management.* New York: Harper & Row.

Suleiman, Ezra N. 1974. *Politics, Power, and Bureaucracy in France.* Princeton: Princeton University Press.

Sylos-Labini, Paolo. 1973. "Sviluppo economico e classi sociali in Italia" in Paolo Farneti, ed., *Il sistema politico italiano.* Bologna: Il Mulino.

Tannenbaum, Arnold, and Robert Kahn. 1958. *Participation in Union Locals.* Evanston, Ill.: Row, Peterson.

Tarrow, Sidney. 1975. "Communism in Italy and France: Adaptation and Change," in Donald L. M. Blackmer and Sidney Tarrow, eds., *Communism in Italy and France.* Princeton: Princeton University Press.

Taviss, Irene, and William Gerber. 1969. *Technology and Work.* Cambridge, Mass.: Harvard University, Program on Technology and Society.

Taylor, James C. 1971. *Technology and Planned Organizational Change.* Ann Arbor: University of Michigan, Institute for Social Research.

Thompson, E. P. 1963. *The Making of the English Working Class.* London: Gollancz.

Touraine, Alain. 1961. "L'organizzazione professionale dell'impresa," in Georges Friedmann and Pierre Naville. *Trattato di sociologia del lavoro,* Vol. 1. Translated by M. Paci. Milan: Edizioni di Comunità, 1963.

1969. *The Post Industrial Society.* Translated by L. Mayhew. New York: Random House, 1971.

1975. "Les nouveaux conflits sociaux," *Sociologie du travail,* 17 (January-March), 1-17.

Veblen, Thorstein. 1963. *The Engineers and the Price System.* New York: Harcourt Brace Jovanovich.

Vroom, Victor H. 1964. *Work and Motivation.* New York: Wiley.

——— 1970. "Industrial Social Psychology," in Gardner Lindzey and E. Aronson, eds., *Handbook of Social Psychology,* Vol. 5. Reading, Mass.: Addison-Wesley.

Weitz, Peter R. 1975. "Labor and Politics in a Divided Movement: The Italian Case," *Industrial and Labor Relations Review,* 28 (January), 226–42.

Whisler, Thomas. 1970. *The Impact of Computers on Organizations.* New York: Praeger.

Wilensky, H. L. 1960. "Work, Careers, and Social Integration," *International Social Science Journal,* 12 (Fall), 543–60.

Willener, Alfred. 1957. *Images de la société et classes sociales.* Lausanne: Université de Lausanne, Ecole des Sciences Sociales et Politiques.

——— and Catherine Gajdos. 1969. "Les cadres en mouvement," in Alfred Willener et al., *Les cadres en mouvement.* Paris: Editions de l'Epi.

——— Catherine Gajdos, and Georges Benguigui. 1969. *Les cadres en mouvement.* Paris: Editions de l'Epi.

Williams, Philip M., and Martin Harrison. 1971. *Politics and Society in De Gaulle's Republic.* London: Longman Group.

Willmott, Peter, and Michael Young. 1960. *Family and Class in a London Suburb.* London: Routledge & Kegan Paul.

Zeitlin, Maurice. 1967. *Revolutionary Politics and the Cuban Working Class.* Princeton: Princeton University Press.

Zorzoli, G. B. 1970. *La ricerca scientifica in Italia.* Milan: Franco Angeli.

Index

281